ZAPPA THE HARD WAY

ZAPPA THE HARD WAY
Andrew Greenaway

WP
WYMER
PUBLISHING
Bedford, England

First published in Great Britain in 2010
by Wymer Publishing
PO Box 155, Bedford, MK40 2YX
www.wymerpublishing.co.uk
Tel: 01234 326691

ISBN 978-1-908724-00-7

Edited by Jerry Bloom and Stanley Hope.

Every effort has been made to trace the copyright holders of the
photographs in this book but some were unreachable. We would
be grateful if the photographers concerned would contact us.

Typeset by Wymer UK.
Printed and bound by Lightning Source

A catalogue record for this book is available from the British Library.

Cover design by Wymer UK
Front cover photo © Lynn Goldsmith / Corbis
Back cover photo © Jay Petitt

CONTENTS

This book is dedicated to:

Lord Tomsett of Chesterfield
(I lay awake nights saying, "Thank you, Fred!")

and

Reginald William Greenaway
(1928-2005)

The Cast Of Characters
Summer 1987-June 1988

The 1988 band

Frank Zappa	Lead guitar, computer-synth, vocals, band leader (referred to throughout as FZ or Zappa)
Ike Willis	Rhythm guitar, synth, vocals
Mike Keneally	Stunt guitar, rhythm guitar, synth, vocals
Walt Fowler	Trumpet, flugel horn, synth
Bruce Fowler	Trombone
Paul Carman	Alto sax, soprano sax, baritone sax
Albert Wing	Tenor sax
Kurt McGettrick	Baritone sax, bass sax, contrabass clarinet
Chad Wackerman	Drums, electronic percussion
Ed Mann	Vibes, marimba, electronic percussion
Robert Martin	Keyboards, vocals (Bobby)
Scott Thunes	Electric bass, Minimoog, rehearsal director (or 'Clonemeister')

The 1987 auditionees

Tommy Mars	Keyboards, vocals
Ray White	Rhythm guitar, vocals
Mark Volman	Vocals (formerly of The Turtles) (Flo)
Howard Kaylan	Vocals (formerly of The Turtles) (Eddie)

And others

Gail Zappa	Wife of FZ
Moon Unit Zappa	Eldest daughter of Gail and FZ
Dweezil Zappa	Eldest son of Gail and FZ
Ahmet Zappa	Youngest son of Gail and FZ
Diva Zappa	Youngest daughter of Gail and FZ
Sting	Guest vocals, formerly of The Police
Eric Buxton	Guest vocals, Zappa fan
Dot Stein	Guest belches, Zappa fan (Dr Dot)

FOREWORD

Wow, what a fabulous book! So much information about Frank and his life that I was not privy to and Andrew Greenaway lets us see a large amount of it. The interviews - all are so open and real - by Mike Keneally, Scott Thunes (whom I had the pleasure of meeting at Zappanale #13 in 2002), Ed Mann, Ike Willis - so many other amazing musicians - Lorraine Belcher and, of course, Frank. The incident about the burp is priceless!

Andrew was concerned that some of the things said about Frank would upset me. I've heard lots of good things and a few bad things about Frank, but that doesn't change the fact that I loved, respected and miss him greatly. Being in business, you don't make too many friends and I don't think he was in it to win a popularity contest. He was there to make music and to do it in a way that not only pleased his audience, but himself. As my big brother, he was fun, funny, handsome, creative and very protective. I am proud to be his little sister.

The '88 tour seemed to be an incredible experience and how I wish I could have been there. 'The Hard Way' is an understatement! Frank was the master editor (I've even thought of him as a ringmaster!) and he knew what he wanted and how to get it. A lot of what I read was familiar to me about the tour, but there were a few things I was totally amused and educated by. For instance, how they learned to play *The Untouchables* theme - great stuff. How Scott Thunes was a leader, both liked and disliked by Frank's band members, and his major respect for Frank. Ike's antics, Robert

Martin's musings and everyone's personal experiences; it was like looking through a secret window into it all.

This is the type of book you would read with lots of munchies and liquid refreshment around, because you'll be sitting for a while, not wanting to put it down. Thank you, Andrew, for bringing us an informative, funny and glaringly real look at life on the road with Frank Zappa. Hooray!

Patrice "Candy" Zappa
June 2010

PREAMBLE

For those of you who might not know...

On Monday 6th December 1993, Frank Zappa's family announced that the American composer, electric guitarist, record producer and film director had *"left for his final tour just before 6:00 pm on Saturday"*. Zappa had succumbed to prostate cancer, the disease that had been developing inside him unnoticed for ten years. By the time it was finally discovered, it was deemed inoperable.

But Zappa's true 'final tour' took place in 1988 with a 12-piece band that had a repertoire of over 100 songs. Musically, the 'Broadway The Hard Way' tour was arguably his most successful - certainly, I would argue its case - but it ended in disarray before it was fully completed and allegedly cost Zappa thousands of dollars. His widow Gail said, *"You can speculate over who was at fault, but the fact is that Frank asked each 'sideman' in the band if they would continue to tour with [bassist] Scott Thunes. What this means is that he gave everyone a fair shot at self-determining if they would be what he had hired them to be and what he was paying them to be - professional musicians. They all declined save Mike Keneally and Scott. Professional musicians: there to do a job and do it correctly - irrespective of the challenges and obstacles that may from time to time present themselves. It was sheer mutiny."*

This book is not a definitive account of events on that tour: surviving band members' memories over twenty years later are understandably now a little hazy and, from my interviews with them for this book, it was clear that many were still trying to come to terms with just why it all went tits up. But it's probably the closest we'll ever get - even though drummer Chad Wackerman, despite my constant badgering (*sorry, Chad - I had to try!*), maintained a dignified silence. I have also tried not to take sides, as all of the guys have been wonderfully candid and friendly towards me. But I was keen for Scott Thunes' point of view to be better understood, and hope that I have achieved that here.

Fortunately, the tour has been exceedingly well documented - on the *Broadway The Hard Way, The Best Band You Never Heard In Your Life* and *Make A Jazz Noise Here* albums, as well as tracks on *You Can't Do That On Stage Anymore* series (Volumes 4 & 6), the posthumous *Anything Anytime Anywhere For No Reason At All* and *Anything Anytime Anywhere For No Reason At All Again* digital download packages, and over half the guitar solos on the *Trance-Fusion* CD - more than six hours of incredible music. And for further reading, there's Thomas Wictor's *Interviews With Really Scary Musicians*, Mike Keneally's *Zappa Tour Diaries, The Frank Zappa 1988 Tour Project* webpages maintained by Pat Buzby, and Den Simm's *Project Documentation* - all of which were invaluable to me in compiling this tome.

Many fans consider the 1988 tour to be Frank's best ever; the presence of horns, percussion and 'stunt guitar', not to mention the Synclavier, gave the band a variety severely lacking in the previous synth-dominated world tour of 1984. The use of 'secret words' made many of the concerts unique, and a voter registration drive during the US shows added a political edge - which Zappa's new songs reflected.

This book attempts to give an insight into the true story behind the best band Zappa ever had in his life. Read it while listening to the music, and marvel at how they managed to pull it off so well, and for so long.

So long.

Andrew Greenaway
May 2010

CHAPTER ONE
You Can't Do That On Stage Anymore

On the evening of 23rd December 1984, Frank Zappa had just had a guitar 'duel' with his 15-year-old son, Dweezil, on stage at the Universal Amphitheater in Los Angeles. They'd played together on a cover of the Allman Brothers Band's classic, *Whippin' Post*. In his liner notes to the subsequent *Does Humor Belong In Music?* CD, Zappa referred to this as "the last song of the last show of the last tour"[1] . Later that night, he put his Stratocaster in the corner of his home studio, where it began to gather dust. Two years later, he hadn't picked it up: "I don't have much incentive to play it. I don't have any calluses anymore. I can still think guitar. But to physically manipulate it, I would have to go back in and woodshed for months on end just to be able to do it. For what? There's really no audience for it."[2] And even if there were an audience for it, he said "I have more guitar solos on tape than anybody could ever stand to listen to, and I figure I did it. There it is, it's done, it's a good solo. How many times do you have to do the same thing?"[3]

On Zappa's longest ever tour of Europe in 1982, shows in Kiel, Germany and Geneva, Switzerland ended abruptly after the crowd hurled objects onto the stage; shows in Saarbrucken, Offenburg and other German cities were cancelled because of the country's then tendency for civil disobedience; and a number of people died during a police-instigated riot at Frank's only ever concert in his father's home-town of Palermo in Sicily. The Geneva and Palermo incidents were later documented on the *You Can't Do That On Stage Anymore* CD series but, immediately following the tour, Zappa announced that he'd never go out on the road again. Would history repeat itself?

Zappa's 1984 'world' tour visited 93 cities in the United States, Canada and Europe over a five-month period. It featured a seven-piece band and, along the way, a number of special guests including the prominent American jazz saxophonist, Archie Shepp. Other guests were musicians Zappa had worked with previously during his 20-odd year career, such as Aynsley Dunbar, George Duke, Johnny "Guitar" Watson, Denny Walley, Bruce Fowler* and Napoleon Murphy Brock - who started the tour in mid-July but left on 1st August.

Vocalist and saxophonist Brock was a part of Zappa's legendary 'Roxy' band in the early 70s, and played on-and-off with both Zappa and synthesizer pioneer and singer, George Duke, throughout the rest of the decade. He returned to Zappa in 1983 to record material for the *Thing-Fish* and *Them Or Us* albums then spent some time in England training Staffordshire Bull Terriers. These days he fronts the Zappa tribute band, the Grande Mothers Re:Invented, and regularly performs at the annual three-day Zappanale festival in Bad Doberan, Germany. Talking about the 1984 tour in 2002, he told me "I could only do the short American leg. I couldn't do Europe and the rest of the tour. When we got back together, Frank said 'Why don't you come and do the tour with us?' And I said, 'well I can't do the whole thing, but I'll do what I can'." Zappa, however, publicly stated that "chemical alteration is not something that mixes well with precision performance"[4] following Brock's exit. And at one of the first shows without him, Zappa said that Brock "had health problems" to explain his absence. When I asked Scott Thunes** about this, he told me: "I loved the way Napi stayed in bed 'til it was time to leave for our first gig without even remotely getting his room ready to leave. We out-of-towners (me, Ray White, Napi) were put up at a residency apartment in the San Fernando Valley. Kitchen, utensils and plates: That type of thing. We were there for about three month's worth of rehearsals and so we were very much 'living' there.

*Born 10th July 1947.
**Born 20th January 1960.

Napi's room was a fucking mess. We were due to leave at, oh, say, noon, and I went to go get him and, bless his heart, he was lying there asleep or something. I went in to wrangle him and it was obvious that he wasn't planning on driving with us in the van, but intended to use his own very large old-school boat of an American car to drive himself. Mistake number one. He very seriously completely missed the entire first sound check. This is a serious no-no and I only did it once in the seven years I played with Frank, and that was for a pretty serious reason (I'd lost my passport) and Frank had even threatened to fine me for it. I told him to go ahead, I couldn't help it. So whatever, dood. He didn't. So for Napi to whip that out at the beginning of the tour was pretty righteous. The next two weeks were repeats of this type of thing. After a while, Frank just figured he was too high to proceed. I have no idea if drugs were involved - I'm just guessing - but you'd have to have a serious priority-issue if you thought that what you were doing was more important than what Frank needed you to do."

But Zappa could be somewhat economical with the *actualité* if there was a good sound bite to be had. Throughout his career, he vehemently objected to the use of drugs, while admitting that he'd smoked marijuana two or three times. But he much preferred to chug on a Winston - his real drug of choice, though he thought of cigarettes as food. Like many of us, the man was full of contradictions. Zappa's bassist for most of the eighties, Scott Thunes, says, "Now, of course, Frank was a pretty private person on many levels, but he was also quite open. How's that for a contradiction? He spent a lot of time describing in detail many of his sexual exploits but never told me if he loved his wife or his kids or music in general. Also, it was known at the time of his discovering his cancer that it was a surprise. Even though it was 'the size of a grapefruit', that doesn't mean he 'knew' about it. He hated doctors and hospitals (thought they were great deceivers) but he went to chiropractic - I'm not sure about them! - and ate as badly as a person in America can eat. Burgers, coffee, and cigarettes, and hated doctors. I'm surprised he lived as long as he did." Bearing in mind the political overtones of the '88 tour and Zappa's later desire to stand for President, there was also something odd when, in 1984, he said, "This is a planet of business. It doesn't matter who's in power, the guys that sells the wheat, the oil and the weapons, these are the guys that control our lives to a large degree and the politicians are just like a stupid charade where the characters change season to season".

Zappa claimed the '84 tour lost him $270,000, and artistically it is generally regarded as not up to scratch. Says Thunes, "1984 was pretty fucked without Tommy Mars, so we auditioned keyboard players and ended up with Allan Zavod, who blew us away with his sight-reading. We were sure we'd found our man. Too bad, the 70/30% correct-to-wrong-note ratio he exhibited at the audition somehow never increased on the correct side, and we were always snapping at each other. It was a dull tour for me, but some nice things happened to me outside the band." The disappearance of Brock early on (for whatever reason), the use of electronic drums and second keyboard player 'Knuckles' Zavod (effectively in lieu of percussionist Ed Mann*, who'd been with Frank since 1977), and the frequent playing of simple/doo-wop songs (*Carol You Fool, Chana In De Bushwop, No No Cherry, The Closer You Are*) and other 'crowd pleasers' (*Bobby Brown, Joe's Garage, Cosmik Debris, Dinah Moe Humm, City Of Tiny Lites, Keep It Greasy, The Illinois Enema Bandit, Bamboozled By Love, Zoot Allures* - which was used to open 53 of the shows) means this tour is also regarded by fans as quite a lacklustre affair which, because of the high quality recordings Zappa was able to make, is bemusingly very well represented on CD and DVD. But would these really be the last live Zappa recordings?

Following the tour, Zappa turned to composing almost exclusively on the Synclavier System**. In December 1986, Zappa

---

* Born 14th January 1955.
** A digital synthesizer and sampler manufactured by New England Digital, first released in 1975.

was asked if he had any plans to go back on the road again: "If I ever go back out there, I'm definitely going to take the Synclavier, [but] it's a massively complicated rehearsal problem. I know other people have had them out on the road, but I don't think anybody else has asked the machine to do what I want it to do, and to do it without fail in a hostile environment. My guys can sync with it, no problem. They latch right on there. But that was in a studio. You take it onto a stage, and you've got monitoring problems to deal with. What the drummer needs to hear is vastly different from what the bass player would need to hear. So now you're into multiple monitor feeds. It's a massive headache. And the solution to each headache is in increments of five figures."[5]

So he had been working with musicians and was no longer completely ruling out another tour, and talked about an idea he'd had for a more conventional 'rock song' that ridiculed President Reagan's Administration, called *Lie To Me*. Around the same time he also discussed composing for particular musicians, prophetically using the example of his early seventies 'Vaudeville' Mothers Of Invention band that featured ex-Turtles Mark Volman and Howard Kaylan (renamed, for contractual reasons, the Phlorescent Leech and Eddie - or Flo & Eddie for short). With a band like that one, he said "you can't get them to do something like *The Black Page*. It's not their style. So whatever you write for that particular band has to be engineered for their assets and liabilities. You design the show around them as people, and the show is the product of who's available to be in the band at the time, and what their level of competence is at the time the tour takes place."[6] The Vaudeville band was only together for two years, coming to an abrupt end when Zappa was pushed from the stage into the orchestra pit of London's Rainbow Theatre by enraged 'fan', Trevor Howell. "He wound up spending a year in jail for inflicting 'grievous bodily harm' on me,"[7] wrote Zappa, whose larynx was crushed in the fall, changing the pitch of his voice forever. He stayed in a leg cast and wheelchair for most of 1972.

Fast-forward to the summer of 1987, and Zappa finally does decide to hit the road again. Mann was one of the first musicians he contacted: "I was in Utah at the time, with Repercussion Unit, and it was a great call!" Thunes says "I was never the first to know when we were going to tour again. I lived in Northern California and got a call saying 'We're touring again.' Thanks, Frank!" Out of the blue, Volman and Kaylan call Zappa up and he invites them to rehearse with his band at a facility in Hollywood. The band comprises Thunes, Mann, vocalist/guitarist Ike Willis', drummer Chad Wackerman'' and keyboard player Mars - all veterans of previous Zappa touring bands. They attempt songs performed by the Flo & Eddie-era Mothers (*Strictly Genteel, Magic Fingers, Call Any Vegetable, Dog Breath, Wonderful Wino, Mom & Dad, Take Your Clothes Off When You Dance, Magdalena*); a couple of later Zappa songs (*Ms. Pinky*, about a 'lonely person device', and *The Blue Light*); and an unrecorded one entitled *Wanda La Rue* - better known to fans as *Jewish & Small* - "a nice, complicated musical tone poem" penned by Zappa, Kaylan told the author. It was performed live just once by the Vaudeville Mothers (on 12th June 1970), when Frank introduced it as *Giraffe*, "a fantasy about indiscriminate use of ovens in America". Mann says, "They did it one afternoon that I know of. It was the most fun I saw them having during that time period - remembering old routines a capella over the mic with Frank. That was cool to behold... they were just cracking each other up - and it was always so great to see Frank laugh like that. They were not there long, though. I think it was difficult for them to fit in - they were not band members - too big for that. But not the stars either; that is Frank only, and Frank was paying the bills. I think right after that, it hit home for them that 'you can't go back again' and so they bailed. Of course, I could be wrong."

In January 1988, just a month before the tour actually started, Zappa did a phone interview with Kevin Matthews of WLUP

---

*Born 12th November 1955.

** Born 25th March 1960.

Chicago and said Flo & Eddie had discussed the possibility of joining the band for a couple of dates as guest artists only, but nothing had been arranged. In 2006, Volman told me: "It was really sad for me. It was all about money. Frank wanted us to get paid very close to nothing. He had brought together all of these great musicians and when the concept of money came up he had a figure in his head, which was a figure from 1972. So, we wanted 1987 money. Frank was paying 1972 money. It was an easy decision to make. We left the project and never looked back."

Kaylan said the same: "Both Mark and I were very excited to work with Uncle Frank again and went to an entire week of rehearsals back at the familiar Sunset Boulevard location* and it was wonderful. We learned new stuff and played through the old music, without charts. Our grey cells functioned... and our memories and voices - we were both in great shape. In fact, the band sounded wonderful and Frank appeared to be truly happy. Then, about five days in, Frank told us all what we were going to earn. Mark and I had to explain to Mr Zappa that, in fact, we made more in one night as Flo & Eddie than Frank was prepared to pay for two weeks with the reconstituted Mothers. And the rest of band agreed. No one expected, after all we had been through together, that this was to be a charity gig or that all the money would be going to Frank and Gail. We had to back out of the gig, regretfully; we did have an entire summer of shows that were already being booked at the time and our agent couldn't reconcile the idea of working for free, just to be in Frank's presence. Yes, it would have been great. And, if we were rich men, perhaps we would have done the tour, just for the memories. Still, it does bug me a bit that it all still came down to money - as it did with every group that Frank ever assembled. It's a matter of what you think you're worth as a human, not as a Mother Of Invention - that's priceless. Are we human or are we Mothers?

* Both Mann and Thunes dispute this. Mann claims Zappa stopped using the Sunset Boulevard facility in the mid-seventies. Thunes recalls that initial rehearsals took place at what is today the Hollywood Mental Health Center ("which makes sense now" says Thunes) on Vine Street in LA. Rehearsals then moved to the Hollywood Center Studios on Las Palmas, where the final touring line-up evolved.

That one special week of rehearsals was one of the best weeks of my life - I didn't need the so-called tour. Frank was the only true genius I've ever known. And one of the nicest guys. This money stuff was never his concern."

Back in 1990, though, Kaylan went a little further: "We did all these cute little projects for kids, and we wrote for television, and we were radio personalities in Los Angeles, and we got very, very mainstream. By the time Frank came back to us and asked us to rejoin the group, we had finally broken all those negative barriers. We didn't work fifteen years to clean up our image to do one tour and destroy it. [Also] the band was never gonna be called the 'Mothers Of Invention,' it was going to go out on the road as 'Zappa'. Well, I won't be in a band called Zappa, or Santana, or Allman, or anything else, and anybody that thinks they are the whole band has a problem."[8]

Around the same time, Frank was asked why things hadn't worked out with Flo & Eddie, and said "because they decided it would be bad for their career... Howard made the statement that he didn't really feel that he could go on stage, at this point in his career, and sing songs about blow jobs, and, y'know, keep his new young audience. And I said 'fine'."[9]

Thunes: "Flo & Eddie were funny and nice. I was so looking forward to working with them. Flo even turned me on to *Clausthaler*, not that I needed a non-alcoholic beer, but I had quite a few *Kaliber's* in my day and I never really liked them. But yeah, I figure their official line about it - that the audiences at the Turtles' reunion shows they'd been playing large venues with - along with other sixties nostalgia acts - wouldn't understand the levels of real-human story-telling in Frank's songs. They were afraid that audiences who saw their shows might come to a Frank show and be appalled at the level of pornography and scatology involved." As well as their concerns about the "poo-poo, cocky humour",[10] the duo apparently also had some reservations about the political content of Zappa's new songs. And just to add another twist, Willis told me "That movie came out, called *Making Mr. Right* with John Malkovich, and *Happy Together* became a mega hit again. So Flo & Eddie had to go take care of those commitments. I know that was a big factor." Whatever their reasons, Zappa had to rethink things.

Mann and Mars had previously attended Julius Hart College in Connecticut and formed a band together called World Consort - playing "old and new jazz, electric stuff and Hindemith, Bartók and Zappa arrangements. It was really progressive and chaotically jubilant music that seemed just right for 1973," Mann told the author in 2004. Mars was subsequently asked to try-out for Zappa's band, all thanks to Mann. He described his audition as "Probably, for me, the worst possible audition. Frank had a toothache and it was solo. I went to his house and everything was going terribly. He would play certain measures for me, then I'd play it, and then another section... doing strange rhythmic things that I hadn't done since college. I just felt I was on a sinking ship but just holding on to everything. He finally said, after about half an hour, 'Can you sing at all?' And I said, 'Well, I probably know about a thousand songs Frank, but I'm so fucked up now with this audition.' He said, 'Yeah, me too!' I said, 'Would you mind if I just improvise? I mean, I can't remember a whole song all the way through; could I just sing and improvise?' He looked up at the sky and said, 'That's the first good thing you've done today. Let's go for it'.[11] All the frustration I felt just blew. When I finished, I ended up with a bit of the *Wizard Of Oz* which just came in and I was playing it sort of McCoy meets Art Tatum. It was wild. I finished it and there was a space of time while he waited and I was wondering how he felt about it."[12] As it transpired, it knocked Zappa out: "He called Gail, his wife, downstairs and said, 'Listen to this guy blow,' and that saved me. My reading was only adequate for what he wanted, but the improv saved me, I'm sure. Then we talked a lot and he said, 'I guess you won't have to work many Holiday Inns anymore.'"[13] From 1977 to 1982, Mars was a permanent fixture in

Zappa's touring bands. So it was no surprise that he was to have been a part of the '88 tour.

But midway through rehearsals, Mars suddenly walked out. Sadly, Mars did not want to revisit that period with the author to discuss his unexpected departure, but a reliable source explained how it went down: "Frank started the rehearsals, and Arthur Barrow was asked to become the 'Clonemeister'* again, as he had been before every Zappa tour after he had quit the band. Knowing too well what an extreme task that was, he declined and Scott Thunes got the job. They started up, with a rather slim group, and a lot of the arrangements were based upon Tommy's keyboards. However, Mars felt bullied by Thunes, and really bad about the whole situation. After a while, Mars had had enough of the harassments and, during a rehearsal - while FZ was present - he stood up, approached the Clonemeister, whipped it out, and peed on Thunes' back. At the same time, he says to Frank: 'Sorry, Frank - can't take it no more.' Zappa hardly raised an eyebrow, and answered calmly 'That's okay, Tommy.' Then Mars left the band, and never returned."

Thunes remembers it this way: "We were playing, and he's on a riser behind me, and he's stinking of gin. I figure he's brought some in the *Thermos* that's sitting right behind my head next to his feet. At one point, apropos of nothing, he complains to me about something. I don't recall the exact wording, but he used 'Nektor', his pet name for me. I think it was something like, 'What did you say, Nektor?' Simple as that. I shook my head with a scowl on my face he couldn't have seen, and thought 'he's really lost it, now'. He wasn't there the next day. Weird. I'm sure Tommy and Frank had some kind of discussion, but I don't know what it possibly could have been." Mann diplomatically confirms that Mars "seemed unhappy" and quit; he certainly wasn't fired by Zappa. In 2006, Thunes said of Mars, "He's a nice guy. I love him. Wished things went better

* Zappa's term for the rehearsal director.

between us, but personalities are what they are. Musically, he's the most advanced individual I've ever had the pleasure of playing with. I wish him double-happiness for the rest of his life."

For the 1984 tour, Zappa ultimately appointed Thunes as Clonemeister - a post previously occupied by Mann (1978-79) and bassist Barrow (from 1980). Barrow's description of the role: "I guess the term 'clone' in the word 'Clonemeister' refers to one aspect of the job which was to transcribe from the albums and perfectly teach to the band the songs that Frank wanted to perform. Rehearsals lasted eight to ten hours a day, with the Clonemeister running things for the first half or so and Frank taking over when he arrived for the second half. I still had to worry about my own bass and vocal parts, but as Clonemeister, I had to know everyone else's parts as well. It was a quite a difficult job, especially when I first took over. I had a portable cassette recorder and taped the parts of rehearsal when Frank was there. At night, after rehearsal, I would listen to the tapes and make notes or transcriptions of what Frank had come up with that day. The next day I would drill the band on the previous day's changes and additions. Frank changed his mind a lot, so it was hard to keep up with all of that constantly shifting information."[14]

"When I saw Frank in 1980," says Thunes, "it seemed to me that he was very happy with just getting the notes right. Everything else is secondary. And I couldn't understand, after all the early Zappa stuff I'd heard, why he would want somebody as straight-ahead as Arthur."[15] Thunes would replace Barrow the very next year: "I auditioned, won the job, then helped Frank audition drummers. This was probably my favourite single episode in the early period of being with Frank. In the studio, 21, just fresh off the boat, and I'm assisting the master in forming his musical future. But it really was quite easy at first. So many drummers came and went during a single day that it was mind-boggling. Every ten or twenty minutes, there was somebody else sitting on the already-set-up drum set. IN, OUT,

IN, OUT, all day long. Some were funny in how limited they were, and how could they possibly think they had a chance? But people will surprise, and some with the least amount of actual talent in drumming - at that level - were the most in-your-face about their abilities. The phrase 'Have a nice one, Guy,' came from a person who'd shown absolutely no abilities in any areas that Frank thought important, and he was given short shrift. He got up without a trace of chagrin and at the door, turned around and said the immortalised words with a smile and a wave of his hand. I wish I'd had the level of self-confidence at that period in my life (or before, or afterwards. When it was important, I mean)."

"We really liked this one guy, and he was "IN" as far as I was concerned. Red hair, glasses, possibly a beard? But he was nice and played the shit out of them drums, he did. One night, a LA-based entertainment TV show crew came up to the house to tape some stuff about Frank, as he was putting out a new album, recording, and putting a touring group together. This drummer and I were there so we were 'part of the band.' I was thinking that things were going rather smoothly but, for whatever reason, one day he wasn't there anymore and we were auditioning again. Chad came in soon after. The main reason I got hired was that Frank wanted to see me work with Lisa Popeil. He'd already 'hired' her, I guess, and wanted to see how we'd get along. She jumped on my back and let me ride her around inside the studio within a few minutes of our meeting. He saw chemistry and was happy. Later, I guess a week into rehearsing, she couldn't follow along on a simple blues (she was classically trained, and a motherfucker at operatic singing and piano playing), and she was gone the next day. I was bummed, but it wasn't my call. Soon we had Bobby Martin⁺. Then we had our band."

In 2006, when the author asked Thunes for more about the session with Popeil, he said, "You mean the time we were in the

⁺ Born 29th June 1948.

bathroom together, making out? I don't recall much about that particular time, so I was glad she mentioned it in song. I fondly recall her soft smooth skin, and her bounteous breasts and her obvious sexual passion, but I'm a gentleman and she's a lady and we don't talk about such things. Also, I can't mention what Frank told me about her without her permission, so that will probably stay hidden until after her death. I love her. She's a sweetie."

Popeil told the author, "Frankly, I don't remember jumping on Scott's back, but why would he make that up! I do remember that I was a pretty free spirit in those days, so I wouldn't put it past myself. The lyric idea in *Lisa's Life Story* was actually to make it seem as though Frank was the 'perfect hunk' but then, at the end, throwing in the zinger 'and blond' to deflate the build-up. So Scott, I love you too, but it was for the Boss."

When Thunes resumed the role of Clonemeistering in 1987, he told the author: "Frank never told me anything at all except what songs to rehearse. I had total free reign about every aspect of anything to do with Clonemeistering and bass playing. Earlier, of course, I was rigidly expected to rock the fuck out of Frank's bass lines but also to follow them to a T and give them eyebrows' where possible. After 1982, it was possible. Once I had the music in me, and made it mine, I owned the bass position and everything to do with it."

Previous Clonemeister Mann says, "I used my own percussion arrangements too, but when FZ came in he would refine various parts within the band - including Scott's." I asked whether he had any advice to pass on to Thunes regarding the role, but he says not: "We have different styles."

' *"Songs written with one idea in mind have been known to mutate into something completely different if I hear an 'optional vocal inflection' during rehearsal. I'll hear a 'hint' of something (often a mistake) and pursue it to its most absurd extreme. The 'technical expression' we use in the band to describe this process is: 'putting the eyebrows on it'."*
[From *The Real Frank Zappa Book* by Frank Zappa with Peter Occhiogrosso (Simon & Schuster, 1990).]

With Mars now gone, keyboard, tenor sax and French horn player Robert 'Bobby' Martin was brought back in. Martin had played every tour with Zappa since 1981, as had vocalist/guitarist Ray White (as well as an earlier stint between October 1976 and March 1977). White joined rehearsals in 1987 but later disappeared. Thunes: "I never found out what happened to Ray. There were some theories, but they don't wash. Drugs? Ray tired of the racism inherent in either the songs or Frank's attitude?" Thunes may just be being mischievous here, but Zappa certainly wasn't a very tolerant person; very dictatorial and rarely admitting he was ever in the wrong, he argued that his song lyrics simply reflected his experiences. So when the Anti-Defamation League of the B'nai B'rith complained about his song *Jewish Princess* - a humorous look at Jewish stereotyping - rather than apologise, he said "such creatures do exist, and they deserve to be 'commemorated' with their own special opus,"[16] and proceeded to write another about Catholic girls. It could be argued that songs like *Nig Biz* and *You Are What You Is*, plus his Thing-Fish character, have racist undercurrents, but Willis and White's involvement make it difficult to substantiate - indeed, Zappa had long worked with 'integrated' bands: his first, the Blackouts, consisted of three blacks, two Mexicans and Terry Wimberly, who "represented the other oppressed peoples of the earth"[17]. As regards his attitude, Gary 'Magic' Marker - who worked with Captain Beefheart & His Magic Band in the late sixties, including on the legendary *Trout Mask Replica* album, produced by Zappa - recently had this to say: "he was such an arrogant asshole. It's not good to speak of the dead that way, but he really was. Some of it was humorous and for effect and some of it was genuine arrogance."[18]

The official line on White's disappearance was that his family home had been burgled. Willis confirms this, and adds: "They were living in San Francisco, and in 1987 things started getting really bad there. So Ray came to stay with me. But then one day he left my house and I didn't see him again for ten years." Nobody but Ray knows the true story behind his vanishing act, but White unwittingly paved the way for long-time Zappa fan, Mike Keneally[*], to fulfil his dream.

Like many fans around that time, Keneally called the Zappa Hotline (818-PUMPKIN) in late September 1987 and discovered that Zappa was in rehearsals with a new band. "My initial thought was 'Cool. I get to see another Zappa show.' But upon further reflection I realised that this would very likely be my final opportunity to work with him. So I called back early enough to get an actual human on the phone the next day. I informed [them] who I was, that I could sing and play keyboards and guitar, and that I didn't know if Frank was auditioning but I was highly conversant with the Zappa repertoire and would love a chance to try out." A few days later, his phone rang: "I was asked by a woman if I would hold for Frank Zappa. 'I understand you know everything I've done. I don't believe you. Get your ass up here and prove it.' Frank gave me a list of some of the tunes the band was soon to rehearse. He said I should come up that evening for an audition, prepared to play *What's New In Baltimore?* and *Sinister Footwear II*. The rehearsal space was enormous. Bob Rice [Frank's 'sample trimmer'] was playing a Synclavier sequence of *The Black Page #1*; I plugged into Ike Willis' rig and chumped along with it. Frank was not horrified. He asked to hear the two songs he'd mentioned on the phone and I chumped through those as well. Then Frank wanted to test my repertoire comprehension and started suggesting random song titles. I presented presentable versions... we harmonised, vocally, on a couple of things. He asked if I knew *G-Spot Tornado* on guitar. I didn't but I had learned *Night School*, so he had Bob Rice get the Synclavier print-out of the score to read along as I played the melody. When I got done one of the famous eyebrows rose heavenward: 'There was only one wrong note'. I started feeling really good around this time. Then he set out the music for *Strictly Genteel* on top of a DX-7 and asked me to play the piano part. I couldn't

---

[*] Born 20th December 1961.

sight read worth a damn, so I squinted at the page and played it by ear. I must have done a reasonable job because at this point he shook my hand and said I was a remarkable musician, and that I'd best return for the rehearsal on Monday so 'the rest of the band can witness your particular splendour'."[19]

The band was expanding: "The Fowlers appeared magically by dint of Frank's hiring genius along with some of their cribbage-playing buddies. I know that they're geniuses and all, but they brought along with them some rather normal performers. I never understood that. But the Fowlers, they had 'it', whatever it is," says Thunes, with reference to the Fowler brothers - Bruce (trombone) and Walt (trumpet/flugelhorn) - and their friends Paul Carman" (alto/soprano sax), Albert Wing[†] (tenor sax) and Kurt McGettrick[††] (baritone sax).

Says Keneally: "Bruce Fowler was in the rehearsal room the night I came to audition, so I'm sure the plan was in place but wasn't explicitly spelled out to me - I seem to recall being surprised the day I came to rehearsal and found that the riser for the horn section had been constructed."

Bruce Lambourne Fowler first played with Zappa in 1972 in his Mothers of Invention/Hot Rats/Grand Wazoo 20-piece big band, and then was briefly part of the 'Roxy' band, and continued playing for a few more years before 'defecting' to Captain Beefheart's Magic Band to play trombone (or 'air bass'). Nowadays he is a composer, orchestrator and conductor for many popular Hollywood films. His brother Walt was a part of the Mothers' tenth anniversary 'elsewhere' band before touring and/or recording with the likes of Billy Cobham, George Duke, Johnny "Guitar" Watson and Flo & Eddie. Carman, Wing and McGettrick had never previously worked

* Born 2nd March 1955.
** Born 31st December 1955.
† Born 19th July 1952.
†† Born 1st July 1946; died 6th May 2007.

with Zappa.

With the line-up now into double-figures, it remained unclear to Keneally whether Willis was to actually be involved, as his visits seemed to him to be more social calls than anything else. "There was about a week of vocalist auditions before Ike officially joined", remembers Keneally, "thank God - the other guys who auditioned were a shockingly motley lot. I remember being stunned that a person of Frank's position in the industry was giving any of these guys a shot - but then he was doing just that for me, wasn't he?" Willis, however, told the author there was never any doubt about his involvement: "Frank always called me and said, 'Okay, rehearsals start on such and such a date'. I knew when rehearsals were starting; Mike didn't. Yes, I was there, but I never hung around. When Frank says be there, I'm there. He didn't allow hanging around: it was time to go to work and I was there. You've got to remember that by the time Keneally came in, there were two different bands: there was me, Flo & Eddie, Ed and Tommy. And Chad and Frank. And Ray. Then, a couple of days later, there was no Tommy, no Flo & Eddie. And then there was Keneally. And Scott and Chad. And Ray and me and Frank. Within a week, there was two different bands. Rehearsals started on 2nd October 1987."

On his first day rehearsing with the band, Keneally introduced himself to Wackerman, Martin and Mann, all of whom received him "with politeness. Then came a tall, head-shaven, impolite force of nature skateboarding into and all around the enormous facility. This combination punk-rocker/Marine drill sergeant on wheels was, of course, Thunes. He skated up to my feet (he was on the floor, I on the riser) and I immediately proffered my hand. 'Hello, my name's Mike Keneally, I enjoy your playing a great deal and I'm pleased to

---

* Keneally told Fred Tomsett: *"There was one guy who was an amazingly accomplished singer technically. He's done a lot of background vocals on albums and stuff; he's incredible. Frank tried to teach him He's So Gay, and there was just no way. It was funny how, to me, having an instant grasp of a melody is something that you just do and don't think about it. But a lot of really accomplished people just need to be so prepared and so contrived for days before they try to sing something, and that's completely against the 'anything goes' mentality that should be a Zappa band."*
[From Hats Off To Mike Keneally by Fred Tomsett (T'Mershi Duween No.32, August 1993).]

meet you'. 'Thank you. What are you DOING here?' 'I'm auditioning to play in the band'. 'OH GOD!' He skateboarded away. Instantly, he returned. 'Can you play *T'Mershi Duween?*' The song had yet to be released officially, though I was exceedingly familiar with it through bootlegs. I'd never played it, and as this was my first day, I didn't want to misrepresent my knowledge of the repertoire, so I told him I didn't know it. He snuffed, huffed and skated away. I began to gingerly piece the *"Duween"* melody together on the guitar. I was playing unamplified, and Thunes was about a football field and a half away, but somehow he heard my unplugged electric over the sound of his racing wheels. 'YOU KNOW IT!' he shrieked, and skated back. He began barking string/fret positions at me and after a minute I was playing the melody to his satisfaction... at least he appeared satisfied because he didn't say anything to wound me, he just skated away once again."[20]

It was well known that Zappa would re-arrange old songs on a whim, or to suit the abilities of the musicians at his disposal, and with such a big band the possibilities were endless. Zappa would also legendarily rehearse a large number of songs before hitting the road so that he could change the set list every night (one of the many things that made seeing him in concert such a joy). The 1988 tour would see over 100 songs performed live, with a further 30 plus played during sound checks (including *I'm The Slime*, which sounded magnificent with the horn section). Unusually, for Zappa, a large number of cover tunes were also played alongside some brand new material. On introducing new Zappa songs, Mann says "I loved the early new songs FZ was introducing in 1977; they were a new compositional form compared with the classics circa. 1974. In 1978-79 I was maybe less enthusiastic: the tunes did not have the same depth. Some of them did. A lot of what went on for that group of material was FZ connecting disparate musical elements simply because they were there. 1981-82 was a fantastic time for new compositions - every one of them. Even *Cocaine Decisions*. Big fun then. While I loved to see the inner compositional sense of FZ alive in the creation of *Jezebel Boy*, etc. in 1987-88, overall there was not much new compositional stuff. Sadly, I must say that the feeling at that time was hollow."

Keneally explains how Zappa went about introducing the new pieces: "Usually by bringing a set of lyrics to rehearsal, and then gradually teasing an arrangement together, a melody or chord change at a time - he would play melodies on the guitar or sing them, dictate notes to the horn section, suggest rhythms, tell us the chords he was hearing, etc. But there weren't any charts presented for the new material, except for some horn charts he wrote in airports and hotels during the tour, several of which were incorporated into *When Yuppies Go To Hell* and a few other occurrences."

"I love writing for horns," Zappa said in 1990, when talking about a series of seven, two-hour videotapes "that show *Jesus Thinks You're A Jerk* being put together from scratch. What I'm thinking is, one day, if I ever get around to it, this would be the best way to show how a song starts from nothing, and then turns into this major spectacle featuring Eric Buxton! But it would take a lot of editing... fourteen hours of rehearsal that has to be squeezed down so that you could see each little section being developed."[21]

Of course, he never did find the time, but it would have been something to see: the song features many musical quotes from songs such as *The Old Rugged Cross*, *The Twilight Zone Theme*, *Entry Of The Gladiators*, *Rock Of Ages*, *The Light Cavalry Overture* by Franz von Suppé, Civil War ditties, *The Battle Hymn Of The Republic* and *I Wish I Was In Dixie*, and *Louie, Louie* (something that cropped up in many, many other pieces throughout Zappa's career), as well as a fragment of Frank's own Synclavier piece, *One Man - One Vote* from the *Frank Zappa Meets The Mothers Of Prevention* album. Lyrically, the song was about controversial televangelists Jim Bakker, his then-wife, Tammy

---

* "Louie, Louie *used to be a really cool tune, the Richard Berry version of it. It had a nice arrangement, and a whole different feel to it. It wasn't until* The Kingsmen *version that it became the* Animal House *joke that it is right now."*
[From *They're Doing the Interview Of The Century* by Den Simms, Eric Buxton and Rob Samler (Society Pages, April 1990).).]

Faye, and Marion Gordon "Pat" Robertson - who unsuccessfully campaigned to become the Republican Party's nominee in the 1988 Presidential election. Just as well, as here is a man who believes he could heal AIDS sufferers, whose prayers could change the course of hurricanes, who called for the assassination of the President of Venezuela, and who once said that Scotland was 'a dark land' overrun by homosexuals. Initially, the song featured a 'Twilight Zone' monologue about Robertson performed by Willis. Willis, though, had trouble memorising it and had to rely on a written version to prompt him. This upset Zappa, who chose to drop the monologue after the ninth live performance. On the released version, the monologue is performed by 'the dynamic' Eric Buxton, a fan who followed the band around the East Coast, getting to know most of the personnel.

Of rehearsing the song, Keneally recalls "While it was certainly work, it was just as certainly exhilarating joy, and there was a lot of laughing going on. Frank was almost always in good spirits during the rehearsal period. It was big, crazy, expensive, mind-boggling fun."[22] According to Keneally, though, Zappa was rarely there for the first several hours of each rehearsal - "which were five-day-a-week, eight-hours-a-day affairs."[23]

Mann confirms: "Frank was feeling weak and tired and also involved in a lot of other business decision making. He was not there much." As Clonemeister, Thunes would run the early part of rehearsals. When he called *Alien Orifice* for the first time, Keneally remembers this as the moment he learned that "picking up FZ tunes off of an album is no substitute for seeing the stuff on paper, especially when it comes to odd groupings, because when I played what I believed to be the weird section after the guitar solo, the other gentlemen of the group found my efforts to be greatly amusing. After my attempt at playing the main "*Alien*" melody in Tommy [Mars]-style block chords limped to a miserable death, Scott padded over to me from his position of authority, seemed to grow several inches and glowered: "That was BAD MUSIC'."[24]

Another time, having spent many hours alone practicing *Strictly Genteel*, Keneally remembers "playing it for the first time with the whole band - that song was, for me, an act of acrobatics, switching from keys to guitar and back sometimes in the space of a sixteenth note - I remember Thunes running over to stand next to me and intimidate me right before the wicked keyboard run that comes right after 'every poor soul who's adrift in the storm', and I nailed it and he gave me the finger and ran back to his station..."[25] Keneally also recalls Zappa arriving at rehearsals and starting a Synclavier sequence of *Mo 'n' Herb's Vacation*. "Scott ran like a motherfucker to find the printed bass part, spread it out on the riser and began to play along with it. For many minutes this went on and no one spoke a word. I watched Scott negotiate that fucking piece, my every sinew suffused with awe. This guy was a dead-on motherfucker and I was NOWHERE near his league."[26] On the fourth day of his audition/rehearsal period, Zappa called Keneally over to say that White's whereabouts were still a mystery, and that as he seemed to be 'doing an okay job' he would be in the band - unless Ray returned. "He extended his hand and I had no choice but to accept the gig on these shaky terms. Even to get that much, though, was a mind-blowing triumph. The rest of the band congratulated me enthusiastically, none more so than Scott, who had not stopped giving me shit for four days solid."[27] Clearly a strange bond between Thunes and the new boy was forming, and before long Keneally was formally onboard.

With the final twelve-piece band now intact, Keneally began to relax and have the time of his life. "Many tunes were rehearsed which did not make their way into the live repertoire. Many hours were spent on a weird, mechanical Devo-sounding arrangement of *I Come From Nowhere*. I sang lead on a medley of *She Painted Up Her Face*, *Half A Dozen Provocative Squats* and *Shove It Right In*, which we rehearsed constantly, then stopped rehearsing suddenly. We rehearsed *Jezebel Boy* a trillion times, then played it ONCE during the tour. One day I spent about twelve hours learning *Moggio* - when I was done, I felt like I'd been skiing for a week solid. When Frank called the tune in rehearsal, most of the guys in the band hadn't worked on it and it didn't sound very promising, so he said, 'Omit that'. The song was stricken from the repertoire that quickly. Scott saw my jaw hit the floor and said 'That's what you call The Clamp'. And no impassioned defence on the song's behalf could loosen it."[28]

The author asked Walt Fowler if any tunes were dropped that he really wanted to play: "We just rehearsed a lot of stuff. I don't remember any tunes that were thrown out - except for *Forty-Four* and *Times Beach*... he asked us if those tunes were playable, or should the computer play them?" *Times Beach* was originally composed by Zappa for the Aspen Wind Quintet - a piece in five movements, two of which appeared on his *Yellow Shark* album, performed by Ensemble Modern. But I'd not heard of *Forty-Four* before. Aware that Keneally had mentioned a Synclavier composition called *Thirty-Five* - which proved "IMPOSSIBLE to play. It eventually became *Navanax* on *Civilization Phaze III*,"[29]

The author asked him about *Forty-Four* A similar scenario occurred he explained: "*Forty-Four* was indeed an unreleased Synclavier piece. As I recall, the song title came from the impossible-to-play rhythmic figure in the opening bar: 44 notes spaced evenly across the bar - I don't remember the time signature though. We probably attempted to play about fifteen seconds of the song in rehearsal before Frank waved it to a halt!"

Most of the band seem to agree that rehearsals went on a lot longer than was necessary. Says Mann, "Progress was very slow, but not due to the players - due to the amount of resistance that was in the air. Every break you got five to fifteen people wandering around the rehearsal space saying. 'Fuck this guy...' growl and simmer." A rehearsal tape from December 1987, without Zappa, however, reveals the musicians to be in fine fettle with Willis, Keneally and Martin handling most of the vocals. Also included were some odd sound effects, triggered by Mann on the Synclavier: "I did all that sound design," he told me in 2004. "Walt Fowler vocalises all the 'Ooowww' stuff - and then I modulated it with a pitch wheel. Bruce did the 'Ooouuueeeouuugggg', not to be confused with Walt's 'Aaaahhhhhhhh' or 'Bep-Bep-Bep'. Those guys just make those sounds anyway - but when I heard it, I summoned them to 'speak into the mic, please'. Ike did the Sam Kinison 'Death Scream'. Those samples kind of became the signature sounds of that tour. The Agony and the Ecstasy: we laughed, we cried - it is all there in those samples."

One person lucky enough to witness the band rehearsing was musician and writer, Billy James (aka the ANT-BEE, who briefly worked for Zappa in the eighties providing rhythm charts). "As memory serves, these were the last two rehearsals before the band hit the road for the fateful 'final' tour. The group was rehearsing at a large soundstage in West Hollywood˙. I remember it being rather informal for the people attending watching the band; there were few chairs, so people just stood or sat on top of the PA speakers and tour cases. There were maybe thirty people watching the rehearsals. I vividly recall at one point turning around looking back at the entrance and seeing Garth Hudson from The Band watching very intently - you could tell he was impressed. The first rehearsal Frank had to leave early due to a dentist appointment. I remember Frank getting ready to leave and then Ike Willis shouting out jokingly, 'okay, short rehearsal - let's go!' Everyone laughed - even Frank. He grinned and said, 'No, no - you guys have to stay and rehearse!' The mood was jovial with an air of excitement about the upcoming tour. I had just sent Frank my textbook on rhythm (which, although never published, was endorsed by Bill Bruford, Robert Fripp, Chester Thompson and Jan Akkerman to name a few) for his perusal a week

* According to Ed Mann, these rehearsals took place at Zoetrope Studios, which is where the final band came together.

or so before, so I briefly spoke with him about it. The next night, Frank was there the entire time rehearsing and, for the most part, conducting the band. I remember how incredibly tight the horn section featuring Bruce and Walt Fowler and Albert Wing was - as was the entire band. If there was eventual friction within the ensemble during the tour, you sure could not detect it from watching them perform. Also, the Synclavier was used quite a bit during the rehearsal; sort of sitting there alone in the middle of the stage playing by itself (sort of) - I believe Mike Keneally was also playing it. Most of the music performed that evening was instrumental. I overheard one attendee say, 'Wow, the music is like floating around the room!' And it was - due to where we were seated (on top of a road case) and the position of the stage monitors and the speakers, the music had a 'surround' sound to it. It was truly magical. I sadly never got to see any of the ensuing concerts, but I'll always cherish the opportunity to attend the final rehearsals and witness a rare glimpse into Zappa's intense rehearsing prowess."

Ensuing concert dates had been arranged for an initial tour of the East Coast of the United States, and then on to Europe. But Thunes had been struggling in his Clonemeister role, with certain band members - principally, the horn players - turning up late for rehearsals. Although they deny this, Wing did admit to the author that they had deliberately tried to upset Thunes before hitting the road. On one occasion, "Walt or Bruce - being sandwiched in between Paul and Kurt sometimes made it difficult to distinguish them due to the similarities in their voices - said something that sent Scott scurrying out to the guard booth in a huff, from which I can't recall; I do recall Scott was kinda pouty after the incident, though." When I asked what he himself did to annoy Thunes, Wing says it was simply a case of "just being there. He tried to get me fired. Scott wrote a piece and asked Bruce, Walt, Kurt and Paul to rehearse it. And I got that. But Frank said 'I like you', out of the blue - words I thought I would never hear come out of his mouth. You just had to be there to be able to understand the vibe."

Thunes vehemently denies trying to get Wing fired, but told Thomas Wictor: "After a while, I yelled and screamed and browbeat and acted like a prima donna fool, and it must have been pretty embarrassing, but I didn't know what else to do. I had bad skills; nobody taught me how to do this. At one point, Ed Mann just said, 'I'm not going to play while you're conducting. I'm gonna wait for Frank. I won't deal with you.' By the time we got out on the road, it was already dead."[30] When the author asked Willis if Zappa was aware of what was happening, he assured him that: "Frank knew what was going on, at all times. Actually, there was one incident where Scott just pissed off Bruce Fowler and everybody in the horn section. And I said, 'Okay, everybody stop. Go to lunch.' And the phone rang. And it was Frank, calling from the house saying 'What's going on down there?' He wasn't even there. He knew what was going on. I have no idea how, because this had just happened, like, less than a minute after I'd said 'Lunch! Everybody take a break; Scott, go over there.' The phone rang and it was our sound mixer, Harry Andronis, saying 'Ike, it's Frank - he wants to talk to you.' And Frank said 'What's going on. Talk to me. What the hell is happening down there?' Less than a minute. He knew exactly what was going on. He was kept abreast of everything. I don't know how he did it... but he did it. Trust me." And it wasn't just Mann and the horn section that had a problem with Thunes, as Willis also explains: "Things started getting really tense between Scott and Chad, so Frank tried to split things up: for the last month of rehearsals, I was conducting the band and Scott was handling the dots on the page. My other job was to sit on Scott and make sure nobody killed him!"

When I asked Walt Fowler about the pre-tour atmosphere, he diplomatically said, "It was good, no feeling of unease at all... everybody was very much looking forward to the tour." Indeed, Zappa himself appeared quite relaxed the fortnight before the tour commenced when he attended a performance of his composition *The Perfect Stranger* by the Juilliard Chamber Orchestra and (on the day before the author's 30th birthday) co-hosted a benefit at the 4D nightclub for the Fundamentalists Anonymous Legal Task Force. The Task Force was co-founded by Jim Luce with the following goals: 1) accountability of religious leaders to their followers; 2) deterrence of future acts of abuse or misconduct; and 3) protection and expansion of the legal rights of religious consumers. The fundraiser on 29 January was devoted to helping disenchanted members of Jim and Tammy's Praise The Lord Club to get their money back*. Zappa's co-host that night was Steve Allen, on whose television show the young Zappa appeared in March 1963 playing his sister's bicycle**. Luce prepared a poster for the event depicting Jim and Tammy behind bars, but "It was so good, people pulled them down to decorate their dorm rooms."[31] Never mind, though; Zappa would ensure the misdemeanours of the televangelists would get plenty of publicity while on the road.

---

* Jim and Tammy founded the PTL Club in the mid 1970s; it collapsed in 1987 after revelations that $287,000 had been paid from the organisation to buy the silence of Jessica Hahn, who had had a sexual encounter with Jim.

** Short extracts from a decent 'print' of this show were included in Chrome Dreams' 2008 DVD, *Frank Zappa And The Mothers Of Invention In The 1960s*. In 2010, the full soundtrack, transferred from the original film, was released by Crossfire Publications as *Cyclophony* on the download-only *Paul Buff Presents The Pal And Original Sound Studio Archives, Vol. 1*.

CHAPTER TWO
Welcome To The United States

When interviewed with his daughter, Moon Unit, by *Playboy* magazine in 1982 following the surprise success of the *Valley Girl* single, Zappa had this to say about touring, "When you go on the road, the more girls who get pooched, the happier the whole tour is. That's the key to a happy tour. The band and the crew that don't get laid when they go out there are the meanest, grouchiest, most unpleasant bunch of people to hang out with. 'Go out and get pooched,' I tell them."[1] It seems Moon herself was not too impressed by this as, 27 years later, she wrote "Our rock royalty of a dad toured for nine months out of the year, cheated on my mom when he was away, but always came back to us, to sleep all day and work all night. When I was little, 'Mom' meant let people be themselves so Dad doesn't leave us for a groupie and we can keep food on the table and a roof over our heads. 'Mom' meant do your own thing, because my mom didn't have time to play with us or teach us conflict resolution - she was too busy making sure my dad didn't leave us for a groupie. 'Mom' meant yell a lot to get us to stop screaming so Dad can sleep so he can work and doesn't leave us for a groupie."[2]

In his autobiography, he readily admits to his bad attitude towards 'typical familyism': "Thanksgiving rolls around, and the kids want to have a Thanksgiving dinner - they lay out the dining room table with all kinds of food... they have to drag me, kicking and screaming, out of the studio to go upstairs and join them. I hate sitting around acting traditional to amuse the little folks who happen to be genetically derived from larger-folks-who-buy-them-sportswear, enduring a family meal, during which I might be required to participate in some mind-numbing family discussion. I eat, and get the fuck out of there as fast as I can. It's the same with Christmas dinner or any other traditional family gathering. I can't stand it."[3] Of course, he never did leave his family. But he clearly led a hedonistic lifestyle, with scant regard for the feelings of those around him; it was all very much about having fun while getting the job done.

During the opening US dates of the 'Broadway The Hard Way' world tour, Zappa was in high spirits and referred to his band as the best in the world. At the end of the first night, during *Strictly Genteel*, he had the road crew come out and dance around on stage wearing aprons, saying "I believe a happy crew is an efficient crew... so, if there are any members of that special species out there that goes for a guy with a wrench in his pocket, take a look ladies: here they are. Meet them at the load-out after the show." He also talked about travelling around the States in a bus with eleven guys as being a "little bit like going to camp; we have some laughs".[4]

In truth, Zappa had two buses for the band in 1988: smoking and non-smoking - or, as Willis put it, "There was the guys-who-loved-to-hang-out-with-Frank bus, and there was the salty old veterans' bus." On the smoking bus with Zappa were his bodyguard and road manager, the Fowler brothers, McGettrick, Thunes and Keneally (who didn't actually smoke). Everybody else travelled on the non-smoking bus.

From his earliest tours, Zappa never really hung with the band and crew that often: usually he stayed in better hotels, as he claimed he needed the space to write music and conduct interviews. Mann recalls other changes in 1988, "The loss of manager Bennett Glotzer[*] was - in my opinion - a big one; Bennett made sure the family feeling was always present. The disappearance of that was felt big time. The new, faceless managers were slick suit-wearing

---

[*] Zappa's personal manager since 1977.

Hollywood hot-shots. Their approach was that Frank was walled off and isolated. Although it was possible to talk with him, he was just never around. The band and Frank were kept apart for much of the tour." Willis agrees: "The 1988 tour would have been my absolute favourite tour only the people who were managing Frank at the time were not my favourite people."[5]

Thunes tells how the tour buses had two lounges, separated by a door. "I got the whole back lounge to myself, virtually every night. On the other bus was everybody else in the band, and every night, all night long, Ike Willis would just be up and down the aisle, hanging out with the different groups of people, talking, talking, talking. Watching the movie in the front, the movie in the back, bobbing back and forth, just driving everybody bananas."[6] Thunes describes tenor saxophonist Albert Wing as another "extremely vociferous talker". I asked Willis about this, who said "Well, I talk to everybody. The thing is, at that point I'd been with the Fowler Brothers' band almost as long as I'd been in the Zappa band. So Albert and I were good friends. That's just us."

Keneally recalls "a lot of great dinners with Scott and Chad during the early stages of rehearsal, me thinking how cool that the two of them were the same age and had come into the band at the same time, and how close they must've been; after awhile, Chad stopped coming to dinner with us, and Thunes and I became allies as the shit started to come down on him."[7] Says Thunes, "for some reason [Chad] decided to agree with the negative energy that was building up on the other side of the highway while our bus is cruising mellowly at 4.00 a.m. and I'm sitting in the back and watching movies and drinking beer and smoking clove cigarettes and just having a wonderful time. Everybody is in the other bus slowly being driven mad with anger [and] frustration. And you could imagine what it was like when we'd stop, and people would come onto our bus, and it was mellow, and they would see me in the back."[8]

But none of this growing disharmony was evident on the opening date of the tour - indeed, though the troubles rapidly worsened backstage, out front the band appeared wonderful most nights. Says Mann, "The reason that the music sounded good was because everyone loved Frank so much and no one, no matter how miserable they were, chose to quit and leave him high and dry." A sentiment clearly shared by the audience who, when Frank ambled onto stage at the Palace Theatre in Albany, New York on 2nd February 1988, and asked "Did you miss me?" let out a huge roar. He advised that they would get to hear the premiere "of a whole bunch of new songs" before the band launched into a vastly re-arranged new-age version of the *Black Page #2*. He then introduced the band - including "the new guy", Keneally, and "my trusted Clonemeister", Thunes.

Zappa had long urged young America to register to vote via notes on album sleeves. And for this tour - which was in an election year - he tried to set up voter-registration booths in the lobbies of his US concerts, asking audiences to go register during the intermission. When the band played the Tower Theatre in Philadelphia, the Registrar of Voters "refused to send over voter registration slips because he said 'we already have enough registered voters.' He liked things the way they were. The other place we had trouble was Washington DC where the comment was made that 'we don't know about his politics and so we're not going to send anyone over.' But... we managed to register 11,000 people.'"[9] Although he was very anti-Ronald Reagan and the Republican Party's policies, he was by no means a Democrat either. But he strongly felt that you had no right to criticise any party if you didn't actively participate. In Albany, he introduced some of his new songs as being part of a 'Republican Retrospective Medley', which "takes us through the whole history of Republican shenanigans, right up to the present time". This starts with an old song about President Nixon, called *Dickie's Such An Asshole* (not performed since 1973, and not actually released on disc until April 1988 on the *You Can't Do That On Stage Anymore Sampler*), which "is followed by a new song called *When The Lie's So Big*, dealing specifically with Pat Robertson's campaign for the Presidency. This is then followed by *Planet Of The Baritone Women*, about male junior executives who carry purses and wonder why their female bosses think of them as a bunch of little weasels. Then we have a song called *Any Kind Of Pain*, which is about women in advertising, followed by *Jesus Thinks You're A Jerk* which deals with Jim and Tammy and, once again, our old favourite, Pat Robertson." After the intermission/voter-registration, Zappa then conducted a 'Presidential Popularity Poll', which had many shouting his name. Zappa had often talked about standing for President - arguing that "even if I didn't know shit from Shinola, could I do any worse?" In the early nineties, he actually hired two political consultants to do a feasibility study on a Zappa bid for President and, in 1991, he formally announced his intention to stand as an independent candidate in the 1992 election. Sadly, his failing health precluded him from taking it further.

It was becoming quite clear that part of his motivation for getting back out on the road in 1988 was political. But also the quality of his new big band and the music they performed must have been another huge factor. As well as the new songs, many old favourites were tinkered with - some quite extensively. *Packard Goose* from *Joe's Garage*, for instance, replaced Zappa's guitar solo with a medley of the *Royal March* from Stravinsky's *L'Historie Du Soldat* and the *Theme from Bartók's Piano Concerto 3* - which he described as "one of the most beautiful melodies you ever heard in your life"[10] (all orchestrated by Thunes, who told me Zappa "tweezed it a bit, so it's not really all mine. But I take credit for it because he stole credit for the music for *Promiscuous*, as bad as it is."). While *Tell Me You Love*

---

* A ham-fisted rap song about President Reagan's Surgeon General, Charles Everett Koop, that was played just the once on tour. Frank obviously thought highly of it, though, as it appeared on the *Broadway The Hard Way* album, and he reproduced its lyrics in *The Real Frank Zappa Book*. Thunes told Den Simms *"Frank just said, 'Do a rap rhythm.' Technically, rap songs don't have any 'music'. So what's the bass to do? I wrote the bass part. Frank never told me what to do on that song. That's my bass line, one hundred percent. I never considered it until Keneally pointed it out. And he's Mr Nice Guy. He's not doing anything to make anybody annoyed. He just said. 'Did you ever think about that?' I said 'No.' I don't give a shit about it enough to cause a stink. I'm not gonna tell Frank about it, or ask for any fuckin' profits, or anything. That's not gonna do any good at all. Frank doesn't have time to take care of everything. There's no need with a piece of music like that anyway."*
[From The Obsessive Analyst by Den Simms (Society Pages USA #9, May 1992).]

Me, originally from *Chunga's Revenge*, had mutated from the 1984 tour's *Don't Be A Lawyer* to the Michael Jackson baiting *Why Don't You Like Me?* Some interesting cover versions were also regularly executed in 1988, including reggae-fied renditions of Ravel's *Boléro* and Led Zeppelin's *Stairway To Heaven*.

Keneally remembers the first gig thus: "It was a very good show and there were witnesses to attest to that fact. If I was nervous at all I didn't notice, and it apparently didn't come across to the audience that I was nervous, because nobody said 'Boy, you sure looked nervous up there'. And it was really fun and easy and it was just very quick; it was over in a flash. During *King Kong* Frank made me play guitar and keyboards simultaneously while singing at the same time, and also had me recite the 'headband' speech from *Teen-age Wind* which I doubled on guitar. "*Stairway*" ended with me on my knees at the front of the stage - all in all a heady experience for my first show with Frank."[11]

They then played three consecutive nights at the Beacon Theatre in New York City: the first was pretty much a re-run of the Albany show, with the notable addition of *Truck Driver Divorce*, during which Frank fired off "an adventurous solo, with Thunes following boldly at every harmonic turn"[12]; the second saw the introduction of a whole raft of songs - Keneally recalling, "Everybody was mad at Scott, because when Frank had written up the set list, Scott was afraid that the band was incapable of playing *Andy* and *Inca Roads* 'cause we hadn't rehearsed them lately. This got around to Frank, and Frank got around to Scott and said 'I understand you're really nervous about *Andy*'. And Scott said, 'Oh, really I'm not, I'm sure we can handle it'. But when it looked like the show was gonna run long, he decided to cut *Packard Goose* and *Florentine Pogen* and *Andy* and *Inca Roads*. So we were sad. But then we went on for the first encore and did *Catholic Girls* and *Crew Slut* which went over wonderfully."

"I guess Frank didn't feel like leaving the stage as was scheduled for that moment, but instead of going straight into the final encore, he said 'Let's do *Andy* and *Inca Roads*'. And he mentioned that the songs hadn't been performed since 1979 in the United States'. It was wonderful. And then we came back after leaving the stage and did *Illinois Enema Bandit*, which is fun from my point of view because I don't do anything on that song, I just play two harmonics over and over on the outro, so I got to dance around and cavort with dental floss and Scott, and wear a funny hat that said 'Don't Disturb Matter'. Boy, just a ton of fun, and that was the best show we'd done so far."[13]

The third saw many items thrown on stage by the audience which Zappa commented on, occasionally changing song lyrics to accommodate. *King Kong* was interrupted after the mixing console shorted out when someone dropped their drink over the balcony onto it, but they managed to continue playing and, for the encores, all of Zappa's children joined the band on stage. First came Diva, who was serenaded by her father on *The Closer You Are*. Her sister Moon then came out and the siblings danced along to *No No Cherry*. Brother Ahmet cavorted with them during *The Man From Utopia Meets Mary Lou*, then they proceeded to start doing cartwheels across the stage.

Finally, "Dweezil came on and did a solo in *Whippin' Post* which he was totally unsatisfied with," remembers Keneally. "Sounded fine to me but he was really unhappy about it. So he went away, and at the end of *Whippin' Post* we were supposed to go into *I Am The Walrus*, as per usual, but Frank was telling everybody that we were gonna go right into *Watermelon In Easter Hay*. And I realised that if anyone on stage should know that, it's Bobby, so I said to Scott 'Tell Bobby, tell Bobby', and Scott didn't see fit to tell Bobby until Bobby had already closed out *Whippin' Post* by singing 'You know, sometimes I feel that I AM...' And then Scott yelled to him that we

---

* *Andy* was actually performed live for the last time prior to the '88 tour in 1980.

were going right into *Watermelon In Easter Hay*. And then Bobby sang '...not the walrus...' So that was actually very funny, and we went right into *"Watermelon"* then. And the other best moment of the night, apart from Frank singing to Diva, was his last note playing his new Kramer on *Watermelon In Easter Hay*, with the most intense series of harmonic overtones I've ever heard wrenched out of one note - quite cool,"[14]

"That was a really good part of the tour, at the very beginning,"[15] remembers Wing of the show that would prove to be Zappa's last ever in the town he chose to play many of his concerts in. Asked about the audience response so far, Zappa said, "Massively enthusiastic. They really love the band because it sounds bitchin'. And it's a good sounding band... it's like, let's hear some music!"[16] It was quickly becoming evident that this was to be a far more interesting tour than 1984.

After the New York dates, the band travelled to Washington for what some describe as the best shows of the tour, musically. *King Kong* and *A Pound For A Brown* - both instrumentals originally recorded by the Mothers Of Invention for the *Uncle Meat* album - acted as vehicles for improvisation and solos. Keneally said that during sound checks "We rehearsed mostly instrumental stuff, which was encouraging because we haven't been playing a lot of them. We rehearsed *What's New In Baltimore* and *Sinister Footwear* which sounded much better, and *Marque-son's Chicken*, so there should be some variations in the show soon."[17]

These dates also featured two special guests: Daniel Schorr, the Emmy winning American journalist who Zappa coerced into singing *It Ain't Necessarily So*, and Greg Bolognese, who helped with some of the spoken lines in *Crew Slut*. Bolognese was introduced as 'a friend', so when the author met Willis backstage at Zappanale in 2009, I asked about him: " I've known Bolognese since he was a teenager. He used to come to the shows before I joined the band. I met him when he was 15 or 16. And he always used to come to the shows. The New York gang. They always bought the same seats. Front row. I've known those guys forever. And they're still there: Stevie, Eugene, Bolognese, the LaMastro brothers', Jack Conklin... all those guys. Whenever I'm in New York, those guys are there, man. Stevie and Eugene moved to Florida. Colin Romastro moved Upstate, but I see him when I'm in Upstate New York. Greggie still lives on Long Island. Conklin still lives in Manhattan. Joey Psychotic'', he died of a liver ailment about five years ago. The boys, you know? They're very, very loyal."

Onto Philadelphia and, two weeks into the tour, the fun continued (although Keneally's diary reveals that Bruce Fowler asked him to go to his room to talk about some of the problems in the band while they were there). In 1980, the Tower Theatre in Philadelphia was "the birthplace of a marvellous tradition" where Zappa started to collect small articles of feminine underclothing thrown up on stage by girls in the audience. This activity yielded the infamous "Voodoo butter underpants... the pants that nearly broke Tommy Mars' neck"[18] in Chicago. During a radio phone-in in Washington a few days before the Philadelphia shows, Zappa explained that "Voodoo butter is a human by-product which may, in sufficient quantities, infest some of those undergarments that are thrown up onto the stage. To be truly voodoo butter, it must cast a spell on the person who experiences it."[19] Some of these unwashed garments had been turned into a 'panty quilt' by Emily James of Lyons, Colorado and put on display in a Denver art gallery. Zappa urged the continuation of this ritual during the Philly shows in 1988.

At the start of the first encore of the first show, Zappa also raised the subject of 'confinement loaf'. Willis explained to Matthew Galaher, "I read the morning before the show that one of the Senators came up with this idea... what they do in prisons is put

* Colin and Greg LaMaso both grew up with Steve Vai on Long Island; Greg was Steve's roommate at the Berklee College of Music.
** Joey Psychotic appears in Zappa's *Baby Snakes* film, notably during *Camarillo Brillo*.

saltpeter, which is an ingredient in gun powder, [in the food] to lessen the sex drive of inmates. And this Senator was pushing for this to get passed as a law so that murderers, rapists and child abusers will be sort of numbed out of existence mentally. I said 'Look, Frank, you'll love this.' Needless to say, he just dropped a brick!"[20] Zappa told the audience about this and asked, "How long before confinement loaf appears in United States high schools?"[21] Confinement loaf would manifest itself in various lyric mutations subsequently.

For many years, Zappa's bands had altered song lyrics to reflect events and situations on the road, and Zappa would introduce secret words or a phrase for many concerts. This went to some absurd lengths on the '88 tour, with varying degrees of success. His main foil for these would be Willis, who Zappa named his 'jokemeister'. Says Willis "I have a habit of being able to change the words to a tune but they will still rhyme and they would still work. Frank would then laugh and do it back to me and I would do it back. There was a show we did back in Nantes in 1984 and we did almost the entire show by changing the words round, and it still worked. It was great and we laughed all night long. We want to be laughing more than the audience. The audience seem to think it's a written part of the show and it isn't. After all, the band members have to have fun too. It's a good attitude."[22]

But Zappa also wasn't averse to having pre-planned silliness inserted into familiar songs from his huge repertoire. In *The Real Frank Zappa Book*, Zappa tells how he used percussive and vocal sound effects at the end of the '1988 deluxe version of *Peaches En Regalia*'. "When the melody comes in after the second intro, we use 'Fake Devo'*, superimposed on *Twilight Zone* in the rhythm section, while the 'nice little melody' is re-harmonised with an ugly chord travelling parallel. Then there's a short break, and Ike says, 'Whooo-

---

* A musical texture described in *The Real Frank Zappa Book* as "anything absolutely squared off, mechanical, dry and dead-sounding".

oo!' like Count Floyd from SCTV. It doesn't mean anything, but to see Ike Willis pretending to be Count Floyd for one or two beats in the middle of all that is something I find enjoyable - and then, just to make sure that you didn't miss it, when the melody repeats the next time, it stops just a little bit longer and he says, 'Whoooo-oo, whooooooo-oooo!' Of course it's mega-stupid. That's why I like it."[23]

During the second Philly show, Diva and Dweezil again made guest appearances - Diva introducing the song inspired by a story she told her father when she was four or five, *Chana In De Bushwop*. Remembers Keneally, "Set two was scheduled to start with *I Am The Walrus*, but Diva was there and, finally, conscious and in the room long enough to hear *Chana In De Bushwop*, which Frank wanted to play for her. So we started the set with that. She was at the final rehearsal in Los Angeles but fell asleep before we played "*Chana*", and she was supposed to come to one of the shows in NYC and hear *Chana In De Bushwop*, but she got pissed off at her brothers and sister and said 'Well, I'm not going to the show.' So she didn't hear it that night either. This night she was there and ready, so Frank stuck it in the middle of the show where it wasn't originally scheduled. However, Scott's girlfriend also wanted to hear *Chana In De Bushwop*, and she just happened to leave the auditorium right when we played that song. And Scott was sad about that. Somebody's always missing when we play *Chana In De Bushwop*."[24] And if you did not attend that show, you will have missed for sure the one and only live performance of another new song, *Jezebel Boy*. Keneally says the song was rehearsed about "200 times in LA before the tour started, so I don't really understand why we only played it one time. I suppose it's such an 'LA' song that it just never felt right to play it anywhere else."[25]

For the Saint Valentine's Day performance (referred to as the 'freebase show' in US fanzine Mother People), Zappa invited Brother A. West - real name, Andrew West Reid Jr. - to perform an evangelical monologue, to 'drive out the demons' and 'create some balance' to proceedings, during the improvised section of *A Pound*

For A Brown. Introduced as a member of the Reagan administration, he came out and "berated Frank and berated the audience and explained how it was important to spend money on arms for the Contras, and took off his overcoat," explains Keneally. "He was wearing fatigues, and said 'I'll be going down to Nicaragua as soon as this performance is through'. A good selection of clichés presented with a lot of energy, it was really quite impressive. The audience was screaming and throwing things at him, and during the break it became clear to Frank that a lot of the people thought he was for real, so the next set began with Frank assuring the audience that the guy was a friend of his, and not to hurt him if they happened to see him later on."[26]

Zappa was introduced to West by Jeff Stein, who worked on Dweezil's *My Guitar Wants To Kill Your Mama* video. "I saw some of his work. He did some logos for me and some other illustrations: he did the album cover for *Broadway The Hard Way*, and then he did illustrations for the [*Real Frank Zappa*] book... he'd come over and we'd go chapter by chapter through the book, and I'd tell him my ideas [on] how to illustrate what I was talking about. Then he would do sketches, and some of them were not approved by the publisher; they felt the illustrations were in bad taste."[27] West went on to become an award-winning children's television artist who, in 2006, was imprisoned for sexually molesting a six year old girl, as well as possessing and producing child pornography.

Hardcore Zappa fan Den Simms attended that Valentine's Day show, and knew that his seat near the front offered him his best chance to request that Zappa conduct the audience as a musical instrument (something he'd demonstrated on an Australian TV show in 1973). "That morning, I hit up a supermarket for cardboard, various vegetables and dental floss, and I used these items to fashion a large heart with the initials 'FZ' spelled out in the centre with carrots. I figured this would, at least, get his attention. I added the note with the list of 'not so normal requests'. The main intent was at the bottom of the note: '...or blow off all of the above and conduct the fucking audience.' I had no idea that he would honour the entire list!"[28]

Keneally takes up the story: "Among the requests was to have the band do a dance number a la *Approximate*, to sing something a capella, to have Chad sing, and to have Ike do a solo performance with his percussion paraphernalia. And all of these things occurred. First Frank conducted the audience with his various hand signals, as seen on *Video From Hell*, and then Frank held his microphone up to Chad and Chad sang *The Love Boat* theme, which managed to find itself into several other tunes during the show. For the band dance, a bunch of us went up to the front of the stage; there was Scott, Ike, Paul, Ed, Bruce and myself, I'm not sure whether Bobby was there or not - Bobby and Ike were feeling poorly from the night before, they'd been up all night, and it was great that they both got the first solos on *Pound For A Brown*, they were barely able to remain upright. Back to the dance number: Paul had a copy of the music to *Approximate* and put it down on the floor, and we read that and danced the music. There were some people from the audience who joined us, including one transvestite whose name I can't recall. It may have been Sparky. And then Ike played with his toys, including the ray gun I'd given to Ed, his honker, his beeper, his bdlmbdlmbdlmbdlm - I can't remember the name of that thing, the thing that goes bdlmbdlmbdlm when you say 'ointment' in *Florentine Pogen*. And for the a capella performance, Frank, Bobby, Ike and I sang *The Closer You Are*, punctuated by Frank conducting the audience. And that went over well. Frank continued conducting the audience periodically throughout the rest of the set."[29]

At the 16th February show at the Bushnell Auditorium in Hartford, Connecticut, Zappa was rumoured to have received a death threat. While *Jesus Thinks You're A Jerk* was now bereft of its 'Twilight Zone' monologue, the show went on... and on. Keneally: "The first encore was *"Walrus"* and *"Sofa"*, at which point Frank made the announcement that as partial compensation for those members of the audience who were late getting into the auditorium, because of extensive searching procedures and exceptionally complicated registering to vote procedures, the show was going to be made longer, and he whipped *Cruisin' For Burgers* on us at that point; we weren't expecting to play it. But I was very happy to do so because it's such a totally, totally cool song, and tonight was its tour debut. One of my favourites, maybe my favourite song to play."[30]

After the second show in Hartford, Keneally records that he went back to Willis's room and "Ike was being terribly complimentary, saying that of all the puppies whom he has seen come and go, only Chad has rivalled me in terms of making a powerful first impression. Ike is taken with my abilities and my attitude, and lack of ego when it comes to being told by Frank to play something. I just play it like I'm supposed to do. No big deal to me, but apparently other people have bridled at the idea of playing the parts which are dictated to them without immediately embellishing upon them. I'm more than happy to play the stuff as written."[31]

On the first night in Boston, Zappa announced that the show would be tailored to appeal to musicians since they were playing near the Berklee College of Music. Unfortunately, the concert then featured a number of flubs: firstly, alto saxophonist Paul Carman, who had been told specifically by Zappa before the show that he kept screwing up a melody at the start of *The Black Page*, went out and got it wrong again. Carman tried to redeem himself by inserting the correct line in his solo for *Stolen Moments*, drawing a rousing ovation from both band and audience. During the encores, Robert Martin - Curtis Institute graduate, 1971 - then forgot the words of the fifth verse to *Advance Romance*, prompting Zappa to announce "Paul Carman, ladies and gentlemen!", and then to extend proceedings as "We have to stay after school after that one!". Oddly, on the second night in Boston, Zappa dedicated *Yo Cats* to all the Berklee students in the audience, but the band pretended to play along to pre-recorded music (yes, they do what all the big rock groups have done for years - they 'lip-sync' it) while Willis sings the song.

Zappa fan Dot Stein was living in New Hampshire at this time and attended one of the concerts at the Orpheum Theater. "I borrowed my mom's car and drove there with my friend, Jenny Jupiter. The show was incredible. From the first minute to the last I was glued to the speakers. I couldn't stop listening, even to go to the bathroom. After the show, we were sitting in the car and this huge snowstorm was building up. Suddenly somebody was pounding on our windshield, and I recognised Scott Thunes. He was yelling 'Hi, my name is Scott!', as if we didn't know! He told us he had been so busy giving autographs that he missed the tour bus when it left. He wanted to know if we knew our way around Boston and if we could take him to the Holiday Inn. Scott was really friendly, and we talked all the way to the hotel like old pals. When we got there, he invited us up to his room... so we were hanging around in Scott's room, watching TV and sending out for pizza. Scott got treated to a foot massage from Jenny while I massaged his back. Then Jenny and I had the idea of starting a burping contest. We are both like queens of burping. So we were burping and having fun until two in the morning while winter snow piled up outside. Scott offered that we could stay in his room. I warned him that he shouldn't think that anything was going to happen between us. He said he had a girlfriend, and that was the last thing on his mind. We got cosy on the double bed, Jenny and me on one side and Scott on the other, and he behaved himself like he promised. Before I fell asleep, though, Scott let me have a peek at his tour calendar. With his permission, Jenny and I wrote our names on the guest list for every single concert for the rest of the tour. We also both wrote down our telephone numbers for him. I think Scott was a tad lonely, since everyone in the band hated him except Frank - and that was all that mattered to Scott anyhow. I thought Scott was a kind of arrogant, talented, young rebel."[32]

Thunes tells me that he and Stein were in fact lovers on the tour.

And she now confirms this: "He had a girlfriend at the time, so I wasn't sure he wanted the truth out there. Scott has a HUGE penis. Massive. The guys in the band hated him more for that than being teacher's pet. Thing is, we never fucked, I just blew him all the time, sadly! Wish we would have. For some reason, men seem to think getting head is not cheating."

Thunes adds: "The girlfriend I had was, oh, fourth back from the wife I have now, not including rock girls this and home-girls that. Water under the bridge, and all that. Dot was fucking hot. I was extremely lucky and enjoyed my time with her immensely. Unfortunately, things happen and on the road you can go from hot loving to 'who's that over there?' in about two minutes, let alone the days we spent together. This says nothing at all bad about Dot, but merely the proclivities of the testosterone-laden amongst us. And the first part, where she says I lay between them platonically, is true. It was the next time I saw her that things progressed, rather rapidly, to extremely hot sex. Always such a generous person. I will treasure my time with her for, like, always."

Around this time, the heat was on Pentecostal preacher, pioneer of televangelism and cousin of Jerry Lee Lewis, the Reverend Jimmy Swaggart. During the previous two years, Swaggart had exposed the sexual indiscretions of Marvin Gorman and Jim Bakker, two of his fellow Assemblies Of God televangelists, who Swaggart feared were taking away his audience and donations. In 1987, Swaggart had appeared on Larry King's TV show and stated that Bakker was a "cancer in the body of Christ." In retaliation, Gorman hired a private detective to follow Swaggart. The detective found Swaggart in a Louisiana motel with a prostitute. On 21st February, Swaggart tearfully spoke to his family, congregation and TV audience, saying, "I have sinned against you, my Lord, and I would ask that your precious blood would wash and cleanse every stain until it is in the seas of God's forgiveness." On a New Orleans news show a few days later, the prostitute in question stated that, while Swaggart was a regular customer, they had never actually engaged in sexual intercourse; she said he liked to watch her undress. As a result of all this, Zappa had begun to change many of his lyrics to refer to the saga. In Boston, the secret word was "Just the tip". And at the Mid Hudson Civic Center in Poughkeepsie a few days later, Zappa opened the show with "Did everybody hear the great news today? Jimmy Swaggart under investigation! One day every one of those cock-suckers'll get caught! Now, I understand in the case of Mr Swaggart that he claims that it was not multiple encounters with many prostitutes. Apparently only one sweet young thing, and he did tell Cal Thomas of the Moral Majority that the sex act itself was not fully consummated. However, he did admit to doing something pornographic with the girl. Let's use our imaginations, ladies and gentlemen...", as the band launched into *Stink-Foot*.

Although suspended by the national Assemblies Of God for one year, Swaggart returned to his television pulpit after only three months, stating, "If I do not return to the pulpit this weekend, millions of people will go to hell." Despite subsequently being caught with another prostitute some three years later, Swaggart today presides over a worldwide multi-million-dollar Ministry, comprising radio and television programmes featuring his wife, son and grandson.

As Zappa rightly continued to drag Swaggart's name through the mud on stage, some unusual cover tunes were being performed during sound checks. Before the 27th February show at the Royal Oak Theatre in Detroit, these included six Beatles' songs: *Lucy In The Sky With Diamonds, Strawberry Fields Forever, Paperback Writer, Taxman, Norwegian Wood* and *Within You Without You*. Explains Willis: "Frank was a good friend of John Lennon. In 1980, when we were on tour, we were just about to go on stage in Milwaukee* and that's when we heard that Lennon had just been killed. When we came to the 1988 tour, Frank one day just came into rehearsal and asked if we knew

* On 8 December 1980, Zappa in fact played the Arlington Theater in Santa Barbara, California; the band had visited Milwaukee in November.

any of those Beatles' tunes because he'd never played them and he'd never heard some of them all the way through."[33]

That evening they actually performed straight versions of *Norwegian Wood* and *Lucy In The Sky With Diamonds*, as well as regular tour encore, *I Am The Walrus*. Says Keneally "The length of the encores combined was probably just as long as either of the sets proper. So we got in a lot of playing that night, and it was a good show. But the great show was February 28th, Detroit #3. That day we rehearsed *Norwegian Wood* with new lyrics, which Frank basically wrote on the spot regarding Jimmy Swaggart, and if it was to be retitled it would probably be called *Texas Motel*. Frank was on a roll, and *Lucy In The Sky With Diamonds* quickly became *Louisiana Hooker With Herpes*, and then *Strawberry Fields Forever*, which might also be newly entitled *Texas Motel*. Vivian [Mike's then wife] was there for that sound check too and was writing down all of Frank's new lyric changes as he blurted them out. We had quite a lot of fun."[34]

"We put that together in one afternoon," confirmed Zappa, "It's a mini oratorio. We did it because a lot of people already know those songs and it would be absurd to hear this band playing *Norwegian Wood*, *Lucy In The Sky With Diamonds* and *Strawberry Fields Forever*. And that's how the thing got started; I said it would just surprise people if we did it. So we started working on it in rehearsal and I decided to re-write the words to those songs and make it all about Jimmy Swaggart. We took all the basic facts from the news story on [him] and just changed the appropriate words and came up with this medley that has been making people laugh so hard since we put it on stage. It gets an unbelievable response. *Louisiana Hooker With Herpes* is a good sing-along song!"[35] Mann "was so happy to be able to play the *Lucy In The Sky With Diamonds* riff on the glockenspiel!"

In addition to Zappa's acquaintance with Lennon - which included a guest appearance (with Yoko Ono, natch) at the Mothers'

---

* Fans usually refer to this as *Norwegian Jim*.

Fillmore East show on 6th June 1971 - Zappa easily coerced Beatle Ringo Starr to appear in his 1971 film, *200 Motels* (as Larry the Dwarf, "dressed like Frank Zappa"). It is well known that the Beatles were fans of Zappa's music (Paul McCartney once described the Beatles' 1967 album *Sgt. Pepper's Lonely Hearts Club Band* as 'our *Freak Out!*', and Lennon and George Harrison sent Zappa a telegram on hearing the Mothers' *Cruising With Ruben & The Jets* - which, in turn, inspired McCartney to write *Oh! Darling* for *Abbey Road*), so it was odd that after asking for permission to lampoon the *Sgt. Pepper* sleeve on *We're Only It For The Money*, Zappa said the release of his band's album was delayed due to McCartney. "I never understood why Zappa blamed me for not being able to use the "*Sgt. Pepper*" sleeve," he said. "I told him I'd write to Brian [Epstein, the Beatles' manager] to ask [EMI]. I don't think [they] would have stopped them, or even could have stopped them."[36] Zappa's response to McCartney saying, "That's what business managers are for," was "No, that's what artists are for: to tell the business managers what to do!"[37] The "*Money*" album was finally released in March 1968 - less than a year after "*Sgt. Pepper*" - but with the parody of Sir Peter Blake's iconic front sleeve on the inside.

The Beatles' medley was performed again at the next two shows in Muskegon and Chicago, where Zappa met another pop icon: former Police-man, Sting. "It was kind of odd, because I'd never met him before and I just ran into him at the hotel," Zappa told DJ Kevin Matthews. "I invited him to the show, because they had a day off. And he came down and he watched the first part of the show from the audience. Then, during the intermission, he came backstage and I asked him if he wanted to come out and do something with us. First, he said no - he didn't think there was a way that he could do it with us. And I said 'Oh, there's no way that you can lose because this band will always make you look good. We'll just make up what we're gonna do,' and I gave him a yellow pad and a pen and I said, 'Here, just write out what you're gonna do and we'll do it: no rehearsal'. And so he did it."[38]

Sting joined the band for a rendition of *Murder By Numbers*, the B-side to The Police's single, *Every Breath You Take*, which won 'Song of the Year' and 'best pop performance by a duo or group with vocal' at the Grammy Awards in 1984. Sting introduced it by saying "four years ago, Jimmy Swaggart said this about me: he said 'this here song by The Police, *Murder By Numbers*, was written by Satan! Performed by the sons of Satan! Beelzebub! Lucifer! The Horned One!' I wrote the fuckin' song, alright?" In fact, Sting co-wrote the song with Police guitarist, Andy Summers, although his music was effectively replaced by an impromptu vamp based around Oliver Nelson's jazz standard, *Stolen Moments*.

Keneally talked with Sting backstage and "was struck by the fact that he admitted to being nervous about singing with us. He's one of less than a handful of people I've met whose charisma is absolutely undeniable, whose presence completely changes the energy in a room the moment they step in. One of the others, of course, was Frank."[39] Mann's meeting with Sting was fleeting: "As he was leaving, a lot of us were standing around to say hello and he very quickly shook everyone's hand and said 'You are a good musician', 'You are a good musician', 'You are a good musician', 'You are a good musician'... etc." Wing told me "I tried to engage Sting in casual conversation; a full length mirror commanded his attention, which provided a more convivial atmosphere for him." Another noteworthy moment occurred that night during the Synclavier section of *A Pound For A Brown On The Bus* when Willis exclaimed, "Let's hear it for Grammy winner, Frank Zappa!"; the previous night, Zappa had won the award for 'best rock instrumental performance (orchestra, group or soloist)' for his *Jazz From Hell* album. "Accidents will happen,"[40] Zappa told Kevin Matthews.

Before the next show, "during the huddle, Frank read to us a note from Sting saying that he really enjoyed playing with the band, thanks for accommodating him, he would really like to help Frank out with registering voters in America as long as Frank helps Sting to get Thatcher out of office - which Frank found very intriguing - and the note ended with 'Please mail me the sheet music for *The Idiot Bastard Son*,' you won't be sorry. Love, Mr. Sting'. Frank called him Mr Sting on stage. Let me think of some other things I might not have mentioned about Sting; during one of Frank's guitar solos, Sting came over to where I was and looked at all the underwear surrounding me and said 'What the hell is this?' I said 'It's gifts from the audience,' and he took down a bra and put it on his head. Sting obviously had a very good time, his note seemed to verify that. Also, at the huddle, Frank had a photocopy of a review of the first Beacon Theatre show from *Rolling Stone*, a magazine which has not traditionally been all that favourable towards Frank, and this was a very good review. Frank couldn't believe it."[41]

That second night in Chicago was Wing's most memorable gig of the tour: "That was the night I met Randee Pollock. I met her at the Limelight VIP room. Later, we exchanged info. Randee was actually Plan B: a backline guy caught me hangin' with his little sister after the show and he told her to go home. I tried calling her a little later, but then I met Randee. A few days later, Randee and I made plans for Burlington…" Randee became a permanent fixture on the tour after that and caused Wing to be late for one rehearsal, that he'll admit to: "Had I not faltered running from parking lot to the stage; cost: one day's pay. What happened earlier that morning: priceless!" When the author asked Willis if Randee was a hanger-on, he said "Oh, I remember her: she followed us. My God, that's right. Definitely hanging-on there!"

Another song was about to be introduced to the expanding repertoire: in Chicago, the band had made its first attempt at playing the theme from the late-50s prohibition-era television series, *The Untouchables*. Zappa said "I think that's a great piece of music. That's a genius TV theme, and I've always liked it. I said, 'We should play

---

* Sting had serious plans to release a live album from his show at the Wiltern Theatre in Los Angeles on 27th July 1988; this would have included his one-off performance of Zappa's *The Idiot Bastard Son*.

The Untouchables'. But nobody could remember exactly how it went. So Laurel Fishman* went to a television station, and got a cassette, this TV station was running *The Untouchables* there, and talked somebody at the station into making a little audio cassette of the theme. We brought it back to the sound check. We listened to the cassette through the speakers that played into the room. The horn players went over and stood next to the speakers and they listened carefully and each guy picked out his own part out of this thing, and they sketched out their parts, and that's how we learned *The Untouchables*. That proves its fun to do music, if guys just think about music when they're in the band. But the minute they start thinkin' about stuff that is not music, I mean, maybe even in Chicago these guys are sayin' to themselves, 'What the fuck do we have to do this for? Do we have to go over and stand in front of this speaker and figure out what the third sax part harmony is to *The Untouchables?* Jeezus Christ! I'm a jazz musician! Should I really be doing this?' But the net result for the audience, I think they get off on it, and so there's a time to decide, 'Okay. You're a jazz musician, but you're here to entertain people too'."[42]

Regarding the role of the five-piece horn section, in 1988 Zappa said "Basically what they're being asked to do is not to play chords, or harmony parts behind guitar solos. They play a little eight-bar figure that makes the transition between the body of the song and the guitar solo, that's not all that's required of them. The rest of the time they're playing really complicated parts that are challenging to them, so that keeps 'em on their toes. Other groups that go out with horn sections, their basic function is to play the little punches and pads and boop-boop-boops in between what the electric instruments are doing. That's not a very gratifying life for a horn player to just play a few notes and spend the rest of the night banging on Latin percussion instruments. We don't do that."[43] A year later, he would explain the expanded '88 line-up a little more

---

* A long-time Zappa fan/'band aid', whose exploits with guitarist Steve Vai were documented in the song *Stevie's Spanking*.

economically: "the orchestration was far more luxuriant for some of the older songs than they were originally recorded, simply because I didn't want to have eleven guys standing around onstage with nothing to do."[44]

At the next show in Cleveland, one of the horn players got to do a little more than play his instrument: during *Let's Move To Cleveland* (the refrain for which naturally received a huge roar), trombonist Bruce Fowler recited the following strange monologue: "It happened right here in lovely Cleveland a long, long time ago. About three hundred and thirty million years ago, in fact, in the Upper Devonian. There was a really nice intellectual kind of a Placoderm type of a fish, and he was real creative, and he was just having lot of fun living...living his life gently along here in the Upper Devonian Peninsula you've got here. And suddenly, out of nowhere, came a band of religious fanatic sharks. And they organised themselves in crazy, fiendish groups. And just ate everything, leaving nothing for this talented creative Placoderm type fish. And it just brings tears to my eyes that you may let this happen again in 1988. I don't know what to do about it! It's driving me wild! I can't hardly stand it no more! I might have to play an out-of-tune note or something! I JUST CAN'T STAND IT ANYMORE! OH GOD! OH GOD! OH GOD! OH GOD!"[45] Fowler, a keen rock and fossil 'hunter', later explained that he was working on a poetry album, "I did something on the 1988 tour in Cleveland about the fossil fish from Cleveland. They're these armoured fish from the Devonian period. I knew we were going there and I called up the museum and spoke to the expert in the fish who told me something about them. Then we had to start talking politics. Generally I agreed with Frank about politics. I thought he was a brilliant spokesman about freedom of speech. I could really get behind what he was talking about. I'm sure if we hadn't had the demise of the band, I'm sure that could have happened even more."[46]

In his tour diary, Keneally notes "We left Cleveland on the

morning of 6th March. Bob Stone* had made a cassette copy of the show in Cleveland the night before and, while on the bus, a bunch of us sat in the back lounge and listened - me, and Bob Stone of course, and Chad, and Albert and Paul - to what we had done. It sounded good. Occasionally I headed up to the front of the bus where Bobby Martin was reading, and I'd lay down up there. Ike and Ed were both sleeping. It was a nice bus ride. Uncharacteristically quiet, because Ike was sleeping... I'm thinking that I may be switching to the other bus, because when Ike is awake there's no rest to be had."[47]

That evening, at the Veteran's Memorial Auditorium in Columbus, they premiered *The Untouchables*, and the Secretary of the State of Ohio, Sherrod Brown, bestowed an honorary Secretary of Statehood on Zappa: "I told them I would accept this honorary award if I could participate in the foreign policy of the state of Ohio. I figured that if there's any border disputes between Ohio and Kentucky, that I could mediate. And the guy told me that Kentucky wasn't the problem, it was Pittsburgh."[48] he advised Kevin Matthews. A film crew from *60 Minutes*** was present to capture Zappa's acceptance speech of "Thank you. May the force be with you." A fan complained about the crew's presence on stage, but Zappa said "They're not in your way. What're you missing - somebody's aura? Look, have pity on them. They have to stand up here where it's loud. They're from New York. It could hurt them." During rehearsals earlier that day - which usually ran from four in the afternoon until six - Zappa "mentioned that Jimmy Page and Robert Plant might be popping up sometime to play *Stairway To Heaven*, and he said it would be nice to do *Shapes Of Things†* for Jeff Beck when he shows up in London. So Frank looked at me, and I figured out the chords and we did a reasonably good instrumental version of *Shapes Of Things* with Frank playing the vocal melody on the guitar."[49] Zappa was also

---

* Zappa's recording engineer for most of the 1980s.

** A US investigative TV news magazine, which has run on CBS News since 1968.

† A song written by Paul Samwell-Smith, Keith Relf, and Jim McCarty, originally recorded by The Yardbirds during Jeff Beck's tenure, and released as a single in 1966.

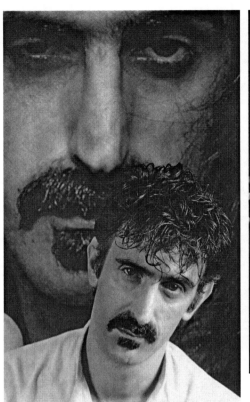

Above: Zappa plays Zappa in 1987, shortly
before embarking on his final tour.
(Lynn Goldsmith / Corbis)

Before the 'Broadway The Hard Way' tour commenced,
a gruelling rehearsal schedule took place in West
Hollywood with a band that was already starting to
fracture - although FZ seemed very relaxed at the time
that these photos were taken. *(Lynn Goldsmith / Corbis)*

The secret word was "rehearsal".
(Lynn Goldsmith / Corbis)

Below: Frank prior to the tour as co-host of a benefit for the Fundamentalists Anonymous Legal Task Force, an organisation devoted to helping people get their money back from Jim and Tammy. They were lampooned on 'Jesus Thinks You're A Jerk', a new song that was regularly played on the tour and subsequently released on the 'Broadway The Hard Way' album.
(Lynn Goldsmith / Corbis)

Left: 20th March, Rothman Center, Fairleigh Dickenson College, Teaneck, New Jersey.

"What's the secret word for tonight? - Golden pheasant."
(Ken Windish)

Below: Yo Cats!

Relaxing with a couple of feline friends in April '88 during the brief break between the U.S and European legs of the tour.
(Lynn Goldsmith / Corbis)

Shut up 'n play yer guitar.

Above:
At the Rothman Center, Fairleigh Dickenson College, Teaneck, New Jersey, 20th March.
(Ken Windish)

Left:
In keeping with his new found interest in politics, and dealings with the establishment FZ adopted a far more conservative dress code during this period of his life, even at some of the gigs.
(Lynn Goldsmith / Corbis)

Rothman Center, Fairleigh Dickenson College, Teaneck, New Jersey, 20th March.
(Ken Windish)

Insets: Anyway The Wind Blows: Clockwise from top left:
Paul Carman, Albert Wing, Walt Fowler, Bruce Fowler, Kurt McGettrick...
or, in Thunes' words, "those fucking asshole horn players." *(Stanley Hope Collection)*

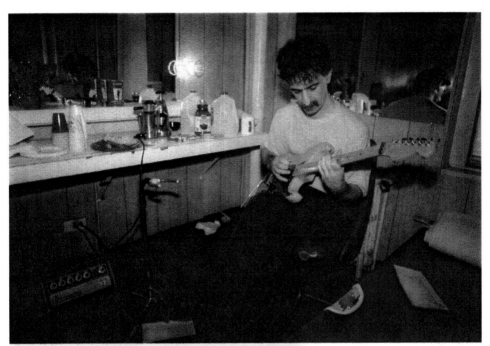

Above:
A rare moment of solitude
backstage during the U.S leg of
the tour.
(Lynn Goldsmith / Corbis)

Left:
FZ whips it out. Despite vowing
he wouldn't tour again, not only
did he give his fans what he
wanted but also knew that many
loved him first and foremost as a
guitarist.
Many of the solos from the
'Broadway The Hard Way' tour
were posthumously released on
'Trance-Fusion'.
(Lynn Goldsmith / Corbis)

Liederhalle, Stuttgart, 24th May.
(Chris Coulson)

miffed that an unnamed [in Keneally's tour diary] band member turned up late for rehearsals, at around 5.30. During *The Illinois Enema Bandit* that evening, Frank changed the lyrics to include "Paul, are you guilty?" and "Let that asshole sax player free."

The next day - a day off - Keneally records his pleasant walk through the 'art section' of Columbus, meeting up with Thunes and, later, Carman: "...lots of galleries and art supply shops, and there was a jazz club there called The Major Chord, and it was evident that this was where things of a more bohemian nature were likely to go down. I kept walking and took note of graffiti on the walls, including one recurring character called Mr. Yuk', he was all over the place - obviously somebody's little trademark graffiti thing. I had my first ever *White Castle* burgers, and the perfect type of just-artificial-enough vanilla shake that I remember from my childhood, and then I finally made it to the record shops which were right next to Ohio State University. I went to a place called Singing Dog and got a nice set of four 7-inch Zappa interview picture discs in a big plastic carrying case for twenty bucks. Continued walking, found a two-story record store where the upper floor is called School Kids and the lower floor is called Used Kids, and one of the guys in School Kids recognised me from the show the night before, and we talked for a while. I got a local paper called *The Scene* which had a nice interview with Frank, and also the *Rolling Stone* with the Beacon Theatre review in it. Then I went down to Used Kids and got a Hatfield And The North CD for seven bucks, happy about that. And then I was walking back, trying to decide if I was gonna walk back the several miles to the hotel - it was dark by this point - or try to flag a cab or something, there appeared Scott, who had also been browsing, looking for CDs. We went into a bar and talked for a bit, had a real good time. He was in a good mood. We went to an arcade where he played several car games, and there was one game in the arcade that sounded like every ten seconds somebody was going

---

*Mr. Yuk is a trademarked graphic image, created by the Children's Hospital of Pittsburgh, and widely employed in the United States in the labelling of poisonous substances.

"Mike. Mike". It was an electronic voice saying something, but it sounded like it was trying to get my attention and that was disconcerting. But I had a very good time with Scott. Scott and I continued walking and walking and walking and saying surely we're not walking all the way back to the hotel, and then we got to the hotel. In the hotel bar we found Bob Stone, a pair of Fowlers and Paul. Poor Paul is having a bad couple of days: he lost his leather jacket in the bar two nights before in Cleveland, and here in Columbus he had just misplaced $100 from his wallet, so he was feeling a little poorly. Also he had hoped to record one of the shows, he got a brand new tape recorder, and he left it on 'pause' the whole night. Poor Paul. But he's got a beard, and it's looking good."[50]

On to Pittsburgh, where Zappa suggested adding the patriotic *America The Beautiful* to the repertoire. Keneally says the band "whipped up an arrangement pretty quickly. It sounded really nice. During this sound check I put a Mr. Yuk drawing on Scott's amp, thinking that he'd recognise Mr. Yuk from his walk around the University area the day before, but Scott didn't know who Mr. Yuk was and actually got offended until I owned up to being responsible and explained what it was."[51] It seems this episode fleetingly passed as a joke because, a few nights later, Zappa introduced Thunes as Mr Yuk on stage. Thunes today, though, has no recollection of this incident at all. The show itself in Pittsburgh was relatively uneventful save for Zappa stopping it midway through *City Of Tiny Lites* to remonstrate with a security guard: "Wait a minute! What is this fascist over-supervision that we see going on in the audience? Do we have dangerous people in the audience? What's going on here?"

At the next show, in Buffalo, individuals in the band gave musical hints at another new, well-known song about to be added to the repertoire - and Zappa too mutated the *Penguin In Bondage* lyrics to "and he might just box your doggie and leave you a little dried-up *Boléro.*" Thunes relayed a story about researching the tune to

Thomas Wictor: "Every city I go to, I always find the music store. That's what I do. I've got five hours to kill, I might as well find the music store and see if there's anything there. Frank had this little project - he wanted to do the *Boléro* - so I found the sheet music to *Boléro*. At the same time, Mike Keneally is calling his wife, desperately attempting to get her to go find one and then fax him a copy. Which he did, and that's the one we ended up using for the arrangement. Mine was for my own personal use, and I'm sitting there looking at it in the hotel lobby, waiting for the bus, and Paul [Carman] asked me if he could see it. I said 'Fuck off. Get your own.' And anybody who knows me at all, they know how to deal with it. Chad would've gone, 'Oh, come on! Lemme see it,' and I would've handed it to him. But Paul... I have no use for anybody who has no use for me. If the only reason you want to talk to me is to see my sheet music, fuck off! No! Absolutely not. I'm not going to play that easygoing 'everybody's mellow' game. I don't need you; you don't need me; don't pretend you do."[52] The song was formally introduced on 21st March at the Landmark Theatre, Syracuse, but Zappa wasn't too happy with the early performances: "By the end of the European part of the tour, they really had it down, and they were playing it well. They weren't playing it that well in the US because it was still a fresh arrangement. We played it all over Europe, and it was a major hit in the show."[53] By the time the band got to Europe, it bore its now familiar (to Zappa fans) reggae arrangement.

It's quite difficult to gauge the atmosphere in the band from Keneally's tour diaries as he was (and still, to this day, very much is) a happy, optimistic, upbeat sort of a cove. And it would appear that on stage at least there was very little sign of any discontent. During the encores at the Memorial Auditorium in Burlington, Zappa forgot the words to Obie Jessie's *Mary Lou*, asking, "What's the outro?" On returning to the stage, he quipped "I've just received a note that says I should stay after school for that one!" to the amusement of the rest of the band. Keneally notes, "It was a wonderful show. This was our first hockey rink gig, and it sounded great. And everybody was great, and it was a wonderful show."[54]

Trey Anastasio of Phish agrees: "His interplay was always with drummers. In a lot of jam-style guitar playing, the drummer sets off a groove, and the guitarist riffs off another guitarist or keyboard player. I saw Zappa at Memorial Auditorium in Burlington, Vermont, on his last tour, in 1988. He did this guitar solo in *City Of Tiny Lites* where everybody in the band dropped out except drummer Chad Wackerman. I was in the balcony near the side of the stage. When Zappa turned his back on the audience to play with Chad, I saw this huge smile on his face. They were ripping together, and he was blissed out. Zappa was a huge influence on how I wrote music for Phish. Songs like *You Enjoy Myself* and *Split Open And Melt* were completely charted out - drums, bass lines, everything - because he had shown me it was possible. And when I went to Bonnaroo with my ten-piece band, we did two covers, Charlie Daniels' *Devil Went Down To Georgia* and *Sultans Of Swing* by Dire Straits. In both songs, I had the horn section play the guitar solos, note for note. I never would have thought of doing that if I hadn't seen Zappa do *Stairway To Heaven* in Burlington, with the horns playing Jimmy Page's entire guitar solo, in harmony."[55]

But it seems Keneally played a big part in that particular arrangement, as he reveals on his website: "Frank had been playing an improvised solo in the middle of the song the first few times we played it; one day I showed Paul Carman the notes to Jimmy Page's original solo, and the next time Frank called the tune, Paul and I started playing the solo in unison, without warning Frank about it first. He listened until we were finished, then stopped the tune and said 'Okay. Now show it to the rest of the horn section'. Audiences used to explode when that part of the song popped out. And to anyone who saw the East Coast shows where I ended the song on my knees at the front of the stage - Frank made me do it. I swear to God!"[56]

So, just over a month into the tour and on the surface all appears to be going well. But on Sunday 13th March 1988 - the day American porn star John Holmes became stiff for the last time - at the Civic Center in Springfield, a formal band meeting was called to air some issues. Thunes thought it might be something to do with their hotels being too far from venues so that when they returned from gigs the kitchens were closed. But instead, the unassuming Wackerman announced to Zappa that the horn players felt the rhythm section wasn't supporting them during their solos. "I look around. How many people are in the rhythm section? There's... Chad... and there's... me,"[57] says Thunes. McGettrick chipped in with, "Yeah, Scott, when we're playing lines together it'd be really great if you could come over to my side of the stage."[58] Then Carman, "Yeah, Scott, we don't feel like you're playing behind us - we feel like you're just going off on some other tangents while we're playing."[59] Thunes says this was true, but thought that "was part of the idea of getting a bunch of disparate elements on stage and seeing how they blend. This is how I play; this is how you play. I'm not used to playing behind five horn players a night and having to support them on their solos. I got hired to support Frank."[60]

Zappa then asked Thunes what he thought about all this, and he says "I am in shock. I had no idea this was going on, and I'm very, very upset."[61] When Mann tried to pipe-up, Thunes cut him off with "Wait a minute! You! Don't talk to me. You have a personal agenda with me that has nothing to do with this band. I don't want to hear what you have to say, and if you say a single, 'nother word, I'm leaving this room. Don't!"[62] Mann tried to continue, so Thunes picked up his bag and left. He sat alone at the side of the stage for about twenty minutes, when Frank joined him and said "We're all in this together. We're all trying to do the right thing; we're all trying to have a good time here. Some people are a little bit harsher than others, and you're the harshest of them all. You know, I've never met anybody who's so caustic as you, and maybe you wanna think about that."[63] Thunes agreed, said he'd try to mellow out, and broke down in tears. "From that point on, I was persona non grata. Absolutely 100 percent."[64]

CHAPTER THREE
Playground Psychotics

While Keneally did not record any more diary entries in the US after the 'wonderful' Burlington show, reviews of the Springfield gig give no indication of any tensions within the band - referring to Zappa's good mood, his amusing interaction with band members, and the monster improvisational sections, Zappa fanatic Jon Naurin summed the gig up by saying, "FZ and Ike (Willis) are in high spirits throughout the concert, and we get a good dose of humour. This, in combination with the great guitar solos and the *Pound For A Brown* improvisation, makes this one of the best shows of the US tour."[1] In his autobiography, Zappa wrote, "If I'm in a bad mood, I try not to share that with the audience - at the same time, I'm not the kind of guy who can put on the 'Mr. Happy Face' and pretend that all's right with the world - acting out a lie is even worse than telling it."[2]

Thunes says that four of the band members approached him immediately after the showdown to say that they had had nothing to do with it - that they did not agree with what had been articulated. The four were: Ike Willis; Albert Wing (who told the author "I liked having Scott there for this reason: the adrenaline factor; it was like I had something to prove - like 'look at me, I'm still here'. Whatever Frank's decision was, I told him that I supported him no matter what the outcome; during lunch earlier that day, I realised it was the beginning of the end for the band. I predicted it."); Robert Martin (who also confirmed to the author, "I had a better relationship with him than most of the rest of the band, partially because he respected my heavy classical background"); and Mike Keneally (with whom Thunes "ended up hanging out with the whole rest of the tour. Best friends... we went out to restaurants every night; it was absolutely no problem."[3])

Perhaps the reason for Zappa's seeming ebullience was that he had other things on his mind: after the show he met up with Lorraine Belcher, his 'buxom red-haired companion' from his early years. Belcher had remained friends with Zappa since they first met in 1964 and began a relationship at his Studio Z in Cucamonga. In March 1965, after the pair were coerced into making a 'party tape' for an undercover agent from the San Bernardino County vice squad, the studio was raided by the police and Zappa was found guilty of 'conspiracy to commit pornography.' He spent ten days in Tank C at the County Jail (a period immortalised in his song, *San Ber'dino*) and the pair slowly - though briefly - drifted apart. Belcher told me "I lived in Laguna for a while. Frank closed Studio Z and moved to Echo Park, where I would stay with him sometimes. It was a chaotic time. Then I moved to Seattle for a while. Frank couldn't find me. So he put out *Lumpy Gravy*, which was my nickname for him. There was a little cartoon guy inside the album cover saying 'write to us' with the address in New York. I had married some guy I'd only known for three weeks, to get away from the rock 'n' roll life in LA. I sent a little note to him saying 'I am married but still recognisable', and he called a few days later. When I picked up the phone, Frank said 'I thought you'd see that'. The Mothers then played Seattle three times in nine months. Frank and I would sit alone together backstage, saying 'What are we going to do?' He had married Gail, who was pregnant with Moon. So he came up with the brilliant idea of me divorcing my husband and moving in with them in LA. Shocking. Even more shocking was, I did it! But I said, 'I want my own room'. We never touched each other the year I lived there with them. I moved back to Seattle for a few years, but we still saw each other, as I would fly down there sometimes for a visit. It was five years before Frank and I were intimate again, which destroyed the relationship with Gail when she found out."

They continued to meet over the years and, in 1988, Zappa

invited Belcher to the Springfield show, for what would be their final meeting. "I got his phone message, and raced back to my house in Chester to change my clothes and zoom to his show there. The show was great, I thought. Afterwards, we went to an Italian restaurant which closed for his arrival. However, the owner's family and friends were over in the bar, and some of them came to the table one at a time to pay their respects. He was very gracious to them, and was open to visiting with them a bit. Some other people joined us for dinner, but I can't remember who they were: two other people were at the table... maybe his bodyguard? I just can't remember. We wanted to be alone, of course. I was surprised to see Frank drink a beer! A dark ale, I think. Back at the hotel, I had to go get my own car and park it in the lot, so when I arrived in the lobby I had no idea what name he was registered under. They wouldn't let me up to the room! I had to loiter around in the lobby for at least fifteen minutes 'till someone I knew walked by. It was pretty funny: they thought I was a groupie. We laid around on the bed for a long time in the beginning, watching CNN and talking about the world. Then he told me some proud papa anecdotes about his kids. Whenever we got together, we always spent the first hour or so catching up on all our 'hot poop', as he called it. He was extremely comical and ironic that night. He was playful and funny, which was usually his type of foreplay... that's all I need to say about that. He was going on to play Rhode Island, and wanted me to follow him there. But I had something else I had to do that night. I was so sorry I didn't go. He did say he was 'over' touring - he was tired of it. And I thought then that he looked tired. When I left, it wasn't like either of us thought that was the last time we'd see each other. But I did feel really sad for some reason when I left... I do remember that. I felt terribly melancholy all the way home in rush hour traffic."

Although that was the last time Belcher ever saw Zappa, he did invite her to join him in New York - "as he was coming alone" - for the Zappa's Universe tribute shows at The Ritz in 1991. Sadly, due to ill-health, he never made it there, and Moon finally made the first official statement regarding his cancer. But that's jumping ahead.

The next show Stein and her friend Jenny would attend was in Portland on 15th March. "Scott called me the day before. He wanted to know if we were coming to the show. 'If you want to,' he said, 'you can come down at 4:00 and hear the sound check.' I was beyond thrilled, just about ready to flip out. Jenny and I drove to Portland, and Scott met us at the entrance. He was all excited to see us. He took us up to the front row and told us to sit quietly, not to make a sound. I was drinking *Diet Coke* and suddenly, right in the middle of *Boléro*, I just had to let loose this huge burp. You could hear it all the way through the huge, empty concert hall. The band stopped playing and they all stared at me. Frank looked down at all the people in the first row and demanded to know who did it. Of course nobody wanted to take the blame and get thrown out, so everybody was just looking straight at me. I raised my hand and admitted I was the one. 'Come up here,' Frank said. It was still as quiet as a church. I went up there pleading. 'Frank, I'm so sorry! I promise never to do that again.' I was in total fear. He just looked down at me and asked, 'Can you do that again?' He explained that he wanted to sample my burp and use it in the show. So there I was, standing up on the stage with ten musicians waiting for me to burp. 'Well, go on, burp,' Frank said. 'I can't just burp on command,' I told him, 'I need *Diet Coke* and some time.' 'Get her a coke,' Frank told a stage hand. 'No, it's gotta be *DIET Coke*, Frank.' 'Okay, okay - get her a *DIET Coke* then!' After about ten minutes, the band grew tired of waiting, but then I let out three long, loud belches and the keyboard player recorded them."[4]

These huge sampled belches, together with those of Frank's nephew Jade Teta[*], were then used on stage during the rest of the tour ("whenever he wanted to send up Jim and Tammy," Stein told the author). Stein is now a professional masseuse, with a dedicated team of assistants who handle clients in almost every major city in

[*] Zappa told Society Pages: "*Jade has the ability to burp very loud and very long, and he can also burp words. So, when he was here visiting in '87, we had a sampling session. I stood him in front of a microphone, and let him do an assortment of burps, and then gave him a list of words and phrases to burp, and some of those were put into the Synclavier and that's what ya heard...he could do it just by gulping air.*"

the US and Europe. She told *The Sunday Times* "Zappa gave me my nickname, Dr Dot, because he referred to me as the doctor."[5] When the author asked her if she was massaging in 1988: "Yes, but I wasn't professional back then - I didn't have a table. I massaged the whole band - on chairs, on the floor, everywhere. But Frank wouldn't take his shirt off - he couldn't relax, he was a workaholic. I just massaged his hands. Ike wouldn't take his shirt off, either. But Scott was a big massage fan. It sounds kind of surreal now, but at the time it didn't seem that way."

Willis remembers another incident in Portland: "Chad said something to somebody in the crew and Scott made one of his offside comments. Chad said 'That's it. I've had it.' Within minutes, Frank knew about it and called us to his dressing room for a meeting. He said 'Hey, I'm not gonna put up with this. I don't like rocking the boat. This is a very expensive tour. A very long tour.' After, I told Scott 'You've got to stop doing this, man. You've gotta stop; you're pissing too many people off. Stop!' And, like I said, Frank told me to sit on him and make sure they don't kill him. Those were his words. 'Please, try your best.' And on that day in Portland, he got away from me for about five minutes: Said something to one of the guys in the crew, set them off; set Chad off."

During the show itself, more notes and undergarments were passed up to the stage, including one pair of pants in a plastic bag "Must be a good one," Zappa commented, "Who's this from? John Holmes, ladies and gentlemen!" After much laughter, Willis added "They're still moist!" And you thought I threw that line in about Holmes in Chapter Two purely for comic effect, didn't you? Also offered-up was a hymnal. Said Zappa, "A girl walked up to the stage and handed us a Christian songbook. And so I thumbed through it and handed it to Bobby Martin to sight-read... *Stainless The Maiden*. If you're gonna pick a Christian song, how about *Stainless The Maiden*, huh?"[6] Further mentions of both Holmes and "*The Maiden*" were made throughout this particular show, as well as Zappa's pointed ad-lib - "Let's be sophomoric for a while!" - during *Jesus Thinks You're A Jerk.*

The next night, at the Civic Center in Providence, Chad Wackerman was the star of the show. Fan Jason Gossard recalls, "While the rest of the band seems to have decided to make this a mellow, laid-back affair, turning in relaxed yet satisfying performances, the drummer decides to go a little crazy. Pulling off his best Vinnie' imitation, Chad spends the night playing hide-and-seek with the One, messing with Frank's casual solos, forcing some wicked energy into a very carefree evening."[7] Also of note was Zappa's interjection, during *Who Needs The Peace Corps?*, "Y'know, they believe in the devil in this here town." He later explained: "I had done an interview prior to the show with some local television station and they're the ones who told me that they had a Satanism squad, or something related, but with the police and Satanism. It's just ridiculous."[8]

For the next show, Zappa presented a "special St. Patrick's Day programme", which essentially added a medley of *When Irish Eyes Are Smiling* and the theme from *The Godfather Part II* - as well as an opportunity for audience members "who think they are Irish to come up" on stage "in order to dispel the ethnic myth that people of the Irish persuasion are not particularly sexy" by making a sex noise.

The 'Irish Godfather' was repeated at the Memorial Hall, Muhlenberg College in Allentown on 19th March - though, by all accounts, the playing that night was comparatively lacklustre. That was the show where "I blew my lid on mic at Thunes," remembers Mann. It was during the improvised section of *King Kong,* over a Synclavier backing, Mann intoned "For those of you who might not know... the whole is the sum of its parts. For those of you who

---

* Drummer Vinnie Colaiuta played with Zappa between 1978 and 1980 and, according to *The Real Frank Zappa Book,* got the grand prize for being able to conceive of, and identify, Zappa's polyrhythms *"fast enough to play a complementary figure on the moment".*

might not know... no single part can be a whole all by itself, unless it's a fucking black hole. For those of you who might not know, belligerence is obnoxious. For those of you who might not know... the Nazis were never that popular anyway!" Thunes responded by flipping him the bird, while Zappa's reaction was to sit shaking his head, softly laughing. Thunes clarified things recently when he told the author, "At the end of the huddle we always held before the gig, I uncharacteristically fell back into Clonemeister garb (uncharacteristic only at that point in the tour: I'd learned to keep my own council... at least until that time in Spain, but I'm getting ahead of myself) to say something about some piece of music that was being incorrectly played by some or all of the band. I must have said something like, 'For those of you who might not know, the last chord is an F#,' or 'For those of you who might not know, the segue between _ and _ has three counts, not four.' It must have been something important for me to even speak to those guys at all. So Ed slung my own words back in my face. Extra credit. Ouch."

At the time, Mann vigorously denied that his rant was a response to Thunes' huddle comments, and now says of the incident, "I think Frank hated and loved me for that. I think that was two nights after Thunes ran around the back and put the head of his bass up Bruce's ass while Bruce was taking a solo. Later that night, Bruce punched him full on in the chest. When I was unloading on-mic, FZ was smiling and egging me on with hand gestures. But then FZ did retaliate against my outspokenness: a few nights later, last US date in New York, he said to me 'No more vocal samples!' which were my domain. These had of course become a signature by then - but then listen how up in the mix he put them! They kind of define the mood of the tour. When we got to Europe, he said 'use the samples' - go figure. Those samples were the mouth piece for those who chose not to speak directly to the situation. Jesus, there is a lot more - a lot of drama. Silly now, my parts included. Looking back I cannot understand why I did not quit early on, FZ or not."

Thunes recalls the atmosphere on stage around this time - how "from behind, I can feel them. I know exactly what's going on, and I'm attempting to create music through the distressing surroundings that I find myself in."[9] How the negativity affected the band's playing: "I know for a fact that [Wackerman]... told the sound guy to have me completely out of his monitors, which is why in 98 per cent of our downbeats, we're wrong. If I have a drummer who is not playing with me or is playing against me, or their agenda is more important than the larger good, then there isn't anything for me to do except pull back, which is what I did quite a lot. I overstated my sadness; I wore my heart on my sleeve, and for many months of that tour I stood there like a robot. And fans would come up to me and say 'You looked like you were having a root canal.' And I'd say 'You have no fucking idea!'"[10]

It was not all doom and gloom as, on the night of Mann's outburst, Wing took part in a bogus wedding service with Randee Pollock. Super fan Eric Buxton, who was by now getting regularly name-checked on stage, recalls it was "in a drunken stupor. They were sticking together for the whole tour, and they wanted to get married. And Bruce Fowler is supposedly an ordained minister. There was a whole bunch of girls from New Jersey, who were having a bachelorette party, and we were just hanging around the hotel, getting ready to go to sleep, nothing to do. Bobby Martin said, 'I just found this whole room full of girls who want to hang out and drink and party.' We went to the room, and we had a rippin' party all night long, and it climaxed with this marriage ceremony. Bruce performed the ceremony, and he ate the pages of the Bible that he was reading from. He ripped them right out and started chewing on them, and that was the marriage ceremony."[11] Zappa wasn't aware of this at the time - "They didn't tell me that part. I'm sure that woulda wound up on stage. They always leave out the good stuff."[12] - but the next night, while introducing the band members, Zappa did announce that "Albert got married, sort of, yesterday. So if any of you are worried about whether or not you could acquire Albert for your plaything after the show, forget it! Albert is ensconced, ladies and gentleman. That's right, and I know you're really happy about it." I recently asked Wing about it, and he replied "The faux marriage, you'll have to ask Bruce Fowler about that; he was the brain-stormer on that one! I have a vague idea, but tell Bruce that I think I know why, and would not in the slightest be offended by his reasoning behind all of it."

At the end of the show the next night, Zappa asked the Syracuse crowd "how would you like to hear the world premiere of something we were working on this afternoon? Well, it's not perfect yet, but we figured we'd try it out on you because you need it, y'know? There's still a couple of rough edges here, but hold that in abeyance; I think the basic message will come across." As noted in Chapter Two, this was to be the band's first, tentative performance of *Boléro*. The Syracuse show replaced one scheduled to take place in Virginia, which was scrubbed following local objections from anti-rock advocates of the Parents Music Resource Center (PMRC).

The penultimate concert of the first leg of the tour took place in Towson, Maryland - not too far from Zappa's place of birth. Zappa and Willis were both in good spirits, and the band played *Honey, Don't You Want A Man Like Me?* for the one and only time this whole tour (Zappa saw the performance good enough to include on a later volume of his then just started *You Can't Do That On Stage Anymore* CD series). During the show, Zappa spotted a security person in front of the stage and had a few pleasant exchanges with her. During

---

* The PMRC was an American committee formed in 1985 by four women: Tipper Gore, wife of Senator and later US Vice President Al Gore; Susan Baker, wife of Treasury Secretary James Baker; Pam Howar, wife of Washington realtor Raymond Howar; and Sally Nevius, wife of Washington City Council Chairman John Nevius. They were known as the "Washington wives" – a reference to their husbands' connections with the federal government. They convinced record companies they should put "Parental Guidance: Explicit Lyrics" labels on albums to warn of explicit lyrical content. In September 1985, the Senate agreed to hold a hearing on 'porn rock'; representatives from the PMRC, three musicians - Dee Snider, Frank Zappa, and John Denver - and Senators Paula Hawkins and Al Gore testified before the Senate Commerce, Science and Transportation Committee on "*the subject of the content of certain sound recordings and suggestions that recording packages be labelled to provide a warning to prospective purchasers of sexually explicit or other potentially offensive content.*" During his statement, Zappa asserted that "*the PMRC proposal is an ill conceived piece of nonsense which fails to deliver any real benefits to children, infringes the civil liberties of people who are not children, and promises to keep the courts busy for years dealing with the interpretational and enforcemental problems inherent in the proposal's design.*"

the first encore - *The Illinois Enema Bandit* - Bob Rice (Zappa's computer assistant) produced a filled enema bag, which he tried unsuccessfully to get various band members to use on the security lady. On approaching her himself, Rice was surprised when Zappa stopped the show mid-guitar solo to reprimand him: "Wait just a minute. Who in the fuck authorised Bob Rice to try and give this girl an enema? Bob, c'mere. That's totally above and beyond the call of duty. Apologise to her right now. A truly schmucky thing to do. Don't do it again. Now get the fuck out of here!" After the show, Stein says Zappa "promised seven of us who were backstage at just about every concert of the tour that we would get a reward for our loyalty. He said he wanted us all to come up on the stage and dance with him and the band. The only catch was we had to put on these bright yellow aprons and orange mitts."[13] And so, at the Nassau Coliseum, Uniondale on 25th March 1988, during *Packard Goose*, Zappa introduced 'The Long Island Ballet Company'. "I told my friend Chris that she absolutely had to come to the show and take a photo of me onstage with Frank. Aside from the birth of my daughter, this was the high point of my rock and roll life."[14]

Before the second set, the band sang *Happy Birthday* to Wackerman. Zappa also had Andrew West perform his mock evangelical monologue once more. Thunes recalls "I had invited an old Marin County friend who'd moved to New Jersey (I know, it was in Union City, but he drove out there to see me). He'd become a hard-core Christian Born-Again-er, and during the A. West section, I could see him in the front row with his head in his hands. I was pretty disgusted and pissed, not really knowing how far gone he'd, uh, gone, and after the show, I tried to find out what was going on with him. But it all became moot when I got to his truck and it had a Pat Robertson for President bumper sticker on his, uh, bumper. I was shocked and dismayed and asked him what was up with that, and he stated that Pat was going to 'help the children'. I bid him farewell and the next time he called me I blew him off. We're still friends."

All of the encores that night were covers. For the first - *Stairway To Heaven* - Zappa had his son Dweezil come out and replicate Jimmy Page's guitar solo. Dweezil stayed on stage to duet with his father on *Whippin' Post*. At the start of the show, Zappa had read a letter from Mario Cuomo, the Governor of New York, congratulating him on his efforts to encourage audiences to register to vote; he ended his last ever rock show in the US with a rendition of *America The Beautiful* and a cry of "See you in the Fall!"

CHAPTER FOUR
Shall We Take Ourselves Seriously?

"One of the interesting things about our European audience, especially in Germany - when we first started playing in Germany, we had a large part of the audience in certain cities that were close to US installations, where the GIs would come to the shows. In some cases it would be thirty to forty percent of the audience would be GIs. So we looked forward to doing those cities because we could do more songs where we could talk to the audience, 'cause we knew people understood what we were talking about. But today, when we play in Germany, the bulk of the audience that comes to see us is German. We have a very low turnout of US servicemen because, today, US servicemen like heavy metal."[1]

For some reason, despite being proudly American and writing many US-centric songs, Zappa wound up with a far more fervent fan base outside of his homeland - particularly in Europe. Asked why he thought this was, he told *Playboy* magazine that "Germans, in particular, have a history of supporting new composition. They also have a viable contemporary tradition of new music that gets funded and performed regularly."[2] He went further, telling *High Times*, "I think the lack of airplay that I've had in 25 years of doing music in the United States is amazing. I don't think there's anything wrong with the music that I make. I don't think there is anything in it that would cause it to be undeserving of broadcast airtime, but for some reason it never gets on the air. That's not true in Europe; I've had hit records over there. The largest selling single in CBS's history in Scandinavia was a song called *Bobby Brown Goes Down*. The same song was a big hit in Germany. They don't have problems over there with what I say and what I do. But for some reason, in this country, somebody has said, 'We can't let this man on the radio.' What could happen if you play my records on the radio? Something terrible?"[3]

Well, some terrible things had just happened on the US leg of Zappa's 'Broadway The Hard Way' tour but, as Keneally - ever the optimist - wrote at the time, "For me, the good far outweighed the bad. I felt it was a triumphant tour, and I think that things are going to be better here in Europe. Already Frank has put the clamp on any negative factors that might be affecting the music, and the first two days of rehearsal have gone really well."[4]

Mann, though, later told US author Greg Russo, "By the time the band got to Europe, the vibe within the organisation was terrible. [And] things were to get much worse with the addition of several English record company reps who were assigned to travel with the band and do promotion in each town. These individuals, along with the newly appointed English road manager, seized upon the obviously bad band situation as kind of a game to play, in the form of creating and spreading rumours within the organisation that would serve only to increase the misery and friction."[5]

The first European dates took place in France, Belgium and Germany. From the very start of this leg of the tour, *Stairway To Heaven* sported a new reggae arrangement ("which is far superior to the old one,"[6] claimed Keneally). Zappa had been fond of creating reggae arrangements of his own songs for a number of years. He had been using hand signals in the sixties to introduce sudden time changes or events on stage. And by the eighties, these visual cues had become something of an art form - helped enormously by the calibre of musician he then employed. "Twirling my fingers as if I'm piddling with a Rasta braid on the right side of my head - that means 'play reggae',"[7] he wrote in his autobiography. A bemused Wackerman recalls Zappa doing just that for the first song of one show in Indiana in the early eighties... and then the next: "I just see him get this big grin on his face, and he did it for the entire show!"[8]

the drummer recalls.

At the first concert in France, Zappa told the crowd, "You will be hearing some brand new material tonight. We hope you can understand the words. And for those of you who will not understand the words, there are old songs that you already know the words to." The new material comprised just four songs (*When The Lie's So Big* / *Planet Of The Baritone Women* / *Any Kind Of Pain* / *Jesus Thinks You're A Jerk*) played back-to-back, midway through the set (the first with no intermission); at the next two shows, in Belgium and Germany, just two newies were performed. Zappa didn't regain confidence in playing his recent compositions or lengthy instrumentals until the band hit Cologne. This may in part have had something to do with the venues they played in - the Sportpalais in Gent, for example, is traditionally used for indoor cycling and is not renowned for its great acoustics. But it was clear from the huge cheer that greeted Zappa's announcement that there would be an intermission during the Berlin show that he had concerns about the audience's grasp of the English language. Behind the scenes, though, he had written a new horn chart and had been experimenting with inserting it into another new piece that started with four synthesizers playing a simple chord progression and contained some heavy metal guitar; this would be something he'd tinker with throughout the European leg and parts of it (recorded at various locations) would ultimately be edited into the piece we now know as *When Yuppies Go To Hell*. At one press conference, he was asked how he'd been utilising the Synclavier on the road. Referring to a section from this new piece, he said, "Certain notes in the sequence pop out and, when they do, the horn players imitate those notes. So they're playing along with the machine. The machine is blended into the live performance in that way."[9]

It was at the Deutschlandhalle in Berlin in 1978 that David Bowie approached Zappa's then guitarist, Adrian Belew, asking if he would work with him after the tour. Belew duly did, and then went on to play with the likes of Talking Heads and King Crimson. The incident in Berlin became a part of Zappa folklore which, in 1982, spurred him on to get keyboard player Mars to forge a letter from Bowie to Vai and Thunes; this had them both believing for days that Bowie wanted them in his band. Thunes had relayed this story to Keneally, who subsequently got his own 'Bowie letter' which he "knew hadn't come from Frank, it was evidently not his work, but it was a not bad facsimile of a letter which David Bowie might well have written to me if he'd seen me play and wanted me in his band. It ended up being from Ed and Chad. On the bus to Cologne, I showed the letter to Frank and he was wildly amused by it, and everyone began hatching a plot to get Albert in on the game. I think Ed was a little bit disappointed when he found out that I didn't believe the letter for a second, he didn't realise I'd already been aware of the tradition. But it was a lot of fun."[10]

At the show in Frankfurt, Zappa seemed in an impish mood, introducing Thunes to a very enthusiastic crowd as "everybody's favourite bass player," and, during the encores, commenting, "Now that we've succeeded in messing up a Led Zeppelin song, let's fuck with the Beatles!" The next night in Cologne saw the premiere performance of the new piece that would ultimately become a part of *When Yuppies Go To Hell*, which was referred to at the time variously as the *'Dessicated Number'* or *'New Song'*. And then the band left mainland Europe for the UK.

The last time the author had seen Zappa in action was at the Hammersmith Odeon in 1982; I'd seen him six times since 1977. But, because of my impending nuptials, I couldn't justify seeing him in 1984. Even though I'd not long been a father in April 1988, there was no way I was going to miss him this time though. Of course, in those days there was no Internet and access to information on Zappa's releases and concerts could only really be gleaned from the weekly music papers. But even this was not particularly detailed, and so I had no idea who was in his touring band, although I figured there'd be at least one or two familiar faces. Also, my Zappa obsession back then was being somewhat reigned-in by my new family commitments. So the idea of attending more than one of the four UK shows sadly wasn't on the cards - especially as I would be attending another gig the day before his first Wembley show. So I cut out the ads in the press, read what interviews with the man I could find and contented myself with seeing him again soon.

No such concerns hampered Al Stone, who attended three of the four UK shows - including the first one in Brighton, on the author's mother's 58th birthday. Take it away, Al: "As soon as I discovered the dates of the UK leg of the tour, I was on the phone to friends and regular concert companions - Michael and Daniel - to see if they wanted to come. As I expected, the big decision was how many nights can we manage to get to. The three of us had enjoyed an outing to Brighton to see the Kronos Quartet, so we decided that a trip to the seaside would be an essential start to our '88 tour experience. Obviously, if we were prepared to drive the 50 miles to Brighton, we would also have to make the shorter journey to Wembley so we decided to book for the first night there as well. And my wife, Nadja, decided to join us at this closer-to-home venue. As the day of the Brighton show approached, I began to hear a few snippets about the band - there was a new stunt guitarist, Ike was in it and, something I was really looking forward to experiencing, there was a brass section. Even armed with this knowledge it was still a surprise when I realised that there was a BIG BAND on stage and I wasn't prepared for the 'showman' style Zappa who got the band to start into *Stink-Foot* before walking, to rapturous applause, out on stage. It was a treat to hear from the start that the arrangements sounded really rich with a big brass section. Zappa's glassy Strat tone, which was relatively clean compared to earlier tours, was a surprise and, in keeping with the sound, his playing - while still in that uniquely Zappa vein - lacked some of the edge I had come to expect from recordings and previous concerts. Another thing I wasn't prepared for was the interval. I'd got used to the

Hammersmith Odeon gigs, where you were greeted by a warning/guarantee notice stating that Zappa would play a long show without an interval. I was used to surprises from Zappa, but I hadn't been expecting Beatles' tunes and *I Am The Walrus* gave me a big thrill. One of the things I loved about Zappa's shows was the mixture of new material and new arrangements of classic (Zappa) songs, and I'd got used to hearing bits of other peoples songs interjected into these. But the number of covers that the '88 band played was an unexpected revelation. The arrangements on these covers were as detailed and powerful as those for Zappa's own material, and to me this indicated respect and affection for these pieces. If "*Walrus*" initially appeared to be an isolated treat, this was disproved by the encores. It seemed like we were getting an insight into some of the non-Zappa repertoire that he considered worth the trouble of putting the Zappa stamp on."

In his introduction, Zappa had said, 'it's a great pleasure to perform once again for people who can understand what the fuck we are talking about and, simply because in theory you can understand what we are talking about, we will be doing some new songs for you tonight.' Having said that, the first set was mainly comprised of old familiar songs - save for a second run through of *Dessicated*, which Zappa cut short after a soprano sax solo and failed attempt at conducting the crowd. The second set, though, included all of the new songs in the 'Republican Retrospective Medley', during which a member of the audience tried to endear the English to Zappa once and for all by hurling a plastic pint 'glass' on stage, hitting the Synclavier. Zappa momentarily stopped the band to glare at the 'fan'.

"Uh-uh, no,' reprimanded Frank. The twist? An echo was miraculously put on the 'No' and it was bounced around from channel to channel. After a suitable pause, the band picked up again - funny that the line they stopped on was 'You will make a mistake...' Uncanny. Not surprisingly, the line was replayed with a renewed vigour and purpose,"[11] wrote Matthew Johns in British Zappa fanzine, T'Mershi Duween. The British, of course, had long-since earned a special place in Zappa's heart as a result of two specific incidents: firstly, when Trevor Howell pushed Zappa off the stage into the orchestra pit of the Rainbow Theatre in December 1971, nearly killing him; and secondly, when Zappa tried unsuccessfully to sue the Crown for breach of contract after a Mothers' show at the Royal Albert Hall was cancelled on 'possible obscene material' grounds. Also in attendance at the Brighton show was Tim Summers, who saw another extraordinary moment, which, "for me will be the most amazing thing I ever heard Zappa play; right at the peak of his solo on *Sharleena*, a string broke with a tremendous bang over the PA - and he played the rest of the solo entirely with hammer-ons and feedback."[12]

The all-non-Zappa encores were: the Beatles/Swaggart medley, the mighty Zep's "*Stairway*", and Ravel's *Boléro*. In his diary, Keneally notes that Zappa "heard from the British record company that they are interested in releasing a CD single of *Boléro*, so he was trying very hard at these English shows to get a really good version of *Boléro* on tape, and this one wasn't it. There was some really horrible stuff going on in the one section with [name deleted] particularly." It was one of the sax players that cocked-up, is all this author knows.

The record company was Music For Nations, who had just released Zappa's *Guitar*, an album of solos recorded between 1979 and 1984 and (with the exception of three tracks) excerpted from live performances of Zappa songs and bequeathed bespoke monikers of their own. This was a sequel to his earlier *Shut Up 'n Play Yer Guitar* set, and was nominated for the Best Rock Instrumental Performance; it lost out to Carlos Santana's *Blues For Salvador*. After finishing work on Monday 18th April 1988, the author bought a copy of this on CD from the Virgin Megastore in London's Oxford Street before catching the tube to Wembley Park; never ever dreaming I'd be writing about this now, that's for sure.

I got my ticket as soon as the date was announced, and managed to score myself a seat in the centre of the third row with a tremendous view of the band. You only have to see one of the clips on *YouTube* (even a poor quality one) to witness the awesome power of this amazing group of musicians performing the new age version of *The Black Page*. From my vantage point, the sound was absolutely amazing, and I've attended many concerts at the Wembley Arena, before and since, and never heard anyone sound so good ("Yeah, well, we have Harry Andronis, a Chicago native, to thank for that. He's our house mixer. He does a good job,"[13] Zappa told Kevin Matthews). It may just have been good fortune, having such a great seat, as Zappa himself announced that he was "so glad you could make it to help absorb some of the horrible echo in this room tonight."

Al Stone's experience too differed from the author's, as he'll tell you in a moment. But I'm centre stage now. Yes, me. Everybody look at me. At this time I was oblivious to the fact that Zappa had been playing freshly minted songs, and remained that way until some months later. On their first London date, every song the band performed was originally released in the seventies or earlier - with the exception of *Teen-age Wind*. But the arrangements had been really spiffed up, with the horns adding some real oomph to the likes of *Disco Boy*. I remember thinking how healthy Zappa looked. So little did I know.

During the intermission, I went for a leg-stretch and who should I notice, about to leave the Arena? None other than Robert Plant CBE, who I had seen at the Hammersmith Odeon just the night before. As a long-time Zeppelin fan, I just had to try and talk to him. The security guards happily let me out to give chase. I told him how much I'd enjoyed the previous evening's encores with James Patrick Page - especially B.B. King's *Gambler's Blues*. He was with a young lady and was naturally a little pre-occupied, but he scribbled his name on an Abbey National till receipt for me and I watched him dive into a waiting car with his female escort. Didn't even say goodbye. No, that's not true: he was more than polite and it really helped make this evening extra-special for me.

Those who have been spoiled by listening to all of the many audience recordings from the 'Broadway The Hard Way' tour describe this particular show as uninspired. But I think if listened to in isolation - and I believe this applies to every single one of the concerts - you can't help but be impressed by this amazing big band. Sure, I now know that there were some truly stunning performances along the way, but even an 'average' '88 show knocked spots off of anything else around at that time. Or any time. As I re-entered the auditorium, the band were back on stage and Zappa was soon singing *I Ain't Got No Heart* from the very first Mothers' album. True, there hadn't been too many real surprises in the set thus far. But it wasn't long before the Synclavier and weird array of vocal samples were being utilised during *Big Swifty*. And then came new boy Keneally's big moment, as he sang *Who Needs The Peace Corps?* "For some reason, Scott and Ike had congregated on stage directly in front of me,"[14] he recalls. But with a cry of "Will you guys get out of my way!" Keneally managed to get to the front of the stage to perform the song's closing monologue. This incident caused Zappa and his jokemeister to heckle him mercilessly.

At Zappanale #20, the author asked Willis about the mischief he and Zappa got up to on stage during the tour - asking if he had any particularly fond memories: "Oh, just too many," he said. "We just had so much fun. I'd be at my mic, singing, playing, trying to do my job, and Frank would sl-i-i-i-i-de over to me, and suddenly he's right there and in the middle of a verse, he'd say something, and I'm on the floor. Then, of course, now I've got to get him back. And we could go on like that all night long. As the tour progressed, it would get more and more like that. That was the hardest tour!" - all said with a huge grin on his face.

The audience were clearly enjoying things too, and Zappa perhaps misconstrued the cheers that greeted Robert Martin's mock lounge singing of *I Left My Heart In San Francisco*, when he commented, "I think we've discovered that this is the only audience in the world that really wants to hear that song, so let's just do it to them." Throughout the tour, Zappa had been referring to Tony Bennett's signature song as one of the ugliest things ever written. Probed on this by Den Simms of Society Pages, Zappa said "Oh, I'm just joking, that's not the ugliest. I think *Happy Birthday* is one of the ugliest songs ever written!"[15] After Martin reprised his snatch from the 23rd most historically significant song of the 20th century, the band thundered into *Peaches En Regalia* from Zappa's most popular album in the UK - to huge cheers. What came next nearly blew my mind: *Stairway To Heaven*. I sat in awe as the band played an almost faithful reggae rendition (if that's possible). I was completely taken by surprise by the inclusion of this song in a Zappa set, as were most of the audience. By quoting from the *Teddy Bears's Picnic* and *Dance Of The Cuckoos* (aka *The Laurel And Hardy Theme*), was he actually taking the piss? As the song approached its hard rocking finale, Frank stepped forward with his Strat... only for the horn section to play Jimmy Page's famous guitar solo note-for-note (as Trey Anastasio revealed in Chapter Two). I was gobsmacked. Whatever statement he was making about this classic rock song, after running down the band member's names, Zappa signed off with a friendly "Thanks for coming to the show. Good night, Robert!" But, but... Percy's slipped out, I wanted to shout*.

Of course we called them back, and were treated to more amazing cover versions (*Boléro* and *I Am The Walrus*). By this time my head was spinning so much, I couldn't even put a name to *The Illinois*

---

* Mike Keneally's wife confirmed that Robert had just left the building - he told Society Pages *"My wife was sitting right next to him, and at one point, he said to her, 'Can you hear the bass?' because Wembley has such horrible acoustics. My wife said that she couldn't hear the bass, and he goes 'Yes, it sounds rather strange in here, doesn't it?' Of course, my wife was trembling, 'cause Robert Plant was asking her these questions. Maybe it was because the sound wasn't too good, but he took off before we played 'Stairway.' But it was nice of him to make it over, even for an hour."*
[Society Pages USA, Issue 6]

Enema Bandit, a song I'd heard many times before - and even more since. Before *Boléro*, Zappa had said, "If you're enjoying this tonight, it'll be a completely different show tomorrow night." But still this thicko didn't take the hint. The very final song of the night was *Strictly Genteel*, which originally appeared in Zappa's movie *200 Motels* and contained the line, "Lord, have mercy on the people in England, for the terrible food these people must eat." He introduced what was an amazing instrumental rock band version, thus: "This song was first played by the Royal Philharmonic Orchestra, and then later by the London Symphony Orchestra. And now, we're gonna play it right!"

In attendance that first night were Roland Orzabal (of Tears For Fears) and Bill Bruford, who Keneally described as "a sweetheart of a guy, not at all the ogre I've been led to expect by various articles. He remarked that Ike and I seem to have a good time on stage together, which is true."[16] Pete Townshend was reputedly there the next night, and Bruford again too - for the sound check, anyway.

Okay, now it's time for Mr Stone to give his impressions of Wembley: "It didn't take more than a few bars of music to remind us that this was Zappa and he was not going to simply go for a repeat of the previous day's programme. Unfortunately, it also didn't take more than a few bars to remind us that the acoustic of the arena is crap. However the quality of the playing and the music, together with the excitement of hearing a bunch of different pieces to the previous day transcended that and I was soon absorbed in the show and ignoring the shortcomings of the space. I've heard so many recordings, official and otherwise, of various shows from the 1988 tour that I can't put hand on heart and say I remember particular parts of the performance from that night. All the subsequent listenings, reading of reviews and discussions with others who were there have conspired to produce a composite memory so I can't accurately recall impressions of most pieces. I do however distinctly remember the mixed feelings I got when *Strictly Genteel* started. I was thrilled that they were playing a piece I loved, but I was also convinced that it would be the last number of the evening as it is such a brilliant piece to end on. Yes, it was the end of the first Wembley concert, and supposedly also the end of my 1988 tour experience. I had heard a band who played a huge repertoire of fantastic music brilliantly and I wanted more. After all they were playing Wembley for a second day, but how would I present my need to go to the next night to Nadja? As I was mentally grappling with this she turned to me and said something along the lines of, 'that was such a fantastic show, I wish my son had seen it. Any chance we could get tickets to bring him tomorrow?' Oh, yeah there was a chance, and all I had to do was to give the people I worked for the final evidence that I was nuts, by telling them that I needed to leave early for the second day running to go to my third Zappa concert in a row. In fact I needed to leave even earlier than the day before so that I could be front of the queue for returns when the box office opened. And front of the queue I was, getting the three tickets that would ensure that I provided my stepson with the very best musical education possible. In fact Zappa was far from his thirteen year old musical taste but music had meant a lot to him from a young age. I found out years later that this concert had left him with a lasting impression. In an interview he gave to an online dance music magazine to publicise one of his DJ-ing gigs, he mentioned 'Zappa Wembley 1988' as a formative musical experience. There were others of his generation there who had discovered Zappa's music and in a queue during the interval that night I heard two kids who were too young to have been around when the original albums came out agreeing how great it was to hear *Oh No* and the *Theme From Lumpy Gravy*."

"When that second Wembley show was over I knew it really was the end of my '88 tour experience. If I had known then that it would be the last chance to see Zappa with a touring band nothing would have stopped me from going to Birmingham the next night, but as we compared our experiences on the way home I was enthusing about how amazing it was to have heard three such different concerts, each full of highlights, and we were all sure that even though we might have to wait a few years for the next tour, Frank would be back again because he was a master of live concerts and, after all, it was one of the things he lived for wasn't it?"

Al neglects to mention that during *Dickie's Such An Asshole*, "Ed made a mistake on the diddle-uh-dit-dit diddle-uh-dit-dit, and Frank didn't let him get away with it. He made him do it three times total until it was at least reasonably accurate, and then we went on... much to the horror of several people in the band. Turns out later that several members of the band thought that Frank was in a really bad mood and I just thought that he wanted to hear the songs played right. Seemed to make sense to me,"[17] wrote Keneally. This incident later prompted a lyric change when, during *Any Kind Of Pain*, Martin sang "Accuracy sounds good." For the second encore, Frank introduced his eldest son, saying "Dweezil is going to play the guitar solo on this special version of *Chunga's Revenge*." Of course, Frank joined in, but you have to agree with Keneally that the lad "did a wonderful job. After the show, I was talking to Dweezil in his little room backstage and Frank came in and gave Dweezil a big hug and told him that he was a musician now, boy, because it was the most demanding backing that he had ever had to play a solo over. At least with Frank, and he pulled it off really well. Frank said it was great. It was a nice moment."[18] God, why didn't I go?

One fan who did witness the last of the UK shows in Birmingham was none other than the editor of this book: "Like the author I wasn't too impressed with the previous tour in '84, which had been my first experience of Zappa live. Slightly surprising given that I had been introduced to his music in 1969 as a mere six-year old, courtesy of my eldest brother Richard. Having grown up to the sounds of *Uncle Meat*, *Weasels Ripped My Flesh* and *Hot Rats* from such a young age had certainly ensured that my musical upbringing was a colourful one. By 1988 I had most of Zappa's catalogue but I certainly wasn't prepared for what I experienced on what would be his final tour. Despite my disillusionment with the '84 tour and less than a hundred per cent enthusiasm for most of the albums that had been released during the ensuing four-year period, I had decided to get tickets for a couple of shows. The first was the opening night at Wembley and it was a huge improvement on what I had witnessed at the Hammersmith Odeon in 1984. Twenty-two years on, my memory of that first show amounts to very little, but I do recall the set-list impressing me; in particular the inclusion of *Mr Green Genes* and *Peaches En Regalia* and being taken aback at the inclusion of *Stairway To Heaven, I Am The Walrus* and *Boléro*. That said, I knew that Richard was in for a treat. He was generally one of those that Zappa once described as thinking the only good stuff was the early material. He was particularly fond of *Mr Green Genes* and our mutual favourite Zappa composition, *Peaches En Regalia*, was going to be the icing on the cake for him - especially as it wasn't performed during that '84 gig we attended."

"Little did I know as we headed off to the NEC on that April evening that we would witness what was almost an entirely different set. As I had been the one who had got the tickets, I was delighted that we had excellent seats in the fourth row and somehow it felt like my way of thanking Richard for introducing me to Zappa's music almost twenty years earlier. All I remember repeating as each of the first few songs were played was 'they didn't play this at Wembley!' As it then dawned on me that Zappa might not play *Mr Green Genes* or *Peaches En Regalia* they suddenly launched into *Cruisin' For Burgers* from *Uncle Meat*, which delighted Richard no end. Amongst my most vivid memories of the evening was a lengthy instrumental section (although I don't recall which song) where Zappa conducted the band, pointing to the guys at random to take solos. As I later learned, not only were they playing different sets each night but aside from having to learn so much stuff they also had to improvise when required, and at this show it was there in abundance: a truly phenomenal experience to witness. My other memory that sticks with me to this day was a moment during what I think must have been *Hot Plate Heaven At The Green Hotel* where one audience member appeared to be heckling. As it came to Zappa's solo, he focused his eyes upon the offending audience member and stared at him without hardly moving a muscle for what seemed like an eternity. He virtually wrung the guys neck during an awesome and lengthy solo. Fortunately, despite the huge variation in the set-list, *"Peaches"* was once again played, probably because Zappa was well aware of just how popular the *Hot Rats* album was in England. It certainly ensured that Richard went away happy and we both marvelled at the amazing standard of musicianship we had witnessed."

At a press conference during the UK shows at London's Dorchester Hotel, Zappa did little to hide his disdain for the rock 'n roll writers he once described as "the worst kind of sleaze"[19]. He was asked by one journalist whether the band's performance of Stravinsky's *Royal March* predicted speed metal. Zappa snapped back, "No, because my rendering of the *Royal March* was made a long time after speed metal was invented." "Oh, but it was rather fast," said the hack. "It was very fast. You wait till you hear our version of Ravel's *Boléro*. Of course, we play it as a reggae." When asked what he enjoyed doing most in the music business, he said "I enjoy playing with my band." And the least? "What, do you mean, next to doing a press conference?"[20]

During the four UK dates they played, the band performed over 60 different songs. Zappa was also fiddling with the arrangements of some of his old compositions: in the very first issue of his Zappa fanzine, T'Mershi Duween, Fred Tomsett reported that he "had got down to Wembley early enough to be able to hear the sound check. FZ spent a long time taking the band through *Cruisin' For Burgers*, writing a new middle section as he went."[21] This was utilised during the second Wembley show, but by the time he got to Birmingham, Zappa had changed it some more. Also in Birmingham, *More Trouble*

With Fabio Treves, waiting to hear from Mayor Pillitteri about his proposal for a World Cup football opera. *(Maki Galimberti)*

Left: Whether on stage or in the studio, Zappa invariably had a cigarette in hand...
(Lynn Goldsmith / Corbis)

Below: In the studio with the late Bob Stone, engineer on the 'Broadway', 'Best Band' and 'Jazz Noise' albums. *(Lynn Goldsmith / Corbis)*

Above: In Italy with everyone's favourite bass player Scott Thunes, and a cup of coffee.
(Fabio Treves)

Overleaf: Italy the hard way. *(Fabio Treves)*

Insets: Keneally and Thunes.
Mike Keneally was the only band member who stuck by
Clonemeister Thunes when Zappa gave them the ultimatum.
(Stanley Hope Collection)

Mike Keneally

Scott Thunes

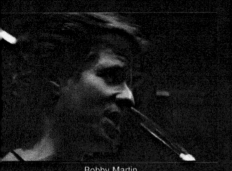

Bobby Martin

Ed Mann

Chad Wackerman

Ike Willis

Main photo: Soloing in Italy. *(Deepinder Cheema)*

Insets *(Stanley Hope Collection)*

Below: "Ladies and gentlemen - Ike Willis."

My fabulous wife:

Left: Relaxing with Gail.
(Lynn Goldsmith / Corbis)

Below: An executive kinda guy.
(Lynn Goldsmith / Corbis)

Following the tour Zappa wasted no time in documenting it on record, or more to the point, the relatively new medium of the day, compact disc, releasing five discs worth of recordings from the tour within three years of its conclusion. Did they ensure the returns on the $400,000 he claimed he lost through cancelling the remaining scheduled dates?

Every Day sported a new mid-section introduced by Zappa during the afternoon rehearsal for that show; Keneally remembered Zappa saying "he wanted to put something new in the middle because he was thinking of using it as an opening song. So we tried it with *Dessicated.* That didn't quite work, so Frank just started making up a new thing. Just wrote it on the spot there."[22]

It was actually very reminiscent of the vamp from something he'd 'made up' just before going on stage with violinist L. Shankar in 1978 for the Halloween shows in New York - which was eventually released on *You Can't Do That On Stage Anymore, Vol. 6* in 1992 - called *Thirteen* (which is "sub-divided 5/8 and 4/4, if you wanna clap your hands."[23]). At the end of the Birmingham show, Keneally could not fail to remember, "there was a guy in the front who was giving me the thumbs up saying, 'Great show!' and everything, and he was wearing the coolest purple and green hat. I said, 'Great hat!' and he tossed it up on stage and said - dramatically - 'It's yours!' So I gave him a guitar pick, and walked back happily wearing my hat, and nabbed one of the big old posters that was up on the wall advertising *Guitar*. So I had a hat, and a neat poster, and I was thinking that everything was just about as cool as it could be, and then in walks Scott with Andy Partridge and Dave Gregory [of XTC]. Mere words can't do justice to how neat this was. Suffice it to say that they mentioned to us that they would be in Los Angeles recording when we got back, and Andy suggested that it might be cool for me to come in and do a little guitar work on their album. Uh, this is obviously unbelievably fantastic. So I'm just going to stop talking about it." Keneally is a huge fan of XTC's, and included both a snippet of their *Mayor Of Simpleton* and a song written in tribute to the band (*Open Up!*) on his very first solo album, *hat.* - which also features a cover shot of Keneally w-e-r-e-i-n-g (never mind) the very titfer thrown up on stage at the Birmingham show.

One of the major things the UK shows lacked was any secret words. Well, the band more than made up for this on its return to mainland Europe. On the afternoon of the next show in Würzburg, West Germany, Zappa was introduced to country music legend Johnny Cash, who agreed to sing with the band that night. Unfortunately, Cash's wife (June Carter) then became ill and he was unable to do so. But the band had rehearsed both a heavy metal version of *I Walk The Line* and a reggae rendering of Cash's biggest hit, *Ring Of Fire* (co-incidentally, co-written by Carter). And so - at the end of a blistering brass enhanced *Heavy Duty Judy*, and in response to a banner in the audience - Zappa advised that the night's secret word was 'ring of fire' and asked how many people would like to hear the song even if Johnny wasn't going to sing it. The audience's response made it clear that the band should definitely play the song. So step forward, Mr Keneally: "Since I managed to do a serviceable Johnny Cash impersonation in the sound check', Frank asked if I would be willing to do it during the show and I said, 'Sure.' So *Ring Of Fire* was not initially written into the set list, but it got stuck in... just called on the spot. And the words 'ring of fire', and little musical bits of *Ring Of Fire*, managed to find themselves in almost every song that night. It was very funny."[24] They had so much fun that they ended up performing the song twice more: for the first encore, Zappa introduced it by saying, "Boy, it sure is a shame that Johnny couldn't make it tonight. We really missed him down here. He would've gotten a big charge outta this shit. In fact, the sickest thing we could do this evening is play that fucking song one more time! I'm gettin' to like that song a lot. Everybody now!"; and, for the third encore, he said "In answer to a rapidly diminishing number of requests, we just can't help ourselves - we have to play it again." That night, the Zeppelin classic mutated into *Stairway To Fire*. Wing told me "I did my best not to lose it - *Ring Of Fire* was that funny." Keneally adds: "At least half of that show ended up being sung in fake Johnny Cash voices by the whole band. Pity the poor Würzburgians."[25]

---

* On his website, Keneally subsequently wrote, "*I will always contend it sounds more like Mr. Ed.*" [http://www.keneally.com/allaboutmike.html]

After the gig, the band drove to Bremen and sort-of enjoyed a day off. According to Keneally, Bremen "was very cold, and very sort-of gray, and almost modern, but not. The buildings were fairly worn, and it was like a city that wasn't quite thriving. And when we arrived there, it was on a Saturday, and everything was closed. We went to McDonald's and got a Big Mac, and we went back to the hotel and relaxed for awhile. And realised that we had to go and get something better to eat. And we went and tried to go to a steakhouse, but you needed reservations to eat there. So we went to a little restaurant nearby, and we wandered about the mall that was adjacent to the hotel, and couldn't really go for much in the way of walks, because it was quite cold [and] everything was closed." The show the next day saw the last stab at *Dessicated*, and Greek composer Iannis Xenakis - together with a mumbling sound - became the secret words.

At the sound check in Copenhagen, they rehearsed another new song, *Rhymin' Man*, which Zappa had just written especially for Keneally: "he told me on the bus ride to Copenhagen that he'd written a Johnny Cash-type song for me to sing, and Bob Rice kept telling me how that was a big step, to have a song written especially for you, and I'm sure that's true." The song is about the Reverend Jesse Jackson, and partly redressed the balance after all the Republican bashing on the tour. It also included short extracts from a whole host of traditional and/or popular songs, including Chopin's *Marche Funebre*, *Happy Days Are Here Again*, *Entry Of The Gladiators*, *Havah Nagilah*, *Hail To The Chief*, *La Cucaracha*, *Frere Jacques*, *Hallelujah*, *I'm A Bum* and The Knack's *My Sharona* (which Zappa heard being rehearsed in the studio next door when he was recording the *Joe's Garage* album). During his lengthy interview with the guys from the US fanzine, Society Pages, Zappa asked if they recognised the snippet from *Mississippi Mud*, which follows the line "Dipped his hands in the doctor's blood and rubbed it on his shirt like playin' with mud." When they said they hadn't, he said this was because he was so old, "I've heard more music, and more kinds of music than the average listener today. I lived through a whole musical area that most of the fans that listen to it now, they never heard those songs. So things that would seem automatic to me, as a visual aid so to speak, you'll never know. I mean, you've probably never even heard *Mississippi Mud*. One day, in an old movie, you'll hear that song, and you'll go, 'Uh-oh! It's *Rhymin' Man'*." And it's that sort of attention to detail that makes Zappa's work so endlessly fascinating for many of us - you find yourself listening to a song on the radio or hearing a phrase on TV and start singing one of his songs. Anyway, back in Copenhagen, sitting in the front row was Danish school teacher and hard-core fan, Ole Lysgaard*, who Zappa had gotten to know over the years. In his liner notes to *Joe's Menage*, Lysgaard wrote "Frank opened the concert, dedicating the show to me, asking me to stand up, saying that he hoped I especially would enjoy the program of the evening (which I, strangely enough, did very much)."[26] That night, Willis sang *Mr Green Genes, Florentine Pogen* and *Andy* in his guise of the Thing-Fish.**

Onto Lund in Sweden where journalist Geir Meyer-Johansen was lucky enough to attend the sound check. He recalls how hard the band had to practice the new songs; Zappa was drilling Keneally especially, wanting him to play some country-ish things on one of the new songs (probably *Rhymin' Man*). Keneally also noted, "we did a medley from *The Mystery Disc, Box 2. Wedding Dress Song*, and *Handsome Cabin Boy*†. We started working on that, really pretty, really nice. Just a quartet version, Frank, Scott, Chad and me."[27] Meyer-Johansen says Zappa ended up alone on stage, trying out new guitar

---

* In 1978, Zappa gave Lysgaard several cassette tapes, including one of part of his 1 November 1975 concert at the College of William and Mary in Williamsburg, Virginia. In 2004, Lysgaard sent the tape to Zappa's widow, Gail, who decided to officially release the recording as *Joe's Menage* [Vaulternative Records, 2008].

** "*The dialect comes from a black poet at the turn of the century by the name of Paul Lawrence Dunbar. I told Frank about this guy because that's really where the dialect from Amos And Andy comes from. Dunbar used to write his poems in that dialect, exactly the same way you see it written in the libretto on Thing-Fish. I always thought that was great and pretty funny.*"
Thing-Fish Rap by Evil Prince [T'Mershi Duween, #54, October 1996].

† "*I love sea shanties, I thought they were really good melodies, so I arranged them for a rock and roll band. We used to play 'em all the time. I used to really love to listen to sea shanties and folk music. When everyone else was listening to Cream, I was listening to A. L. Lloyd and Ewan McColl. These were two old guys who used to record together, trying to replicate the original instrumentation of sea shanties. Some of the words were absolutely unbelievable. Handsome Cabin Boy is a song about the bogus certification of sailors. A girl goes on a boat dressed as a boy, and gets pregnant. The lyrics are all about who done it. I loaned the LP to Beefheart, and he probably still has it.*"
[From the liner notes to Zappa's The Lost Episodes (Rykodisc, 1996).]

sounds and playing "some marvellous solos". Zappa quoted from *Handsome Cabin Boy* during his guitar solo that night on the opening *Black Page #2*. Of the rest of the show, Pat Buzby said *A Pound For A Brown* "starts in a straightforward vein with an exciting Albert Wing solo and a typical Robert Martin one, but things get weird abruptly when Ed Mann gets his turn. The bizarre musical environment here apparently moves FZ to burst into song, and so we get the only *Dangerous Kitchen* of the year. This set is quite well-performed, but suffers from a set list that lacks many of the more exciting '88 items. That changes with the first encore, *Cruisin' For Burgers*. Here we get perhaps the definitive rendition of one of the great rediscoveries of the year, a perfect showcase for the majesty of this band and a number where FZ's new sedate soloing style truly makes sense, suggesting mature dignity rather than a lack of energy. This is one of the great moments that only this tour can provide, and explains why the '88 outing deserves a place on the list of great FZ tours in spite of its flaws."[28]

For some reason, the secret words during the Scandinavian leg of the tour were reaching new heights of silliness. In Oslo, one was "shausage" which, as readers from the UK over a certain age will know, came from the long-running BBC TV programme, *That's Life*, which occasionally would feature performing pets. Prince the talking dog became an (arf!) "over-nite sensation" when he was featured saying a number of words and phrases, thanks to having his jaw manipulated by his owner. 'Shausages' was the one that really captured the imagination and, when Zappa was told about this, he relayed it to the rest of the band. The audience that night in Oslo also joined in the fun, sometimes second-guessing the lyric changes. This was the only show of the tour that Zappa was unable to record for posterity as the recording truck broke down. They finally premiered *Rhymin' Man* that night, and another odd thing happened when Zappa noticed his guitar was out of tune and he had Walt Fowler play a trumpet solo during a "Fleetwood Mac version" of *The Torture Never Stops* (a song that over the years produced very many memorable solos from Zappa).

After the show, Keneally observed "there was a lot of unhappy band-ness going on, that is, just people not enjoying themselves generally, which is a real shame. But I love it, you know, I'm having a good time all over the place. So I was cool. But, unfortunately, there's a lot of disgruntlement in this band. If only everybody could be happy. But, sigh."[29]

Finland being regarded as the home of Santa Claus, the band had some fun the next night with the secret words 'reindeer' and 'Rudolph' (Zappa ran down the band members as Dancer, Prancer, Donner, Blitzen, etc.) At a concert in Helsinki fourteen years earlier, Zappa had responded to a request from the audience to play the Allman Brothers Band's *Whippin' Post* by saying "Oh sorry, we don't know that one... hum me a few bars of it... just show me how it goes, please, and then maybe we'll play it with you."[30] Dismissing it as a John Cage composition, the band then played a revised version of a fan favourite which, on *You Can't Do That On Stage Vol. 2: The Helsinki Concert*, is named *Montana (Whipping Floss)* due to its hastily amended lyrics. By the eighties, Zappa had learnt the Allman's classic and it regularly became a concert closer, thanks to Martin's belting vocals. In 1988, it finally received its belated Zappa premiere in Helsinki - and of course the lyric got changed, as Martin ended it with "I believe I am the walrus," while the band launched into said Beatles' classic. What larks!

Now we're into May 1988, and I think I'll hand over to another special guest: Morgan Ågren, Swedish drum virtuoso with the Mats/Morgan Band. Morgan has been a drummer since he was four, and he joined forces with blind keyboard player Mats Öberg in 1981 while in his early teens, and Mats was just nine. They formed a Zappa cover band in 1984, called Zappsteetoot, and... well, I'll let Morgan tell you about the next show at the Johanneshovs Isstadion in Stockholm:

"In 1988 when Frank came to Stockholm with the 'Broadway The Hard Way' tour, me and Mats got to meet and play with Zappa on his gig in Stockholm, as guests! Mats' uncle (jazz pianist, Bernt Egerbladh) had contacted Frank's tour leader and informed him about us, that we were in this band called Zappsteetoot, that Mats had listened to Frank's music since he was eight years old, and that he knew all of his music. So when Frank got to hear about us, he said he wanted to meet us. Mats and I sneaked in to Frank's sound check and afterward Frank's tour leader came out and told us Frank waiting for us backstage. We walked to Frank's room, and there he was - our teenage idol and major influence! We shook hands and sat down on a couch. Frank started to ask us how we were doing, which of his material we knew. etc. Mats and I ended up playing on our knees and singing. Frank said, 'Do you know this? Have you played that?' After a while, he said, 'Well, I'm amazed that two young guys from a little town called Umeå know so much about my music.' Then, turning to Mats, he said, 'You have listened to my music so much - you should know what I look like.' Frank took Mats' hand and laid it on his forehead, and Mats began to feel how Frank looked! And Frank said, 'Don't forget the famous nose!'"

"Frank was so incredibly nice to us and we had a wonderful time. We also gave him a tape with our own music, including one Zappa piece, *T'Mershi Duween*, which surprised Frank because it wasn't released at the time, but we knew it from a bootleg. Frank didn't listen to the tape; there wasn't even a tape recorder there, but he said, 'Maybe we should do something...?' We didn't have a clue what he was thinking. He scratched his head and said, 'Would you like to come up and play *T'Mershi Duween* as guests? We're gonna do *Big Swifty* tonight, and in the middle section of the song there is this open part where everything can happen! So if you walk behind the stage when you hear the *Big Swifty* theme, I'll introduce you after a while - okay?' The thing was that it was only thirty minutes before the show, and the audience was already inside the hall, so no time to try the keyboards or the drums. What sound will be on the keyboard? What kind of sticks does Chad use? Questions natural for us to ask ourselves before going up on stage with Frank Zappa facing a crowd of 10,000 people."

"To me, most parts of Frank's show were hard to enjoy - I had other things on my mind. We were soon supposed to go up and play, and I couldn´t even remember the fucking song that well either, so I had to think about how it really went. We had only played it once before, a year earlier - the version we gave to Frank on tape. When the *Big Swifty* theme came, we left our seats and walked backstage. After convincing one of the guards that we were about to go up and play with Frank, my next problem was I desperately needed to go to the toilet. I had lost the ability to feel needs like that - I had other things to think about."

"Another five minutes passed and I really had to go. I started to feel pain, I got totally confused; what would happen if Frank introduces us for 10,000 people, and I'm at the toilet unable to even hear him? No thanks. I even asked a guy from the crew if I could make it. As if he would know! But now I just had to do it, I was in such pain I probably wouldn't even play properly. I told Mats, 'I got to go, you wait here.' Mats was sitting on a case just behind the stage. I ran backstage, found a toilet, finished my business and, just as I opened the door from the backstage room, I could hear Frank introducing us. I ran like a maniac, grabbed Mats' arm and we went up on stage. Lucky us - I was fast!"

"A huge round of applause welcomed us. We were at home, and a lot of people knew about us. The applause just got even louder as I walked Mats over to Bobby Martin's keyboards. Bobby said, 'Here's a Yamaha DX-9, and here is the Yamaha electric grand - good luck!' The band kept a reggae beat going during our entrance, which was good; if it had just been silence it would have felt strange, but now we could sort of start our jam from the groove already going. I led Mats behind the keyboards and adjusted the mic stand a little, then

I walked to the drum set. A guy from the crew came from nowhere and put a new pair of drumsticks in my hands. Luckily they were the same model I used to play at the time. When Chad saw me coming, he stood up, but kept the beat on the hi-hat. I sat down and continued where Chad left off."

"Mats and I soon started to loosen up to something else. We had to do our thing, so we just jammed for a couple of minutes, like we always used to. The drums felt okay, the keyboards too, I think. I felt high up there, it was just totally amazing. I don't like using standard phrases, like 'a religious feeling', but this was something else, it really was. I was in heaven. Much because of the fact I could see Frank standing in front of the drum set with a BIG smile holding his conductor stick. He really liked what we were doing, and that gave us a big kick. We missed a little during the *T'Mershi Duween* theme, but we had probably never played as good before as we did then. Scott played along a little and so did Ed and Mike. After we finished, I left the drum seat, and ran to get Mats away from the keyboards, because the *Big Swifty* theme had just started again, and Bobby Martin was about to play again. But Mats was sitting in his way; he was waiting for me to pick him up! I got Mats and passed Frank as we were leaving the stage. Frank stopped conducting just for a second to applaud us, and the audience followed with even more volume than before. We walked off the stage and got back to our seats to see the rest of the show."

"At the end of the show, Frank introduced the band like he always used to, with a chord in the background, saying, 'Ike Willis, Scott Thunes... AND... Mats Öberg and Morgan Ågren. Thanks for coming to the show, hope you liked it. Good night!' We were sitting in the audience listening to Frank Zappa - introducing us! When they came back for an encore, Frank grabbed the microphone and said, 'Those guys were great!' So guess if we were excited! After the encores, we met in Frank's room backstage again. He said we have to do this again sometime and we exchanged addresses. Frank told us that he was looking for a new drummer and keyboard player, and then he just kind of stared at us without really saying anything more. I think he wanted to tease us a little bit too, because he was obviously talking about Mats and I. Frank even wrote down some notes on a piece of paper which showed his way of notating drums. He gave it to me and told me to get used to it. Then it was time to go home; go home and wait for the phone to ring..."[31]

Keneally was also very taken with the duo: "When Mats and Morgan came on to play, I started playing *Sleep Dirt*, and Mats was playing over the changes a bit. Then, they launched into a free-form duet jazz-type thing with Mats, Tommy Mars incarnate, playing unbelievable stuff, scatting along with it, and also playing the stuff that Tommy Mars used to use a harmonised keyboard for: five-note chords on one key. However, this guy was doing it all manually. Actually, it was like a mutant thing happening. The guy was incredible. Then they went into a beautiful version of *T'Mershi Duween*. Frank was beaming, and I was very deeply affected. I hadn't seen any kind of commitment to match this devotion to the music like that in a very long time, and it sort of reminded me what it was about. Very, very cool stuff. Frank obviously was impressed also. After *Big Swifty*, we went into *Joe's Garage*, which to me sounded horrible in comparison to those guys. Depressing."[32]

He confirms that Zappa took their contact details, but they had to wait a few years: the call did eventually come, and the pair ended up being part of the core band - with Keneally and Thunes - for Zappa's Universe, four concerts that took place at The Ritz Theatre in New York on 7th-10th November 1991. The concerts were to have been hosted by Zappa himself, but at a press conference on the afternoon of the first show, Moon advised that, "Although Frank was looking forward to being here... his doctors have diagnosed prostate cancer, which he's been fighting successfully and he has been feeling well... [but] there are occasional periods where he's not feeling as well and it's really unfortunate it happened to coincide with this event."[33]

The concerts included splendid renditions of most of the new songs Zappa had written for the "Broadway" tour as well as numerous special guests, including Steve Vai, Dale Bozzio, Denny Walley, Penn Jillette, and Dweezil, Moon, Diva and their cousin Jade (who provided most of the sampled burps used in 1988). In Zappa's absence, Dweezil walked on stage and held aloft one of his father's guitars - much like the Monty Python sketch in which a tearful Dickie Attenborough says, "Sadly, David Niven cannot be with us tonight, but he has sent his fridge."[34] Lemon curry, anyone?

Ågren's recollection of the first day at Zappa's rehearsal facility in North Hollywood prior to the shows is quite revealing: "Mats and I got there first. We set up our equipment and were ready to go maybe thirty minutes before the actual rehearsal, so we decided to go out and wait for the other ones to come. We bought something to drink and sat down on the sidewalk. A car went by, somebody stepped out: big guy with long hair, sideburns, sunglasses... He opened the trunk and picked out what looked like a bass, and I realised it was Scott Thunes. I guess you all have heard a million stories about the man, about his personality, him breaking up the '88 tour, etc., etc. I had never met Scott before. We had been on stage together, but we never met after the show. Anyhow, I guess we would soon know more about him. Scott locked his car and marched up to Mats and me. I told Mats that Scott was there, and Mats totally lightened up. When Scott was facing us, he says, 'Greetings!' and we shook hands. Mats says, 'Nice to be here!' Scott's reply was, 'Well, I'm not sure about that - that we're gonna find out later... it´s too hot outside, I got to go inside. See you.' I looked at Mats with my mouth open, as we started to imagine the attitude of the next two weeks."

"Mike arrived, and when they were ready to play, Mike says 'First side on *You Are What You Is,*' and the next second he counts 'One, two, three, four...' and we're off. And it sounded GREAT! We just ripped it: loud and intense. I could see that Scott liked the way it sounded. After the three songs *Society Pages*, *I'm A Beautiful Guy* and *Beauty Knows No Pain* in segue, Scott put his bass on the floor, threw his pick up in the air, and said, 'GREAT! This is good. Now we won't have to rehearse this shit for the whole week: we can go down to the beach and enjoy ourselves instead!"[35]

And the duo did get to play with Zappa one more time: "He came to two of the rehearsals, and suddenly at one of them he picked up Dweezil's guitar and started to play on two songs,"[36] recalls Öberg. Keneally confirms this: "What made me happy was that the four-piece rock band in Zappa's Universe rehearsed for a week in Los Angeles before we flew to New York to rehearse with the orchestra. Frank came over to watch us rehearse - just me and Scott Thunes and the two Swedish guys. He stayed there for a few hours and really enjoyed himself. To have Frank watch us rehearse that stuff and then pick up a guitar and play *Inca Roads* with us when I hadn't seen him pick up a guitar for a couple of years, that was special. That's my fondest memory of Zappa's Universe, that early rehearsal stage where Frank was hanging out with us and having a good time."[37]

Anyway, back to 1988, and the band has travelled from Scandinavia to the Netherlands. The night before the show at The Ahoy in Rotterdam, Thunes and Keneally went to see Faith No More at The Paradiso in Amsterdam. Keneally recalls some odd coincidences, as "they sang the last part of *Stairway To Heaven*, and then, later on in the show, they quoted the first part of *Norwegian Wood*, and Scott and I were just aghast. Definitely. They were really funny, and they did *War Pigs* as the last part of their first encore. Really, very interesting group, and I bought their shirt because I was so impressed."

"This was several years before Mike Patton joined Faith No More, before they became wildly successful. The night after Scott and I saw them, I wore the Faith No More shirt onstage during the

Zappa show, and a couple of the Faith No More guys were there. Years later, after they became huge, they started hanging around the Zappa planet fairly frequently - Z' played with them on a festival bill in Europe, and their drummer was going with Moon for a time. Anyway, Jim Martin their guitar player told me that seeing me wearing their shirt at the Zappa gig was a huge morale booster for them, a major help at a time when they needed it. That pleased me to no end."[38]

At the start of that gig, Zappa unusually read out the planned set lists for that and the next night's shows at The Ahoy in Rotterdam. It was during the second Ahoy show that Zappa brought up Mann's error at the second Wembley gig: "Ed had a tragic experience a few moments ago. One of the loyal fans in the audience came up and treated him like a war criminal because he fucked up the lick on *Dickie's Such An Asshole* several weeks ago. The people who come to these shows listen so carefully to every little detail that this man was deeply offended by Ed's performance. So to make sure that he gets his money's worth tonight, we're gonna dwell on it for a few moments now, and have Ed actually practice - kinda warm up for that big lick that happens in *Dickie's Such An Asshole*. We're gonna rehearse it right now, ready? Just do it as a solo, here we go..."[39]

After playing it correctly, Mann chimed in with "Or the way we did it that night, which of course was completely wrong. This is how it went..."[40], then played it wrong. During *Dickie's Such An Asshole* itself, Willis fluffed the lyrics, so that night's secret word naturally became 'rehearsal'. Zappa picked up on this theme later on in the show when he amended the lyrics to *The Torture Never Stops* to diss the band ("Who are all these musicians fuckin' around down there.

---

* Z was Dweezil's band with his brother Ahmet (vocals), Joe Travers (drums), Thunes (bass) and Keneally (guitar). During their live shows, the band regularly played a medley of excerpts from classic pop and rock songs that included Faith No More's *Epic* - often segued with the New Kids On The Block's *Hang Tough*. Keneally was supposed to have listed all of the songs included in 'The Medley', but the number varied from gig to gig, as Dweezil told the author: *"Sometimes it's more, sometimes it's less; sometimes we remember songs being in there, and we still count them, but they're not. I think ultimately it is 118, but at one point it was about 122."*

Are they lazy? Are they wasted?" Could it have been some of the catering some of them tasted?"), perhaps reflecting the atmosphere off stage. This was compounded by his "Will that be an aisle or a window?" question during *Crew Slut* - a phrase he often used when talking about having to send band members home for some misdemeanour.

Sadly, Keneally had now stopped recording events in his diaries due to the tensions backstage, but it was slowly becoming evident that all was not well despite some tremendous musical highs. Zappa later said: "That was the first show in the tour where the band really let me down. They really started to play wrong notes. Inexcusable wrong notes. And I started talking about... you know, 'maybe we should rehearse more.' And for two or three days everybody had their nose out of joint like I have no right to tell them that they're playing wrong notes. And in Europe people listen to the notes."[41]

But it wasn't just the band members that had started to gang up on Thunes. An incident that occurred around this time was when someone defaced his laminated backstage pass. "We each got a picture laminate. I took my laminate off and handed it to the guitar tech every night, so it wasn't dangling in front of me, and sometimes I'd pop it on my pants, but most of the time just take it off and leave it there on the tech stand. I came back one night, and somebody had taken a very sharp object and jabbed my picture about ten times."[41] Thunes can't now recall precisely when this happened ("Trying to forget that shit, you know?"), but it was "WAY after the Springfield show." But that wasn't the end of that particular story. Thunes told me "It wasn't until after some weeks of keeping [the laminate] close to me and then after another long while being comfortable again to leave it alone and only then was my face actually cut out. Probably happened by a roadie, unless there's somebody who actually wants to come out and admit it were them."

I quizzed Willis about this and he confided that it WAS one of the road crew. "He pissed off all of the guys in the crew. He pissed off the horn section. He doesn't play well with others, let's put it that way. So the guys in the crew would find ways to upset him. And it wasn't anything specific. He rubbed everybody up the wrong way. I was the only one he really got along with, and I wouldn't take sides, I'd just say 'Don't do this, man. Don't do it.'"

Thunes supported some of Willis's observations when he told Thomas Wictor "although I hadn't done anything to anybody in months, all the guys had turned the crew to their side. Because I don't hang out with the crew that much. I hang out with the guitar tech, but we got thirty people in another bus following us around, bringing up the lights and the equipment, stuff like that. Some of those people I've known for several years, and they're my friends. But other people are just hired for this tour. They don't know dick about me. They just know about my 'caustic sense of humour'. That's it. So that was when I went to Frank and said, 'I'm freaking out. This is too much. I don't know what to do.' And he said... I'm thinking of the term... Jeff Simmons' had a term for what they were doing: 'playground psychotics'. Great! Fine! That doesn't help me. I know they're crazy. I know I'm right. I know I haven't done anything to them in months, at least. That doesn't help. And that was it. The whole rest of the tour was just hell, and then it got worse for Frank."[13]

This may explain why, at the show at the Westfalenhalle in Dortmund, Zappa responded bluntly to a sign in the crowd that there was "no secret word for tonight," - he seemed content to let the music speak for itself, though there were still a few minor lyric changes. This held for the next night (in Hamburg), where the band played nothing composed after 1976, and Zappa made up ("on the spot"[14] - out of frustration?) the phrase "screaming Albanian jizz-weasels" during *The Torture Never Stops*. After the Hamburg show,

---

† Bass player, backing vocalist and rhythm guitarist with the Mothers from 1970-1974. Simmons is one of the very few musicians to share two songwriting credits with Zappa (for Wonderful Wino and Dummy Up), and also have a song written for him by Zappa (Lucille Has Messed My Mind Up); both Wino and Lucille were rehearsed during the '88 tour, but only the latter was actually performed in concert.

some of the band jammed at a local club. Details are now a little vague, though Mann recalls "a big event in a club where Chad and I played all night. I think that Bruce and Walt and Ike came by later on. It was sponsored by Simmons Electronics."

Following a 'forty six hour bus ride', the band next pitched up in Vienna where both Willis and Keneally got a rare opportunity to solo. The band seemed to have regained its sense of humour and, musically, they were enjoying a particularly fertile period - as later evidenced by Zappa's official releases from the tour. During *The Eric Dolphy Memorial Barbecue*, the band paid tribute to local boy, Johann Strauss the Younger, by playing variations on his famous *Blue Danube* waltz. Back to Germany again, and in Munich the secret words come tumbling down... "mud shark"... "ayee!"... "suit"... "moo-ahh"... "preserved minnows"... there's the return of the *Rhymin' Man*, who introduced a lengthy first encore including the largely instrumental *Dupree's Paradise* and *Let's Move To Cleveland*. Prior to most of the "Broadway" shows, Zappa would program a short guitar loop with his digital delay equipment for use during the concert as a backing for his guitar solos; in Munich, Dweezil made another guest appearance during the second encores and duetted with his dad over one of these loops on a piece they later named *Bavarian Sunset*.

On the afternoon of the next show (in Zurich), Mann and Wackerman met representatives from the cymbal manufacturer, Paiste, who presented them with some corporate gifts. The reps also attended the show that night, and Mann wore one of their company's jackets on stage. Struggling for a secret word, Zappa introduced Mann as 'Ed Paiste', which then resulted in an evening's worth of endorsements the company probably didn't expect. On to Bilbao in Spain and, for some reason, lots of references to baseball - including a one-time only performance of *Take Me Out To The Ball Game* that's not nearly as funny as when the Marx Brothers sabotaged Verdi's Il Trovatore with it during *A Night at the Opera* (though Zappa later chose to share this performance on the *You*

Can't Do That On Stage Anymore Vol. 4 CD, which Keneally thought, "One of the most outstandingly absurd things ever to appear on an FZ release"[45]).

The Bilbao show also introduced another new song: not content with mocking the 'The King Of Pop', Zappa also decided to take a pop at 'The King Of Rock'; "Frank came up with *Elvis Has Just Left The Building* for me to sing during the European leg of the tour, at a time when band morale was extremely low. Since I was still the enthusiastic puppy of the band, I was more than happy to accept, which is probably a good thing - the rest of the guys weren't exactly craving more work at that point."[46] Of his delivery, Keneally said "Once I understood the direction , there was really no other way for me to sing those words. It wasn't an affected voice, it was almost as if I was possessed."[47]

Years earlier, Michael Gray asked Zappa if he'd ever liked Presley, and his response went further than John Lennon's infamous 'Elvis died the day he joined the army' quote: "No. I was fantastically offended when he did *Hound Dog* in '56, because I had the original record by Willie Mae Thornton and I said, 'How could anybody do that?' Anybody that bought that record was missing out because they'd obviously never even heard Willie Mae Thornton's. The people that I was hanging out with, the mere mention of Elvis' name would bring about peals of laughter - because he wasn't doing anything: it just wasn't real."[48] Despite these comments and the obvious ridicule he subjects Elvis to in the song, there still remains a hint of affection in the lyrics: Zappa made some pretty outlandish claims about The Beatles too, but still retained some respect for them.

The second show in Spain (in Madrid) was filmed for possible release. Although the band initially performed below par, things really perked up once the secret word madness started during *Cosmik Debris*, or *Airline Debris* as it became (evidently the band had experienced some problems getting into the country, so references to Iberia Airlines abounded).

The airline was mentioned again during the gig in Seville - as were the house mixer's kneecaps. Andronis told the author, "It was the first nice day on the European leg, an outdoor gig and I was wearing shorts. I guess he was amused upon seeing my legs because he gave me shit all during sound check as I walked around for my listen. Then, the show and *Cosmik Debris*. One always had to be careful around Frank. You just never knew..."

And that leads us nicely to the final concert in Spain, in Barcelona, on 17th May 1988. This is the most well known show of the "Broadway" tour due to it being televised. The secret words were 'prostitute' and 'raffle', as Zappa later explained: "The tour had been going on and there's all this strife in the band and the crew was edgy, and all this stuff, and travel in Europe is really very rough for the crew. We had a day off in Barcelona prior to this television show that we were going to do. I decided to throw a party for the band and the crew, and I rented this restaurant and told the promoter there to arrange to get three prostitutes, and prostitutes are a very common thing in Barcelona. I said, 'Get three prostitutes to come down to this dinner and we're going to have a raffle', that any members of the crew that would like to have the opportunity to get their machinery wet with one of these Barcelona hookers, that all they do is enter into the raffle. The girls came to the party, did a striptease and danced. They brought their own music and, this whole bunch of hoopla. It was a straightforward business deal. It was like a 'rent-a-girl' business. And Marque-son the monitor mixer was one of the raffle contestants and he won a girl. And so the deal was that after the dinner the girls were going to go back to the hotel with the lucky winners. But what happened was, Marque-son's girl took off. After the dinner, you see, everyone left and they thought they were going

---

* Marque Coy was Zappa's monitor engineer throughout the eighties. After the "Broadway" tour, he managed Zappa's LA rehearsal facility, Joe's Garage. He was nicknamed Marque-son to avoid confusion with other Marks in the crew.

to meet the girls back at the hotel, and I stayed around for a while at the restaurant."

"About the time I was leaving, Marque-son was returning in a cab, and he was nearly in tears because his prize was gone. This led to a situation where the promoter, who had arranged this thing, assured me that everything was going to be, you know, a very smooth operation, became totally irate that he had been fucked over by the pimp who had supplied these girls, and saw to it personally that Marque-son got his machinery taken care of. It took him an extra couple of hours, but Marque-son got taken care of. And so, all was right with the band and crew the next day for the television show. So, during the show, we're making jokes about the raffle, and Marque-son, and that kind of stuff."

Coy had been with Zappa since 1981, and even had a piece of music named after him when he hung a rubber chicken on one of the microphone stands before the encores at the late show at London's Hammersmith Odeon on 19th June 1982. It was Coy who introduced Andronis to Zappa, the pair having previously worked together in the seventies for Chris De Burgh. By 1988, Coy was well used to Zappa's humour, as he told *Keyboard/Guitar Player* magazines in 1992: "Every time I've gone anywhere with Frank, it's been a chuckle a minute. There's always something new to laugh about. Some of the situations occur right in front of you, and some of them he'll have seen in a newspaper, and that becomes the joke, and off it runs, and then it expands, and away it goes, and you're just sitting there laughing."[49] References to the previous night's incident ran rampant throughout *The Torture Never Stops*, and for *Lonesome Cowboy Burt*, Zappa cleverly changed the "... make their livin' diggin' dirt" line to "... make their livin' rafflin' skirt."

Zappa introduced the Barcelona show in Spanish. Reading from

† *Marque-son's Chicken* from *Them Or Us* (Barking Pumpkin Records, 1984).

a piece of paper, he said "Good evening Catalonia. Good evening Spain. Hello night wanderers. Sorry for my pronunciation, but I have learnt my speech parrot fashion. I want to dedicate this concert to the people who speak and feel in Spanish; 300 million in Spain, South America and North America who, co-operating together and solving their differences, could get to be the Third Power."

Although many would love to see an official release of this concert on DVD (there have been many 'grey-market' versions), it's not a spectacularly good show - as Zappa himself acknowledged, according to Keneally: "He once described the Barcelona video as a 'low priority' for him. It wasn't one of our better performances, so I don't mind it not being available widely. A much better show, which was also filmed professionally, was in Madrid. All the tapes from all the camera angles are in the vault, but there are technical problems which, so far, have rendered it impossible to sync the film to tape. That may get fixed in the future, and I hope it does, because it really is a much better show and no one has seen it yet."[50]

The popular conception is that 'new puppy' Keneally didn't take sides in "the war of the rhythm section"[51], which is why Zappa singled him out in interviews on the band's eventual demise. When I commented on this to Keneally recently, his response was interesting: "I think I'd be disingenuous in agreeing that my stance was 'neutral', although I might have kidded myself at the time that it was." Certainly, in the immediate aftermath of the "Broadway" tour, Keneally and Thunes were the only two of the musicians employed again by the Zappas. Yet Keneally has gone on to work with a number of the other band members since (most notably, Ed Mann in Budapest, Hungary in October 2007, when the pair headlined a tribute to Zappa). And despite Keneally and his wife hanging out with Thunes, the bass player still felt "I was the only guy who was my friend on that tour. I was alone. Europe: no friends, no band, no nothing. And I got Ed Mann coming up to me in Barcelona yelling, screaming at me, 'Don't you understand what a privilege it is to play with Frank? How can you ruin his music so intensely, so blindingly, so egomaniacally?' Constant barrage because I play a lot of lines. I pick a lot of chunks out of the air, and instead of 'playing the bass', I play Scott Thunes's part in the orchestration of the thing. I enjoy playing the bass, when I get to do what I want. And of course the whole idea of being a bass player is you don't overplay, and you play the bass, all that kind of stuff. Frank has had that his whole life. I don't do that; I've never done that. You don't ask me to do it if Frank isn't asking me to do it. So I had to rummage down in my bag and get my headphones out and put them on, and I'm listening to classical music with Ed Mann's mouth going 'Beh-beh-beh-beh-beh.' It was absolutely delicious. I could not understand why a person like that felt he had the right to do what he did. He very strongly felt that and knew that he was right, and there was never any way that the two of us would get together on it. The only thing I could do to make him happy was to stop doing what I did. And I wasn't about to explain to him because he was being pretty negative about it."[52]

Back in France, and a change of order to The Big Medley that had hitherto ran as *Let's Make The Water Turn Black/Harry, You're A Beast/The Orange County Lumber Truck/Oh No/Theme From Lumpy Gravy*. In Montpellier, *Oh No* started the medley and, on its completion (for reasons unknown), Zappa called an intermission - after just forty minutes. Strange. During the show, Zappa threw in a few "moo-aahs" - a phrase first heard in the songs *Be In My Video* and *He's So Gay*. When later asked for an explanation of the expression, Zappa simply said "It doesn't mean anything. It's just a noise."[53] The final chord of *Bamboozled By Love* contained a little quote from the French national anthem... as did Zappa's solo in *Chana In De Bushwop* the next night in Grenoble. That night, one of the encores consisted of Zappa soloing over one of his pre-programmed loops.

* Thunes told fellow-bassist Bryan Beller: *"In earlier bands, what I did was more bass-oriented, playing notes and adding 'eyebrows' where I could. In 1988, Frank gave me no direction. None! He never said no to anything I did."*
[From *Frank Zappa's "Alien Orifice" Scott Thunes's Complete Bass Line* by Bryan Beller (*Bass Player* magazine, 1 April 2009).]

For the next night's show at Le Zenith in Paris, Zappa dedicated the second set to Glenn Ferris, who had played trombone and euphonium with The Mothers Of Invention/Hot Rats/Grand Wazoo on their eight concerts together in September 1972. This 20-piece big band 'split-up' "after the Boston show, in the dressing room, on September 24th."[54] A recording of this final MOI / HR / GW concert was released by VAULTernative Records in October 2007. Ferris had moved to France in 1980 and, in 2000, was appointed a Professor at the Conservatoire National Supérieur de Musique et de Danse de Paris. That second set in Paris in 1988 commenced with *Eat That Question* from Zappa's *Grand Wazoo* album and, unlike the first set, was comparatively secret word free.

For the final show in France (in Strasbourg), Zappa decided to introduce a 'new' vamp (in 21) to *Marque-son's Chicken*. Like the *Thirteen* vamp inserted into *More Trouble Every Day*, this was first created by Zappa around about 1978, after he filed a lawsuit against Warner Bros., which temporarily prevented him from releasing any new material: "There was a period of time when I was kind of locked out of the music business, and since I didn't have a recording studio at the time, and since I didn't have a contract, and I couldn't go into a recording studio, in an act of desperation, I took my four-track and hooked up a bunch of dipshit equipment here in this basement, just like every other garage-band guy would do, and I was making some one-man tapes here. That's where those things came from, from that period when I was doing little rhythm-box tapes in the basement." The vamp was played again the next night in Stuttgart, and this recording ultimately became the title track of the *Trance-Fusion* album (Zappa Records, ZR 20002) in 2006.

In Stuttgart, Zappa announced that the Russians had invited the band to play at the 31st May 1988 summit between Soviet leader Mikhail Gorbachev and US President Ronald Reagan in Moscow. This summit was billed as a celebratory follow-up to their breakthrough summit of October 1987, where the two leaders had signed a groundbreaking Intermediate-Range Nuclear Forces Treaty, eliminating an entire class of nuclear missiles from Europe. In the event, the band was unable to play and the summit itself ended with no further progress on arms control. But Zappa seized the moment to ridicule Reagan's planned Strategic Defence Initiative (SDI), which was to use ground and space-based systems to protect the US from attack by strategic nuclear ballistic missiles. SDI had been nicknamed 'Star Wars' by the media, and the encores that night saw Willis singing "she's buying a stairway to Star Wars", before Zappa kicked-off his loops to improvise a piece called *Star Wars Won't Work* ("It's just an expensive bunch of nothing."[55]).

A couple of unusual audience-inspired moments also occurred in Stuttgart: after playing *I Ain't Got No Heart*, Zappa stopped the show - because "Never have I seen anyone dancing so hard to that song," - and had a lady named Claudia come up on stage and dance while the band played the song again; during the encores, the band were surprised to get a request from the audience to play *Rhymin' Man*. They duly performed it, and followed it with another unscheduled new song (*Elvis Has Just Left The Building*).

Zappa and his cohorts did severe damage to *Stairway To Heaven* on consecutive nights: causing mayhem in Mannheim with the secret word 'cornhole', Jimmy Page's guitar solo was also initially replaced by the theme from *The Untouchables*. "I edited those two versions together, so I have a combination cornhole/Star Wars version of *Stairway To Heaven* which will probably never be released," Zappa later revealed. "See, if you're going to perform somebody's song, and you don't change the words, all you get is a mechanical license. But if you change any of the words, you need their permission, and indications are, so far, that the song has special significance to the authors, and they don't wanna have the words changed. So when we finally do put out *Stairway To Heaven*, it will not have the words changed."[56]

The band's final show in Germany took place in Fürth, and was notable for one of the strangest musical moments of the tour. I'll let

Pat Buzby explain: "About fifteen minutes into the set, FZ decided to throw a curveball by inserting *Ride Of The Valkyries* in place of the *Willie The Pimp* guitar solo, but it sounds like the band missed its cue, because all we get is the Wagner melody played on one synth above a chugging bass line, while Chad sounds like he still thinks they're playing *"Willie"*. Pathetic. However, this hardly compares to what comes next - the '88 band's one, disastrous attempt at playing *Purple Haze* onstage. The parts are there, but it's hopelessly off-kilter from the start (it seems that most of the band is playing at only half the correct tempo), and it basically sounds like one long train wreck. Both the audience and the band sound totally confused. Finally, after two verses, FZ cuts this mess off and jumps in with a solo."[57] Zappa later said; "I remember that some cue got messed up at that concert... we had to bail out of that when I went into a loop guitar solo, which ended that disastrous part of the show."[58] It could also have been that the band was put off its stroke by a large-breasted woman in the audience, who was later invited up on stage and became the butt of further secret word hilarity (my personal favourite lyric change coming during *The Man From Utopia Meets Mary Lou* where the "big fool, big fool" refrain became "big two, big two" - though "maybe later I'll milk her" during *Bobby Brown* wasn't too shabby. Titter.) But Thunes admitted he did lose concentration on stage and mistakes were being made "because Chad and I weren't communicating. And Frank's only enjoyment in the band was doing guitar solos. And those fell apart. He ended up not doing any. Instead of three-hour sound checks, we had two songs, and he would get out of there. He could not stand being in the same room with us. There was no music going on behind him to support him. It was the worst possible combination of events for him. For someone who likes going out on the road, who likes hanging out with musicians, it was really ugly."[59] Before the final song of the night in Fürth, the promoter presented the band with a guitar-shaped marzipan cake, and things were now going to get even uglier.

CHAPTER FIVE
Why Don't You Like Me?

"It had all the band members' names in frosting on it," recalls Thunes of the cake presented to the band, who had now moved on to Austria for the next gig in Linz. "I showed up - coming out of the bus ten minutes later so I wouldn't have to meet the rush of band members coming out, which happened every night - and somebody had taken a knife and drawn a nice little inch-deep line through my name. And of course the best thing would have been to walk away. But I had just had too much. So I took a spoon, and I scooped out Ed Mann's and Chad Wackerman's names. I played back into their hands. I should not have done it, but I did it, and I didn't enjoy it. When Frank had to discuss it with me afterwards, the look I got from him was one of the most painful looks I have ever gotten from him. Out of all the clams I've thrown and all the clamps he's had to put down on me, that was the one... 'I am showing you, Frank, exactly how much of an anus I am. There's nothing worse than what I just did, for me. I can imagine what it feels like to you.' He was one of the fairest people I've ever met. He understands about that kind of stuff. So, I got a couple of good licks in, ah, in song later that night. Frank used it as the basis for the magic word in *Illinois Enema Bandit*, and that was pretty much my getting back at the guys... him giving me a chance to have my story be told in song, about how bad these guys were. But unfortunately, at the very end when he sings about people needing misery in their lives, he's pointing back at me. So he's not gonna let me get away scot-free either."[1]

In fact, the cake and the preceding backstage pass incident were both referenced in Linz; during *Sharleena*, Zappa 'sang' "Let's scratch Scott's face off the cake," and asked "What happened to his laminate? What the fuck goin' on here, children?" As he ran down the band's names, Zappa referred to Scott as "the faceless wonder".

So, quite typically of Zappa, he was able to draw humour from these serious (but stupid) acts. And for Thunes, it was followed by what he described as his favourite part of the whole tour: "You have to find joy in very strange places: I'm sitting in my back lounge on the bus, cruising along the Berlin Corridor, maybe. That's the visualisation I have. And Bruce Fowler wants to know why I was such an asshole. I said, 'I do not agree with that assessment. I am not an asshole: I am me. You don't have to like me, but I am not going to say that I did anything wrong because I have not been told by Frank that I did anything wrong. You guys don't like it, that's fine. I don't wanna hear another thing about it.' He just got talking about it. He spent another two or three minutes; I said "Shut up! I don't wanna hear it. Get out of here!' He wouldn't leave. Mike Keneally and I had been drinking champagne in the back, we were gettin' pretty drunk. And Bruce Fowler would not shut up. So I stood up, and I dropped my pants, and I stood with my cock and balls three inches in front of his face. He sat there for thirty seconds, and he got up. But this is a guy who eats his own boogers. So I don't really worry about most of the things that happen to this guy. And that was it. They left me alone from that point on, thankfully. But nobody ever, ever tried to understand my point of view."[2]

Obviously, Zappa's expectation was that things could continue and the shows did indeed go on. When I asked Wing to recall his favourite concerts, the one in Udine, Italy got a special mention: "You had to be there!" he told me. When pressed, he replied "During the course of the concert, I remember Frank changed a few lyrics, the upshot suggesting it was over for the band; my journal on the tour was stolen by an old roommate."

Zappa did indeed change many lyrics that night, but principally this was to berate whoever was in charge of the house lights (which remained switched on for most of the show) and a popcorn seller wandering around in the audience. Popcorn! Popcorn! Get your fresh popcorn folks.

Wing is perhaps alluding to Zappa's references (during *Stairway To Heaven*) to pay cheques and aisle or window seats. During the third of the Italian shows in Milan, Zappa seemed a little grouchy: when asked for the secret word, he said "You figure it out"; and, before the first encore, he snapped at the audience, "Don't push, please don't push". It was almost as if he was past caring, and the overall quality of some of the shows in Italy did suffer - although, as always, there were still moments of inspired playing and unusual events.

At that concert in Milan, he invited Fabio Treves, 'The Father of Italian Blues', to join the band on stage. I'll let Fabio tell you more: "I hope you'll understand what I feel remembering one of the most incredible meetings in my long artistic career: to know, to talk and to play on the stage with my greatest idol, the GENIUS of Baltimore. And after all these years I remain proud to read the words of FZ who, in his autobiography, calls me an anarchist! In 1988, Frank asked me if it was possible to organise a meeting with Paolo Pillitteri, the Mayor of Milan, asking if his opera, *Dio Fa'*, could be staged at La Scala. I met Frank in Munich some days before the Italian leg of the 'Broadway The Hard Way' tour. I accompanied the Italian promoter, Claudio Trotta, to get to know, for the first time personally, the great American musician."

"We waited a long time before entering the backstage area - and he looked at me for a very long time, because my face was very similar to his! He suddenly understood - he was an incredible mind! - what kind of person I was, and what kind of music I preferred. I tried to explain (I was very excited and sweaty, and not because of

---

* This was Zappa's proposal for a special entertainment event to conclude the World Cup Football Finals in the summer of 1990, and to be financed by the City of Milan and the Italian Football Committee. Its theme (as stated in *The Real Frank Zappa Book* by Frank Zappa with Peter Occhiogrosso, Simon & Schuster, 1990) was: "*Millions of people believe football is God, but, it is said (at least in Torino), 'God is a liar' - Dio Fa.*" It didn't happen.

the temperature in the arena!) that I was a blues musician, a harp player. I told him that I played and recorded with many blues guitarists, just to let him understand that I wasn't the usual fan and nothing else. He laughed, and said 'Don't speak anymore; I think I know you very well!' For me, it was strange listening to those words because I knew that FZ had a particular character. But I was convinced, deep down inside, that he could understand everything and everybody, after just a glance."

"When he arrived in Milan, I stayed with him night and day. Often I was speechless: I was living one of my secret dreams... one of my greatest experiences, and not just musical. FZ understood what I felt for him and for his music and, before starting his show at Palatrussardi, he said to me: 'Hey Fabio, would you like to play your harmonica?' I thought it was a joke, and there was a faint smile on my red face. 'Yes, obviously, maestro,' I replied. 'Be ready, and prepare your harp. Do you know my tunes?' 'Yes, Mr Zappa.' I was 39 years old, but I could not keep from crying, because I knew that FZ was used to playing ONLY with the musicians of his band! So he called me up on stage, presenting me with his low voice, to play *A Pound For A Brown* in Milan and, for the concert in Genoa, he called me again for the song *Big Swifty*. I was in a state of complete ecstasy. But I realised that FZ appreciated my harmonica style: blues, sometimes country and rock, in a very 'Zappian' mood! Craig 'Twister' Steward, the harp player on the *Joe's Garage* album, was one of my favourite players, and so I'm very happy after all these years to think that FZ said 'okay' to one Italian musician. Some years, I met up with Ike Willis and Chad Wackerman again, who remembered my performance!"

For that final show in Genoa, the band also momentarily regained its sense of humour and, for the most part, turned in a blinding performance. Aside from being the last gig of the tour, this is mainly memorable for the secret word 'jellyfish'. A few years earlier, Zappa had befriended Genoan fan and marine biologist, Ferdinando Boero.

'Nando' had named a jellyfish˙ after his hero, and the pair met up the week before the show: "I saw Frank in Turin, and he asked me if I would be in Genoa. He grinned when I said yes. So he was planning this thing for some time. I saw him the day after the show, at Portofino. He called that concert: the jellyfish concert. I dedicated a jellyfish to him, he dedicated his very last concert to me. From an egocentric point of view it is obvious that, for me, that is the most important concert that Frank ever gave. It is also important for non-Nando people, as it is the last rock 'n' roll concert from FZ!"[3]

As can be gleaned from the snippet on *You Can't Do That On Stage Anymore, Vol. 6* (Rykodisc, 1992), the *Torture/ Bonanza / Lonesome Cowboy Burt* medley got very twisted and the band almost lost it. Said Keneally "My personal favourite MK contribution to a Zappa CD occurs in *Lonesome Cowboy Nando*, when I attempt to cram the line 'I describe the little dangling utensils on this thing and tell him to draw it up so that it looks just like a brand new jellyfish' into the same space where I would normally say 'stomp in his face so he don't move no more'. The first time I listened to this song with Frank, he applauded me after that section. One o' them priceless moments."[4]

As well as Nando, Zappa also name-checked Patrick Germanini, the tour manager for Barley Arts, Claudio Trotta's agency ("a great friend of mine," Treves told me). In one interview at the start of the tour, Zappa had mentioned the possibility of the band later playing in countries like Israel; after the tour ended, he talked of "dates booked in the United States - big, outdoor, high-paying gigs... I had to cancel them all."[5] When I spoke to Willis, he confirmed the plans for more shows: "At the end of the Europe tour, we were gonna come home, break for a couple of weeks, and then start rehearsals for the Fall leg, and we were booked until New Year's of the next year. Frank always told me, 'Okay, this is what the schedule is: we're gonna be in blah-blah... rehearsals start on this day...' And then it all

---

˙ Phialella zappai

got called off."

To those outside the band, there was no indication that Zappa "disbanded the tour in Genoa, Italy."[6] The first public statement about the demise of the band came in an interview with *Musician* magazine a few months later, when Zappa said, "At first, I was enjoying playing the guitar again. Then, at the end of the tour, this war broke out between the bass player and the drummer. They hated each other's guts. And so I just spent the last six weeks of the tour trying to wend my way through this garbage that was going on onstage. On a good night, the ideas I had for guitar solos came out. On a bad night, it was me versus the band. The audience didn't really know, but it was another example of the kind of thing that made me want to put the guitar down in the first place. I haven't touched the guitar since we came off the road. If I'm sitting around the house, I don't play it. I don't even think about it."[7]

There was a clue as to his feelings just prior to publication of the *Musician* interview when, on 31st August 1988 on the live TV show *Good Morning Australia*, Zappa was interviewed on the Hollywood set of *Jaws* at Universal Studios, and was very taken with an Oran Utang there which he pointedly said he liked a lot better than most of the people he'd had to work with in the last month. When interviewer Mike Gibson asked if it reminded him of anyone in rock 'n' roll, he added "No, because it seems to be far too intelligent and considerate and sensitive."

Before Genoa, Zappa claimed to have asked "everybody in the band how they felt about this bass player, they all said 'No, we hate him and we're not gonna play on stage with him anymore'."[8] - with the exception of Keneally. But it seemed odd that Zappa should blame things squarely on the rhythm section, as clearly there were other factors involved. When the author asked Mann how Zappa went about seeking the views of the band, he told me, "Just in general talk - 'are you into it?' - no talk of Scott at all, and I was not asking; it was at the end of the European leg - Spain or something. I just said 'sure', and I never heard another word about it. I always presumed his energy was not up to it, as I had seen so much of that in the previous twelve weeks. When this 'cancelled tour' got so much press, my true inner feeling was that Frank was using that to cover that he did not feel up to it; touring was his life. I found out nine months later that he was undergoing diagnoses... that's all I know."

Because Wing was under the impression that things were coming to an end in Italy, the author recently posed the same question to him: "I can't recall if there was an official vote. Sorry, it's been so long," was his reply. But when Fred Banta had earlier suggested that everyone thought Zappa would just hire another bass player, Wing said, "That was the best case scenario to continue the tour, I thought. But then Frank decided that well, you know, hey. And it's his band; he decides who's going to be in the band. And that's basically what happened. He said we're going to continue with this band, and then left it at that."[9]

The author asked Martin if Zappa had sought his views on continuing with Thunes: "Frank never asked me that. I don't think it's something he would have asked anyone. He knew what we all felt through various conversations and made his decision. I remember one night in Europe, Ed and I spoke with him on the phone (we were in different hotels) - I think it was somewhere in Germany. I explained to him how uncomfortable things were getting for everyone both on and off stage, and how the music was being sabotaged on stage (which he knew), and agreed with what others had suggested: that the tour could be saved with a personnel change."

Here it is worth noting that Martin was on the verge of getting married and, as one band member confided in me, wasn't too fussed whether the band continued on or not. When the author pressed Mann on this 'straw poll', he said, "I think the only 'vote' was when

Frank got on the bus with the horn section and asked them if they would perform with Scott. They said no, and simultaneously Frank asked the Fowlers if they could get in touch with Tom to see if he would do it. He said yes - then they too never heard another word about it." Tom Fowler is the bass and violin playing brother of Bruce and Walt, who played in Zappa's *Roxy* and *Bongo Fury* bands. He confirmed to me that there was "a brief period when it may have been one of Frank's options. I don't remember who I spoke to about it - I believe more than one - but not Frank himself." The British Zappa fanzine, *T'Mershi Duween*, also reported that former Mothers' drummer Aynsley Dunbar had put himself forward to replace Wackerman, and also speculated about the possibility of Öberg and Ågren replacing Martin and Wackerman.

Thunes says that when Zappa told him the rest of the band would not go back to the US to play a bunch of dates if he was still onboard, he offered to quit. But Zappa "said 'that's not the problem. The problem is I would have to go into rehearsals again with another bass player.' I said, 'I don't know what I can say. You know? They don't want me; it's a problem. I'll quit.' He said, 'that's not the problem. I like you. I like what you do. I don't have a problem with you, except for all the mistakes you're making...'" So clearly options other than continuing with Thunes were considered, but dismissed.

Some six months later, Zappa had formulated his stock response to questions about the end of the tour: he told the San Diego Union, "It was worth the physical strain to get up there and do it. But I don't know whether it was worth the $400,000 it lost. And I don't want to go on stage knowing that the bass player was backstage, literally in tears, before the show... and the audience doesn't know,"[10]. In a radio interview a month later, he added "I happen to like that guy, and I happen to think that the rest of the band were wrong about deciding to hate that guy; I think it was quite unprofessional. For me, it's a dark moment in American history that the people on the West Coast didn't get a chance to see the 'Broadway The Hard Way' band, 'cause it really was a great band."[11]

Two years later, he was peddling much the same story, but had embellished it somewhat: "Scott has a unique personality. He also has unique musical skills. I like the way he plays and I like him as a person, but other people don't. He has a very difficult personality: he refuses to be cordial. He won't do small talk. And he's odd. So what? They're all odd! They should tolerate each other. Unfortunately the real world doesn't work that way, and I don't want to name who got this thing started, but it turned into a personal vendetta against Scott Thunes. A couple of guys in the band were the ringleaders and were doing such petty stuff. It had gotten to where we had done two months in the US, two in Europe and were supposed to have a short break and do good-paying, large-scale outdoor things all over the US. And by the end of the European part of the tour, things were going astray rather badly."

"I started taking a poll of different guys in the band: 'Do you hate Scott Thunes so much you wouldn't go onstage with him for these gigs in the summer?' and they all said, 'Yes, we hate him, oh, we hate him. He's bad. He's a bad person. He can't play the bass.' They were so convinced this guy was the loser of all time that I had no choice. If you replace anybody in a band that has rehearsed for four months, you've gotta go back into rehearsal. I couldn't replace Scott to assuage everybody in the band who hated him. There's no bass player who could have done that job. The repertoire was so large, the workings of the show so complex, you had to know so much - there was no way. So I had to lose the income of all those dates because the band refused to go onstage with Scott Thunes. That's why I put out *The Best Band You Never Heard In Your Life.*"

"But let me give you the final payoff to this: the band realised they provided for themselves total unemployment. Everybody on that tour got paid but me. I lost $400,000. And within six months I was hearing, 'Man, we made a mistake. Scott's not such a bad guy.' And the same people who hated his guts were running into him in restaurants and saying, 'Scott, I'm sorry, I don't know what got into me,' this kind of stupid, stupid shit. It was just like little children ganging up on a kid at a boy's school. It was really P-U. I'm not interested in inflicting poetic justice on anybody, remember?"

"I like music, and if that band had stayed together all this time, not only would it be the most outrageous touring band on the planet, but I'd still be playing guitar. I pay people to rehearse, so in order to change anybody, I would have to rent a sound stage, which is $2000 a day, stick the band in there and pay them to learn to live with another bass player. And I would resist doing that simply because I don't like the idea of having a whole band ganging up on me, forcing me to get rid of a bass player I liked. I enjoy playing with Scott. So, what's the fucking deal? And one of the most egregious things: one of the sax players who'd been complaining that Scott didn't give him enough support on his solos - after he heard "*Best Band*", he came over here and said, 'Oh, he sounds good, man.' Stuff like that makes me sick."[12]

Martin echoed Zappa's sentiments when he told the author, "My main problem with the situation was that it was affecting the music negatively. Although I know he respected my opinion, I also know he felt pressured, as if it were a mutiny, and finally cancelled the tour rather than be pushed by the band to make a change. Needless to say, we were all extremely disappointed, knowing what an amazing band it was. 'The best band you never heard' became an unfortunate fact for so many people in all the cities that were originally scheduled for the tour and ended up being cancelled. I had a good relationship with Scott, I think largely because he respected my classical background. But the music was the most important thing. I wish I could have convinced him to act differently in the way he related to other band members."

Aside from the laminate and cake incidents, Thunes mentions other 'petty stuff', such as the time Mann "shot a rubber band at my curtain"[13] on the smoking bus. All of this may account for why Zappa effectively turned on the guys he'd known and worked with over many years (notably, the Fowler brothers, Mann, Willis, Martin and Wackerman) in favour of Thunes - he sure as hell wasn't going to be dictated to by musicians he'd hired to play his music. But why did Wackerman turn on Thunes in the first place - someone he'd 'played well' with for six years? Was there a specific incident that triggered it? Wackerman declined to comment for this book but Thunes' conveyed his thoughts on the matter: "I never spoke with Chad pretty much after we got on the road. He was on the bus with the anti-Scott contingent (Ed) and I wasn't. More so, they had a full bus of at least seven or nine or eleven peeps and I had it easy on the 'smoking bus' with only about six or seven. Also, having the back room pretty much to myself pretty much every night when on the other bus there were at least five people in either the front or the back and two extremely vociferous talkers - Ike and Albert Wing - walking back and forth keeping everybody up late and making noise. It would be difficult for a nice person to keep their heads, and I can't imagine Chad not falling for Ed's rhetoric. But it wasn't Chad, so much as him just taking the dominant position. I don't know anything about his mindset. You should ask him! I'd be interested in what he had to say on the matter, seeing as how I never had any negative interactions with him personally. I'm still kind of shocked about it. What a total dick. Taking me out of the monitors? Whatever, bitch."

Given that Wackerman had previously told the author, "Ed and I connected from the first tour that I did with Frank," I asked for Mann's take on it: "It was Chad's fury with Scott - and my willingness to be a voice for it, which Chad is not capable of, except to fellow band mates, but not Frank - that fuelled the fire from day one. I never saw the *Musician* magazine quote. My quibble with Scott was his willingness on a daily basis to treat these great musicians as shit on mic over a huge PA for hours on end. Chad is nice - genteel. Scott hated Chad's guts? I do not know. I read a thing from Scott yesterday about all the mistakes because people were shooting daggers at him*. The perception on the other end was that he was fucking with everyone musically onstage by intentionally jumping beats. The music from the bass matched the body language from Scott at the time of execution. Very difficult to play with. Anyway, the pathos in all of this is any band member who will be willing to sink to the low of dissing another in the press right after the tour was over, which Scott - and Keneally, to my knowledge - did. But, God, it is so long ago that right now it does not matter. At least to me."

Willis put it all a little more succinctly and, perhaps, incisively: "No, there was no specific incident: it just built up over time. It was Scott's way of dealing with people. They were both very young**. And Scott didn't get along with the horn section... the Fowlers, and stuff like that. According to Scott 'I hate horns, blah, blah, blah'. And he was the Clonemeister at the time, so that was another thing."

When it was known that I was writing this book, someone contacted me out of the blue saying, quite authoritively, that they knew why the tour had collapsed: it was all because of Thunes' anger over his brother Derek's death ("he got in a very bad motorcycle accident that eventually killed him (complications from AIDS)" was how Thunes put it to me). I'd never heard it put quite like this before, so I thought it was something I should ask Thunes about. In 2006, just before the Zappa Plays Zappa† concert at the Royal Albert Hall, I had bumped into Thunes's sister, Stacy - an actress/singer, currently living on the outskirts of London, who I'd seen perform with her brother and Keneally and Willis at the Zappanale festival in Germany in 2002. Through her, I contacted Scott about the possibility of an interview for my website - and she

* From *Thomas Wictor's In Cold Sweat* book.

** Thunes and Wackerman were both born in 1960, and spent much of their twenties together.

† *Zappa Plays Zappa* was originally to have been Dweezil and his brother Ahmet presenting and performing their father's music in Europe in 2005 - with "sternly accomplished special guests" Flo & Eddie, and "other people". Ads were prematurely placed in the music press, they appeared on UK TV with their mum, and tickets were sold (the author had a front row centre ticket for a planned show at the Brighton Centre). But Volman and Kaylan had still to formally sign up for the tour. The tour was postponed until the following year, without Flo & Eddie, or Ahmet plus a new bass player. The special guests were initially Napoleon Murphy Brock, Steve Vai and Terry Bozzio. By 2007, these had been replaced by Ray White. Since spring 2009, it has just been Dweezil and the 'other people'.

suggested I ask him about Derek. He duly obliged and, from his answers (plus comments in Wictor's book and in Keneally's tour diary*), it seemed to me that he had a great deal of affection for his older brother. So I probed Thunes to see if the then recent deaths of his father and Derek could have affected his general demeanour at the time. His response: "I wasn't in any state of negativity about anything ever until Springfield. I had a great time being the Clonemeister and kicking jazz-hole ass. It wasn't until Ed harshed my mellow (a California term of some humour) that I understood what was up. Having to deal with the baby antics of Ed made it all the more stupid to try to have a conversation with a person like Chad - who'd say, 'No, I'm fine with you'. Like he'd tell me if there was anything wrong."

I decided to take it a little further, and said his brother's death must have had some bearing on his anger at that time. He responded: "I categorically deny your claim of me being angry, unless you have some proof I'm not aware of. I was always the most balanced person I knew. For several years, before the 1984 tour, I did spend a lot of time in a cafe drinking coffee and smoking cloves and suffering for my art and not getting laid as much as I would have liked (even though I was getting laid plenty, even off the road) and even getting a name for myself (Scotty Boy Blue) that reflected my proto-Goth atmosphere, but really, I was always rather aware that I had it good, that I lived in Marin County, had lots of hot girlfriends and was a great bass player. So getting on the road and having to deal with assholes and idiots made me frustrated and brought up negative self-images, but mostly it was pure irritation at my lot in life. Anger only came out in teeny spurts, such as when the alto player asked me for my *Boléro* score and I jumped down his throat**, complaining that he should get his own. Even then, it was a terse, nasty statement

---

* The 19th February 1988 entry states: *"It's always very touching to watch Scott listen to his brother playing on tape, because he knows every nuance of everything his brother ever played, and he closes his eyes and plays it in the air and grooves to high heaven, where Derek hopefully is."* [1988 Was A Million Years Ago: Mike's Zappa Tour Diaries, http://www.keneally.com/1988/1988.html]

** Regarding this incident, Thunes told Wictor: *"Thinking back to yelling at Paul Carman, it was a stupid thing to do. You do those things; sometimes you apologise, and you move on. This time I decided not to apologise."*

rather than a pure expression of anger. Is hatred an emotion related to anger, or is it just the standard state of mind of the intelligent person who hasn't acquired the peace of mind associated with old age? My brother was dead two years, that's true. But my dad died in 1988. Also, my mother in 1978. So, who am I angry at because they're dead?"

"Okay," I said. "Maybe 'anger' was a bad choice of word. But I was just trying to see if your 'causticity' was higher than usual as a result of the fairly recent family bereavements. It's clear you loved your brother very much, and I wanted to see if his passing was in any way behind the band's demise." I was not prepared for his reaction to this - it surprised me. A lot.

"I'm sorry, Andrew, but the phrase 'It's clear you loved your bro very much' is sticking in my craw. I'm not sure that's an accurate description of the facts. Here's the problem (I guess it's two-fold, but any family matters can be considered complicated by definition): my brother and I had a very chequered past. He was always a motherfucking asshole to me. Really. Older brother shit aside, he did some stuff to me that was just plain sick in its level of debasement and dishonour. Not sexual, just bullying in various ways, some bordering on criminal. And not just me. Every one of our friends has a Derek-was-a-troubled-soul event in their lives. He died early because he was self-destructive and pathetic. That's a good story for a book. Just not mine. Sure, we played in a band together, but we never really got along all that well. Every band had an Oasis-level argument and, in some cases, my brother and I fought physically to the point of bloodshed. On the other hand, sure, we extended our musicality together, we shared hot girls (or 'traded-off' might be a more accurate label), and we spent many hours conversing about important things and smiling and laughing. But see, I can do that with anybody. He never respected me because I was shallow and never worked on my art. (He was driven to succeed and spent many solitary hours working on being a composer. He might have even ended up being good if he'd lived past 28. As it was, he has a pretty good track record, having had both his string quartets played by the Kronos Quartet on record and in concert, and having written four jazz band pieces and some other things. Other composers could die after having done that.) That was because I preferred people to art. Sure, I talk about art being important and people sucking and all, but the most important parts are that hanging out with pretty girls pretty much beats all other forms of activity. That's just me."

"And also, check this: I'm not sure what love is. I know what I feel for my wife and my children, but the rest of the world can go hang. Know what I'm sayin'? Love only goes so far, and after being beat-down by my brother for so many years, I'm pretty sure that any love I ever may have had for him was leached from my soul by the time I started listening to Led Zeppelin and he punched me in my 13-year old face for not telling him whether or not I felt up the young girl who lived down the street. This happened right at the beginning of *When The Levee Breaks*, and I'll never forget lying on the couch in the living room, tears streaming down my face, having to listen to all that slide guitar and heavy drums until I got sick, all because he had an uncontrollable temper AND he wanted me subservient to him. Fuck that guy and all people like him."

Getting bolder, I picked up on Mann's criticism of Thunes, and I asked if his "kicking jazz-hole ass" verged on 'abuse' and, if not, would it be how he'd be happy to be treated himself?

"This question is far too big to answer in an interview-by-email situation. My legendary status as shit-disturber demands that I answer: if I were half as fucking annoying to them as they were to me, then yes, by all means, I should bend over and gladly accept all ass-kickings and 'abuses'. But no, I do not think it ever - during rehearsals - added up to abuse. The Jazzholes were sloppy, selfish,

---

* Derek Thunes' *Blues* appeared on the Kronos Quartet's *In Formation* album in 1993. Coincidentally, Zappa was commissioned by the quartet to write *None Of The Above*, which they performed on radio and in concert several times in 1985.

late, careless, annoying, and outside any manner of looking out for Frank's best interests. As it lies, I should add that I could have been - at times - less 'effortful', and possibly more judicious in my choice of words to certain peoples in my past. Boy howdy, yes, do I have regrets. I'm no angel. But as Clonemeister? I was amazing. Fuck those guys. I'm still waiting for an apology along the lines of Ed's. Of course, I'd love it if they allowed me to apprentice with them in their killer music-scoring career but in my day I've made worse enemies of better, more important people."

All in all, one heck of an exchange. But what of the view from the other side? One band member told me he thought Zappa actually took a perverse pleasure in watching his dedicated musicians being tormented on a daily basis by Thunes. Where previously Zappa had stepped in when similar problems arose, in 1988 he chose not to because he was too tired and just did not want to know about anything except the show. Zappa apparently did state that any problems were not of his concern and he did not care what the outcome was so long as the notes were played correctly on stage ("a real violation of trust, and fucking hell to endure for four months plus sound checks," was how one of the band described it).

Wackerman was allegedly unhappy because Thunes had this way of leading him a merry dance by putting each note just one micro-step ahead of where it was supposed to be. Willis and Mann both describe Thunes as a wildly talented genius of the bass, which meant he was able to physically jab each note at Wackerman like a bayonet, and he had no recourse but to go along with it as, after all, it is the drummer's responsibility to make sure it all works. And work it did, which is perhaps the most surprising thing about the whole tour: at the time, many of the musicians thought it was probably 'sounding like shit', but now they realise it was actually just 'feeling like shit'.

As Mann was one of the principles on 'the other side', it's only fair to let him have his say in response to Thunes comments. When the author interviewed him in 2004 about the possibility of ever working with Thunes again, he told me: "Scott and I are on fine terms and we correspond from time to time. I appreciate his unique sense of humour. I remember his second day in the band - Frank was giving some generalised direction and Scott interrupted and said aloud to me and Tommy, 'Listen up! This applies to you!' I didn't know him then, and I thought '... what the fuck?' - after all, WE were the vets and HE was the new guy. Of course that was arrogant thinking on my part - and over time I began to understand Scott's safety-pin-in-cheek humour - and once you get it, it is pretty funny: almost like performance art. Yes of course I would welcome the opportunity to play with Scott anytime. As soon as the '88 tour was over, I had no hard feelings whatsoever toward Scott. I kind of knew - even at that time - that the problem was something deeper and more troubling and devastating than a simple personality conflict. It was just that no one knew what, and no one could figure out what was up, as Frank was really closed-mouth about everything. But Scott's cool, and we are both very different people as a result of 1988."

More recently, I asked Mann to reflect further on the reasons for the tour ending prematurely. Was Zappa's health really a big factor? And how on earth did they still manage to produce such wondrous music on stage? He now feels that, at this stage, it would be hurtful and childish to name names: "It's time to be heroic. I feel that I know this is the exact reason why Chad will not speak on the subject." Here's his considered summing up of events:

"Fear, loathing, sturm und drang, the best and worst of every musician in the band including Frank, fun, hellish, intense, exhausting; strange new environment with corporate suits as management, loss of Glotzer and his family vibe, loss of Smothers and his saving grace, loss of Frank's normal band-leader style, loss of Howard and Mark, loss of Tommy Mars. Frank clearly not well, self-destructive behaviour all the way around not just Frank, random acts of kindness and cruelty, polarised, unified, sad, tormented, ill; Big energy karmic kick in the ass for all, angels all around, universal love of Frank and his music which is why no one quit the touring band, and no one was fired either."

"The notice of disharmony showed itself in the interaction of the rhythm section, which created a kind of simmering/angry vibe to make music within. It was together but did not feel like a two-way street. However, both these guys are great players, so, go figure. They were riding the wave like anyone else. You could point to any individual and make an '88 tour crimelist, but that would be short-sighted and provide no insights whatsoever besides the story. Everyone has a story. In the end it was a force of energy that was way bigger than all of us put together, including Frank. It was some big twist in the fabric of Karma, and all you could do just to hold on day to day. I used to wonder why the forces drew these particular personalities together at this time, in such a highly charged environment, to experience this traumatic but romantic event? Was FZ such a GOD that his illness manifested itself in the wellness of his band? Or was this his way to begin to step outside of being the long-promoted FZ figure. I know it was exhausting for him but he also loved it, and hated it. War stories of spiritual advancement I guess. It is a real interesting example."

When I first contacted Mann to tell him I had been asked to write this book, he was very enthusiastic ("Fantastic, man. This is always what I hoped to see: people such as yourself who have become historians of the Zappa culture coming into a place of being able to document lots of stuff that is either twisted or misperceived or simply unknown.") You can imagine how I felt, especially as a few days later I got a similar big-up from Keneally, who thought I was "extremely well-suited to do this project and I believe you'll present a balanced overview which I look forward to reading when it's done!" But a few months later, when my work on the book started in earnest, Mann's attitude had cooled somewhat - he was concerned about the possible involvement of certain other 'Zappa authorities'. I was able to reassure him on this, and he continued to be of much help - as have all those I quizzed. I sincerely hope that I have not done any of them any disservice; I truly appreciate their candour and assistance, without which this book wouldn't be worth a buck o' five. What I have attempted to do is document the events of 1988, with those involved telling their side of the story.

Much as Zappa described himself as a reporter, I have done little more than relay the band's on-road antics and after-thoughts. As an example, I asked Wing for any amusing stories. He told me of an incident reminiscent of the stateroom scene from the Marx Brothers' *A Night At The Opera*: "I remember one night, crashing in the lobby of the hotel. On average, one to two people, if they needed a place to crash, would stay with us; this night, Randee invited eight plus... I don't recall the final tally; they were still arriving as I left."

And two hard-boiled eggs. It really does sound like they had a lot of fun on the tour, and the dispute with Thunes was not their main focus. When I talked to Willis backstage at Zappanale #20, he was absolutely wonderful - had a great time shooting the breeze with him - and, unlike Thunes, he didn't see anything divisive about the 'bus situation'. It seemed to me that the real problem was just certain personalities clashing which, in another time and place, would have been better managed. Willis, Keneally and Martin all appear to be easy going types and Wackerman, as Mann says, seems strictly genteel. But according to Thunes, in 1988 Wackerman initially told Zappa he could not work for anything less than $2500 per week, "and Frank was about to pay him thirteen hundred. We ended up with a compromise of two thousand dollars... [for] all the guys that had been in the band before. Everybody else got thirteen hundred."[14] I get the impression that, as Wackerman couldn't be with his wife (he'd only been married for a couple of years then and his Australian wife was expecting their first child at the time), he at least wanted to be well paid and enjoy the tour - but couldn't because of Thunes. Elsewhere, Zappa is quoted as saying "...an argument broke out between Scott Thunes and just about everyone else in the band apart from me and Mike Keneally. The others all decided that they hated Scott's guts; it was very weird. Basically the ringleader of the whole thing was Ed Mann, and he and Chad Wackerman decided that Scott had to go, and they brought about most of the discontent in the band."[15]

Having met and chatted with Wackerman on a number of occasions, I find it very hard to believe he was the actual agitator. And what makes it all the more difficult to comprehend is that Wackerman and Thunes had not only toured together with Zappa, but played in his home studio at the same time between tours. As well as on his own material, Zappa had also recruited the pair to act as the rhythm section on Dweezil's first solo album, *Havin' A Bad Day*. In 2007, Wackerman told me "It was fun. Dweezil played great, and he was young too, maybe 18 I'm guessing. Steve Vai was his teacher and Scott Thunes helped him arrange his tunes, so they had it all planned out arrangement wise before I even heard the music. A good time was had."[*] This was between the 1984 and 1988 tours. So why would Wackerman suddenly start to hate Thunes' guts? Perhaps the root cause was this twenty something punk bass player lording it over the experienced - but lower paid - horn players, some of whom were in their forties. Certainly Thunes' vitriol seems to be aimed more at them than the percussionists.

But who recruited all these guys and appointed Thunes Clonemeister? Blaming the hired hands and then moaning about them publicly when it doesn't work out shows an amazing lack of judgement and unprofessionalism on Zappa's part; in any other walk of life (in 'the real world'), an employer would be crucified for such behaviour (though, as Zappa told Jeff Newelt, "everybody got

---

* In Wictor's book, Thunes comments on the recording of Dweezil's debut "*I personally would not have chosen him (Wackerman) because it was more a hard rock thing... but there were no other drummers around, and so we did that, and it worked out for whatever, ah, goodness that was there.*"

paid... but me. I took the loss."[16]) And he'd faced similar (albeit, less extreme) difficulties before: in *The Real Frank Zappa Book*, he says "musicians tend to be lazy, they get sick and skip rehearsals... get loaded, drunk or evicted and need assistance moving their families around in 'emergency' situations."[17] What was so different this time? Zappa told *Playboy* that prior to his cancer being identified in 1990 "I'd been feeling sick for a number of years, but nobody diagnosed it. Then I got really ill and had to go to the hospital in an emergency. While I was in there, they did some tests and found out it had been there for anywhere from eight to ten years, growing undetected by any of my previous doctors."[18] So the comments about Zappa's health being a factor in 1988 seem valid and, by the time the band were in Europe, Zappa really only cared that his music was being performed correctly; all else he seemed to wash his hands of. And the music was - by and large, and right up to the bitter end - being played wonderfully well because everyone in the band loved and respected Zappa so much.

Although Zappa did play many guitar solos along the way - and included several on the posthumously released *Trance-Fusion* album - they were nothing like the 'air-sculptures' he had created in the late seventies. In his autobiography he noted, "With the 1988 band, I didn't have to play very much in the show, because the focus was on the horn arrangements and the vocals. I didn't have to play fifteen-minute guitar solos, and, really, there's not much of a market for that anymore - the interest span of the audience has shrivelled to about eight bars, and in those eight bars, you are expected to play every note you know."[19] But some that he did play were spine-tingly-dingly - notably the one on *Any Kind Of Pain* included on the *Broadway The Hard Way* album.

And as well as playing the guitar, singing and conducting the band, he also had the Synclavier to play with. Most of the concerts saw some amazing improvisation using 'La Machine': "Each night there would be a sequence, like a complete composition, loaded into the Synclavier, and during the improvised part of the show, I could turn that sequence on. The Synclavier would play a collection of sounds and then the band would play along with it. On some nights we used 'You're Goin' To Hell'; on some nights we used some stuff with the Congress voices; some nights other things. About the middle of the tour we hooked up some wires so that I could throw a switch on the stage and any one of three different musicians on stage could trigger the Synclavier with their instrumental set-up, so that Ed could trigger the samples on the Synclavier by playing the silicone mallets, and if I flip the switch another way, Bobby Martin could trigger it from his MIDI keyboard, or Chad could trigger it from his octopads."[20]

Another Synclavier owner was Michael Jackson, who had utilised it a little more conventionally on his *Bad* album and tour in 1987 (played by Christopher Currell). Coincidentally, Zappa had planned to use an Anglo-Italian rap version of the track *Bad* in his opera, *Dio Fa* (at the end of which "GOD'S nose shrivels to Jacksonian proportions, and HE dances away,"[21]), which no doubt would have provided him with another excuse not to broach the subject of releasing his Beatles' medley from the tour.

In 1991, Zappa told *Society Pages* "I would love to be able to release it, but I don't have the right to release it without permission from the publisher, and Michael Jackson owns the publishing, so after my song about him, I'm not too convinced that I would..."[22] Zappa also commented in his autobiography "Do we really want to know HOW Michael Jackson makes his music? No. We want to understand why he needs the bones of the Elephant Man - and, until he tells us, it doesn't make too much difference whether or not he really is 'bad'."[23] Frankly, following Jackson's death and the ownership of the Fab's back catalogue now expected to be the subject of years of legal wrangling, it seems highly unlikely that a recording will ever be released officially. But we can live in hope. Or even Stanford-le-Hope.

In addition to the wondrous written and improvised music in 1988, there was also the frequent secret word usage to keep the band on its toes and help raise spirits. Mann says "There seems to be so much speculation about the Secret Words. To me, it always seemed like words that would be funny alone or strung together in the context of the music. From 1977 forward, I think the words were either thought of on stage or during sound check. Once FZ got political, in 1988, they became more words that spoke to his point of view."

Their use would often cause band members - notably Willis - to crack-up on stage. Was Zappa concerned about this? Willis thought not: "The only reason I would have an outburst of laughter is because Frank would cause it. Therefore I wouldn't worry about it. It was all his fault. The 1988 tour would have been my absolute favourite tour only the people who were managing Frank at the time were not my favourite people. The 1988 tour - as far as the band was concerned, because it was the best band that we ever had - was the most fun."[24]

One of Wackerman's few comments on the '88 tour came many years later when he told *Downbeat* magazine: "We had 120 tunes rehearsed so it was completely different every night. Frank would change up styles constantly. People might know a tune as reggae, but he might decide to do it as heavy metal. We rehearsed so much that Frank could change anything and the band could do it with confidence."[25]

And because the band was so adept and game for a laugh, Zappa was also able to tinker and (cough) 'improve' some of the arrangements played along the way. One such was the *Torture Never Stops / Theme From "Bonanza" / Lonesome Cowboy Burt* sequence, as can be heard, compared and contrasted by spinning the "*Best Band*" and afore-mentioned *You Can't Do That On Stage Anymore Vol. 6* CDs.

Keneally tells us, *"The Torture / Lonesome* medley was usually great fun to play. Those readers unfamiliar with Laurie Anderson's work might not realise that we're parodying her in the middle section of *"Lonesome"* - 'Sharkey' is a character in several of her songs. I suggested including the relentless 'ha ha ha ha ha ha' vocal part, ripped off from her song *O Superman*, and I came to regret it on some evenings when Frank decided to keep the section going on forever."[26]

The pumping irony of this inclusion was that, some twenty years later, Anderson married her long-time companion Lou Reed - a gentleman with whom Zappa had had a long-running feud. Rumour has it that this all started when Verve released The Mothers' first album ahead of the Velvet Underground's debut, making *Freak Out!* the first concept rock album produced by Tom Wilson in a gatefold sleeve. Or something. Reed said of Zappa: "He's probably the single most untalented person I've heard in my life. He's a two-bit pretentious academic, and he can't play rock 'n' roll, because he's a loser. And that's why he dresses up funny. He's not happy with himself, and I think he's right."[27]

Zappa in turn included a reference to the "shitty" Velvet Underground on The Mothers' *We're Only In It For The Money* album. In 1992, after being told by Danny Houston that Reed had purposely switched venues from London's Hammersmith Odeon to the Rainbow Theatre in Finsbury Park so that he could look down at the spot where Zappa had hit the ground in 1971, Ahmet responded with "I hate him so much... I will kill him with a pygmy blow-dart and poison his system." Ever the diplomat, Dweezil intervened with "...you have to fix that phrase by saying 'If it is true that he said that stuff about my father, then, next time I see him I will kill him with a blow dart.' If it's not true, then he's off the hook for now. But I still hate his music."[28] So it was more than odd that Reed should be chosen to induct Zappa into the Rock And Roll Hall Of Fame in 1995. When presenting the honour, Reed said "I admired Frank greatly and I know he admired me. It gives me great pleasure to give this award to his daughter." Before her acceptance speech, Moon said "Thank you, Lou. I really appreciate that."

I suppose nothing should really surprise us anymore - not even the fact that Ahmet (Reed's would-be assassin and singer of lyrics such as "I'm gonna fuck you in your ass, tongue-kiss your anus for a shit moustache,"[29]) is now working for The Walt Disney Company. It's a mixed up, muddled up, shook up world. But I like it, like it. Yes I do.

CHAPTER SIX
A Very Nice Body

So, how did Zappa choose to document the 1988 world tour? He quickly put together the first official audio release, which featured all of the brand new songs (save for *Jezebel Boy*), plus *Dickie's Such An Asshole* - which first saw the light of day in April 1988 as a recording from 12th December 1973 on the *You Can't Do That On Stage Anymore Sampler* LP and cassette - and a cover of Nelson Riddle's theme from *The Untouchables*. *Broadway The Hard Way* was first released as a nine-track vinyl album through Zappa's mail order label Barking Pumpkin in October 1988, a week before the US elections. By including the full Republican medley, together with *Rhymin' Man*, the album was intended to help the undecided voter (who may have registered at one of the US shows) make up their minds on which way to vote.

Because of its US centric nature, Zappa was in no rush for the album to be made readily available overseas, but seven months later an expanded CD version was issued (by Rykodisc in the US, and Zappa Records in the UK). While this added eight songs - including the afore-mentioned *Jezebel Boy*, and his King Of Pop-kicking re-write of *Tell Me You Love Me (Why Don't You Like Me?)* - for some reason it excised the confinement loaf rap intro to *Dickie's Such An Asshole*. Also, it included Mr Sting's uncredited guest appearance on *Murder By Numbers*, which was part of a beautiful horn-dominated suite that included the old R&B hit, *Bacon Fat*, and jazz standard, *Stolen Moments* (with a lovely trumpet solo by Walt Fowler). While the voices of Zappa, Willis and Martin were familiar to fans, the album opened with *Elvis Has Just Left The Building*, sung by Alfred E. new boy Keneally. Keneally also sang lead on *Rhymin' Man* and "the role of the prostitute in *What Kind Of Girl?*" which, he says, was only "played twice, and constructed during sound checks on the road in response to current events. Those are pretty much the highest notes possible for me to sing. It hurt."[1]

Although Zappa made much of the fact that all of the material released from the tour was "recorded live (no overdubs)", this masked the fact that the perfectionist in him could not allow for many of the songs to be taken from one take at one show. Perhaps the most extreme example of this is *Jesus Thinks You're A Jerk* on the "*Broadway*" album. The track consists of over 20 edits from performances of the song recorded in at least 11 different locations (mainly the US, but also a snippet (5:59-6:15) from the second London show). This song also featured the dynamic Eric Buxton as guest vocalist, reading the 'Twilight Zone' monologue that Willis had had some trouble performing. The piece ended with Frank announcing "this is intermission... see you in a half an hour!" But fans had to wait a couple of years for the fun to resume.

In 1990, Zappa told *Society Pages* of his plans to release his version of *Boléro* as a single - but in just one country, as "the only place in the world where the copyright has expired, and it's public domain, is England. And so, if it's released and manufactured in England, then it could be done."[2] And sure enough, just ahead of the next full album, a CD and 12" vinyl single was released by Zappa Records in the UK comprising "Broadway" versions of *Stairway To Heaven* and Ravel's greatest hit. The back cover had black and white photos of M. Ravel and F. Zappa, the latter looking up from a copy of John Godwin's best-seller, *This Baffling World* - a book about 'the greatest puzzlements of all time and people of extraordinary talents which defy comprehension'. Keneally was baffled as to why Zappa chose to release "technically the two worst songs on the album" to be the

---

* A reference to Alfred E. Neuman, the fictional mascot of *Mad* magazine, whose image features prominently in the Mike Keneally Band's *Dog* DVD.

** As documented by Den Simms, the obsessive analyst.

single: "A lot of people heard that single and said 'Fuck! Is this what the whole album's gonna sound like? They can't even play in time.'"[3] The final part of *"Stairway"* was recorded at the Wembley concert the author attended, and ends with Zappa saying goodnight to one of its now absent composers. Both tracks appeared on *The Best Band You Never Heard In Your Life*, which was issued as a double CD in April 1991 (by Barking Pumpkin in the US, and Zappa Records in the UK). The album featured "big-band arrangements of concert favourites and obscure album cuts, along with deranged versions of cover tunes and a few premiere recordings."[4]

Sadly, once Ravel's estate heard what Zappa had done to their Maurice's major masterwork, they flipped - accusing him of perverting the intent of the composer. Zappa had to make a public apology and temporarily removed the track from *"The Best Band"* in Europe, where the estate's copyright was in fact still effective for another few years. In 2007, Zappa's widow advised that, "since Ravel had no progeny, his heirs were related to his gardener and or housekeeper."[5] The track was reinstated on the 1995 worldwide reissue, which also replaced the cover artwork with that provided by Cal Schenkel, Zappa's long-time artistic collaborator, for the original Japanese release. The album opened with a stonking *Heavy Duty Judy*, edited from two performances in Germany (Würzburg) and the Netherlands (Rotterdam), which ends with Zappa telling the audience about meeting Johnny Cash and asking them if they still want the band to play *Ring Of Fire*. Of course they do, and so once again the first lead vocal is performed by Keneally.

Zappa's liner notes explained the album's title thus: "The 1988 road band self-destructed before US audiences in the south, Midwest and West could hear it perform. It was, however, heard and appreciated by East Coast and European audiences during its brief existence (four months of rehearsal in 1987/1988, followed by a tour, February through June, 1988), and it is from those performances that this compilation has been made. In a world where most of the 'big groups' go on stage and pretend to sing and play, we proudly present this quaint audio artefact. Yes, once upon a time, live musicians actually sang and played this. All material contained herein is 100% live, and there are no over-dubs of any kind."[6]

Against the tracks, Zappa this time noted the various recording locations from which each was pieced together (although these are by no means comprehensive or, in a few instances, accurate). Keneally believed this was the only way to do it as "the likelihood of having one perfect version from one city is virtually impossible, not just because it's difficult music, but you've got twelve humans performing this difficult music, and even if eleven of them do it right, then there's at least one guy who stands a chance of having made a mistake."[7]

And there were possibly other reasons for some of this editing: *Inca Roads*, for example, was compiled from a number of shows allowing for Zappa to squeeze in quotes from his own song, *Approximate*, and that of the Bee Gees' *Stayin' Alive*. This inclusion was another example of Zappa's oft-touted 'conceptual continuity', whereby everything he did - every song, film, book, interview, etc. - was connected. Consequently, many musical themes and lyrics appear in different forms throughout his entire body of work. In this particular instance, *Stayin' Alive* had been quoted earlier during a live performance of *Approximate* in Pistoia, Italy on 8th July 1982 (and subsequently released on the *You Can't Do That On Stage Anymore Vol. 4* album).

Just to take things even further (which we Zappa fans often do!), his son Dweezil released a complete version of the Bee Gees hit that same year on his third solo album, *Confessions*. For what it's worth, Thunes played bass on every one of these three recordings, all released in 1991. Originally, Ozzy Osbourne sang lead on Dweezil's recording, but contractual complications meant his vocal had to be replaced by that of Donny Osmond for the album. At the time,

Zappa senior said of Osmond: "He's a good singer. And he's a nice guy. He's struggling so much with that Donny and Marie image."[8] Happily, the Osbourne version was also eventually released on Ozzy's *Prince Of Darkness* box-set in 2005 (albeit with Thunes' bass and Josh Freese's drums removed, and subsequently overdubbed by Osbourne's musicians - something he'd done on his first two solo albums[*]).

Zappa was a huge admirer of Osbourne and his former band, Black Sabbath, who he was happy to introduce on stage at Madison Square Garden on their *Technical Ecstasy* tour in 1976. Zappa was to have played with the band, but was unwilling to do so without first having a sound check. In his autobiography, Osbourne tells of the time a few years later when Zappa played the Birmingham Odeon and after asked, "'Is there anywhere we can get something to eat in this town?' I told him, 'At this time of night, there's only the curry house on Bristol Street, but I don't recommend it.' Frank just shrugged and said, 'Oh, that'll do, I'll have a go.' So we all went to this dodgy Indian joint - me, Frank, Thelma[**] and some Japanese chick that Frank was hanging out with at the time. I told Frank that the only thing on the menu he shouldn't order, under any circumstances, was the steak. He nodded, looked at the menu for a while, then ordered the steak. When it arrived, I just sat there and watched him try to eat it. 'Like old boots, is it?' I said. 'No, actually,' replied Frank, dabbing his mouth with a napkin. 'More like new ones.'"[9] Ah, ah, ah, ah.

"Best Band" also featured renditions of two other classic rock songs, both recorded during a sound check in Linz, Austria just after the cake incident. Against a repetitive, mechanical sort of fake-Devo horn-punctuated type background, we hear Willis, in Thing-Fish

---

[*] In 1981, Osbourne fired drummer Lee Kerslake and bassist Bob Daisley just after the recording sessions for *Diary Of A Madman* and erroneously credited his new rhythm section on the album sleeve. In 1998, Kerslake and Daisley sued Ozzy and his manager/wife Sharon for unpaid royalties and missing song writing credits. Osbourne's response was to erase Kerslake and Daisley's playing, overdubbing their parts with new performances by bassist Robert Trujillo and drummer Mike Bordin.

[**] Osbourne's first wife, Thelma Riley; currently a teacher in Leicestershire.

guise, and Keneally, as the Man In Black, having fun with Hendrix's *Purple Haze* and Cream's *Sunshine Of Your Love*. Disc Two adds more laughs with Jimmy Swaggart-inspired lyric changes and some more unusual covers, in *When Irish Eyes Are Smiling*, "*Godfather Part II*" Theme, and Theme From "*Bonanza*".

Just under two months after "*Best Band*", *Make A Jazz Noise Here* followed, another two-disc set. Zappa had pondered releasing both sets as a four-CD package, but thought it might be too expensive - plus "there's some people who don't like instrumental music, and some people who don't like some of the weird types of things that are on *Make A Jazz Noise Here*. I separated that from the more entertaining type material."[10]

So now he had released three quite distinct collections from the 1988 tour: a single album featuring all of the new songs; a double comprising the more vocal-oriented, recognisable and humorous stuff; and another double, focussing on the improvised, non-vocal pieces. In 1996, Thunes said "All those albums have blood on every track. There is danger inherent in everything on *Make A Jazz Noise Here*. And *The Best Band You Never Heard In Your Life*... even the standardised performances, even if they were standardised every night, there was danger lurking behind every single note. You had no idea what was going to happen to the energy level or the tension because the tension was always there. In my music, I dig tension because of the modern classical music that I've heard. I know that it can coexist with normalcy. Frank is a big fan of that. But! I don't need to do that ever again. I don't ever need to play in that kind of improvisatory glory again because it has been expressed perfectly in that arena. Why would anybody want to redo, relive this [*Make A Jazz Noise Here*] album? I haven't listened to it in three years. It's got those fucking asshole horn players all over it. It's got them everywhere. I listen to it. I see their faces. Now, when I listen to *The Best Band You Never Heard In Your Life*, it's Frank's music. They're Frank's tunes. Tunes that I grew up with. Tunes that I think are glorious... *Cruisin' For Burgers* [on *Make A Jazz Noise Here*], I never knew that song. I never knew the glorious gloriousness of playing that solo. I love that solo section. And even on this album, he cuts off the last chord. My favourite part of the song is the payoff. And he cut it off and starts *Advance Romance* with the ugliest guitar noise in the universe. I cannot stand listening to that. It's so absolutely painful. It's the exact wrong production decision to make. Hit the chord, then go into *Advance Romance*. But don't replace my favourite bit of music with my least favourite bit of music. And I loved playing *Advance Romance*, but that was wrong. That was a really, really wrong decision."[11]

Conversely, Keneally says of *Make A Jazz Noise Here*: "The stretch of music on disc two from "*Sinister*" to "*Genteel*" is my favourite bunch of released music from the '88 tour. I just love it. *Cruisin' For Burgers* was my favourite song to play on the tour, it made me happy in ways I can't describe. I'm endlessly happy that this album exists."[12] I wholeheartedly agree with Keneally: *Make A Jazz Noise Here* is easily in my top five all time favourite Zappa albums of all time, mate.

When Marxist music writer Ben Watson asked Wackerman about the album four years after the tour, he said "I quite like that record. It's my favourite of the ones I played on with Frank. It's funny because I don't even realise what's on them as it's all stuff from different tours. He chops them up and it's from all different cities, all those edits. It's only recently that I sat down and listened to the whole record."[13]

In his tour diaries, Keneally notes that "The solo on *Orange County Lumber Truck* is always a lot of fun for me to accompany, but Scott frequently gets angry at Chad during that solo, because Chad takes great Colaiuta-style liberties with the groove, making it a challenge to find the 'one' at any given moment, which is fine, but when Chad ends his journey and returns to the 'one', Scott invariably takes exception to its location, because Scott usually tries to keep the rhythm straight while Chad goes off on his forays, but somewhere along the line a discrepancy evolves, and when Chad comes back it makes Scott sound off, which makes Scott a little angry. There's no way to tell who's the culprit, they both have very different conceptions of time."[14]

Picking up on the apparent stylistic mis-match with his rhythm-section partner of seven years, Thunes told Bryan Beller "We didn't have much of a musical connection."[15] How astounding is that to anyone who, like me, can listen to these guys backing Zappa all day long? Pretty damn. Beller, who has been Keneally's pal and bassist for nearly 20 years and was to have been the bass player for the first Zappa Plays Zappa tour that got postponed*, was quizzing Thunes for an article he was writing for *Bass Player* magazine about Thunes' "own personal showcase of what a bassist could do in Zappa's later live setting,"[16] during *Alien Orifice* on the *Make A Jazz Noise Here* album.

Thunes humbly conceded: "I hear the bass doing what's necessary and important for Frank's music. [It's] the pure essence of what I loved about bass inside Frank's music coming to the fore. I did as much as I was required, as much as I was forced to, and as much as I could get away with."[17] Knowing of Thunes' penchant for a bit of the old Béla Viktor János, I asked him if it was his idea for the band to play the *Theme From The Bartók Piano Concerto #3*. "Nope. Frank's," he told me, "He asked me to orchestrate it, and the Stravinsky, for the band." 'The Stravinsky' was the *Royal March* From *"L'Histoire Du Soldat"* which, together with the Bartók on the *Make A Jazz Noise Here* album, were edited from a discarded performance of *Packard Goose* and sandwiched between *City Of Tiny Lites* and the second movement from *Sinister Footwear* - but not on some European releases as, after the *Boléro* affair, Zappa was a tad windy about the

---

* After the tour got deferred, Beller suddenly decided *"it just didn't fit with what I wanted in my day-to-day life, period,"* and was replaced by Pete Griffin.

families objecting to his treatment of these pieces. They never did, and both pieces were reinstated on the 1995 reissue. There seemed to be no such concerns about the inclusion of extracts from *Lohengrin* by Richard Wagner, *Habanera* from *Carmen* by George Bizet and *Festival Overture "The Year 1812"* by Pyotr Ilyich Tchaikovsky (nicknamed 'The Reader's Digest Classical Medley') during the monster mash-up of *Big Swifty*.

I asked Wing what he thought of the *"Broadway"*, *"Best Band"* and *"Jazz Noise"* CDs. "Glad they're not vinyl," he joked. Do you listen to the albums at all, I enquired. "Don't get me wrong, I have checked them all out: very glad to be alive at this time in the universe, hangin', playin' and recording with some of the world's greatest musicians. And Frank. About the vinyl: it's a lot easier to hear parts off a CD; out of the 120-150 compositions I memorised, 60 were never taken down by me; years go by, memories dim and fade, then the high school reunion. You get my drift?"

Ten days after the release of *"Jazz Noise"*, Zappa issued the fourth in his *You Can't Do That On Stage Anymore* live series of CDs (although *MAJNH* is listed as 'Official Release #57' and *YCDTOSA Vol. 4* '#56'). This added a further two tracks from the 1988 tour: *Take Me Out To The Ball Game* and *Filthy Habits*, both largely recorded at the Bilbao show on 13th May, with the former featuring Willis and Walt Fowler playing long time Atlanta Braves of Major League Baseball broadcasters, Skip Caray and Pete Van Wieren. Goodness knows what the Spanish audience made of this.

A year later, *You Can't Do That On Stage Anymore Vol. 6* gave us a further seven snatches from the tour, including: *Lonesome Cowboy Nando* from the final show in Genoa, this time edited together with a Mothers' recording featuring Jimmy Carl Black from 1971; *Make A Sex Noise Here* from the "special Saint Patrick's Day program" in Binghamton, which also brought us the crazy *When Irish Eyes Are Smiling* and *Godfather II* medley on the *"Best Band"* album; and *We're*

Turning Again, Zappa's almost sentimental, nostalgic reflection on the demise of the sixties, which name-checks old 'friends', Jimi Hendrix*, Keith Moon**, and Janis Joplin†.

Before his death, Zappa prepared a third album of live guitar solos that featured nine from the "Broadway" tour - which he named *Trance-Fusion.* When the author interviewed Dweezil in May 1991, I asked if his father had any plans to release their duet on *Chunga's Revenge* from the second Wembley date. He told me "Yeah, it's gonna come out - it was kinda cool. I've heard it once or twice since then. I think it'll be on the next release..." It actually took another fifteen years for it to appear as the opening track of the afore-mentioned guitar album. *Trance-Fusion* ended with another father/son duet, with all of the other tracks being Zappa's in-the-moment compositions edited out of familiar songs (see Appendix II for details).

As if we hadn't been blessed with enough wonderment from this amazing tour, the Zappa Family Trust has more recently given us a further seven tracks - for download only - including the final song Zappa performed live in his home country, *America The Beautiful.* This sported a minor lyric change: instead of 'God shed his grace on thee' was 'The only place to be'. Asked why this was, Zappa quipped, "I'm not sure God did shed his grace on this country."

---

* Hendrix appeared with the Mothers Of Invention on the cover of their *We're Only In It For The Money* album.

** Moon appeared in Zappa's film, *200 Motels.*

† According to Barry Miles, when his wife Gail was pregnant with Moon Unit, Zappa spent the night with Janis at the Hotel Chelsea in New York. [*Frank Zappa* by Barry Miles, Atlantic Books, 2004]

CHAPTER SEVEN
When No One Was No One

In 1989, Zappa told *Rhythm* magazine: "For 25 years I have tried to do something more than wonderful in the United States. And I have eaten shit. I can't get my music played on the radio. I do a series of sold-out concerts and lose $400,000. I wind up with musicians who feel they can do it all without me. Now what is this?"[1] So, what did the fine musicians who worked with him in 1988 actually go on to do without him?

Ike Willis (synth, guitar, vocals): In the year of the "Broadway" tour, Willis released his debut solo album, *Shoulda Gone Before I Left*, and was featured on The Fowler Brothers' *Breakfast For Dinosaurs* - along with Wing, Chester Thompson and Vinnie Colaiuta. His solo album comprised all original material and featured Zappa alumni Ray White, Jeff Hollie (Willis' best friend from college who played sax on the track *Joe's Garage*) and - on the CD-only track, *Resolution* - former Clonemeister Arthur Barrow. Ten years later, Willis released his only other solo recording, *Dirty Pictures*. Aside from a few guest contributions - for example, on Barrow's *Eyebrow Razor* and Stu Grimshaw's *Der Fremde* - he has pretty much exclusively played and

---

* In 2009, Willis told the author: "*Me and my wife and him, we met on my first day in college in 1974. He's my daughter's Godfather. He and I, we started our first band together in our freshman year in college. If it wasn't for Jeff Hollie, I would have never been prepared for Frank Zappa. Jeff was the biggest Zappa fan in our circle. I met him on the basketball court. We go to our first orientation meeting; my wife to be is sitting across the room. So I met her, and then we're hanging out in the dormitories, and Jeff said 'Hey, man - are you into Zappa?' I said 'Yeah.' We were into Zappa, Mahavishnu Orchestra, Return To Forever, The Beatles. And Jeff had all the Zappa albums. My roommate was a Yes freak. So we'd all just sit up there smoking doobies, and listen to our favourite stuff. And Jeff brought me up to speed on all the latest Zappa stuff. So by the time Frank came to our school - Washington University - and did a concert a few years later, I was on the local crew, and we made eye contact. And after a while, Frank takes me to his dressing room, hands me his guitar and says "Do you know any of my shit?" And I said 'Yeah,' and he said 'Well, play me something.' And I could because of Jeff Hollie. So how do you repay your best friend...I mean, if it wasn't for him, there would be no Ike Willis, okay? All through the Joe's Garage sessions, Jeff was there anyway. So I said 'Frank, please, please. He knows all your stuff. You've got to give me this. At least put Jeff on one song.' And it was on the title track: 'Even if you play it on the saxophone,'; that's Jeff. I mean, how do you repay your best friend for doing something like that? It was the only thing I could come up with to really, really repay him for what he'd done.*"

sang Zappa's music since with a variety of cover bands around the world (such as: Project/Object in the USA; the Muffin Men in the UK; Cuccurullo Brillo Brullo in Holland; the Central Scrutinizer Band in Brazil; and Ossi Duri in Italy). He has done this because he says it was Zappa's dying wish. "After the '88 tour, my mom died of cancer. She was the same age as Frank, she was 52. Needless to say it was a serious case of déjà vu when I walked into Frank's room the week before he died. Same as with my mom, got the I.V. thing and lost half his body weight, very weak and in pain and very pissed off. Eventually he just said, 'Well what the fuck, just get up there and kick ass and keep the music alive for me and just keep it going'."[2] Perhaps his most significant first step in helping to keep the music alive was with fellow "Broadway" band members Martin, Wackerman, McGettrick, Mann and Bruce Fowler in the Band From Utopia, who performed a series of tribute concerts in Germany the year after Zappa passed away. A CD and DVD resulted. Willis continued playing with BFU for a few more years (including a concert in Israel in 1997, with Joel Thome & The Shalom BSAL Orchestra) but did not appear on their second album, *So Yuh Don't Like Modern Art*. He is now a regular at the Zappanale festival in Germany.

Bruce Fowler (trombone): Of all the "Broadway" band members, Bruce has without question had the most successful career since 1988 - just scrutinise the credits for most of the films coming out of Hollywood today and you're likely to see his name as the composer, arranger, orchestrator or conductor of its soundtrack (notable movies include *Sherlock Holmes*; *It's Complicated*; *Public Enemies*; *The Da Vinci Code*; *Pirates Of The Caribbean*; *The Simpsons Movie*; *Chicago*; *Chicken Run*; *Gladiator*; *Face/Off*; *Muppet Treasure Island*; *The Lion King*; *Speed*; *Cool Runnings*; *True Romance*; *Misery*; and *Days Of Thunder*). Immediately post the tour, he recorded albums with his brothers, Ed Mann and Chad Wackerman, including his own, *Ants Can Count*. He later became a key member of the Band From Utopia which mutated into the Banned From Utopia. In 2003, Bruce was part of a 'ten years after' tribute to Zappa commissioned by the BBC, with

Vinnie Colaiuta, Tommy Mars, Arthur Barrow, McGettrick, Wing and brother Walt. Calling themselves the Mar Vista Philharmonic, they recorded two improvised pieces in Arthur Barrow's Lotek Studio (*Shut Up 'n' Make A Jazz Noise Here* and *Sad Spangled Banner*) loosely based on a number of Zappa compositions. These were aired by BBC Radio 3 on 4th December 2003. Bruce made a guest appearance on Jon Larsen's *Strange News From Mars* in 2007, and in 2009, Larsen's Zonic Entertainment released a CD of a 2002 jam by the Mar Vista Philharmonic called *No Forest Fire*, billed as the closest "you'll ever get to a new recording by Frank Zappa's last touring all stars band."

Walt Fowler (synth, trumpet, flugelhorn): As well as *Breakfast For Dinosaurs*, Walt played on albums by Wackerman and Mann just after the "Broadway" tour. Like brother Bruce, Walt is featured on many major motion picture soundtracks - including *The Lion King*, *The Thin Red Line*, and *Ocean's Twelve* & *Thirteen*, - and orchestrated music for the likes of *Con Air*, *Twister*, *Pearl Harbor*, *Shrek*, *The Bourne Supremacy*, *X Men 3*, *The Chronicles Of Narnia*, *Transformers* and *The Dark Knight*. From 1989, he did many tours with Diana Ross, and joined James Taylor's band in 2001, appearing on his Grammy-nominated *Covers* album.

Paul Carman (alto sax, baritone sax, soprano sax): After adding Zappa to his CV, Carman formed ESP, an acoustic jazz quartet. In 2000, they released *Even Picasso Couldn't Find Her* on NineWinds Records. Carman has also released a series of Metronome discs, featuring live jazz drumming for music students and professionals to use as a practice tool.

Albert Wing (tenor sax): Wing has done many sessions with the Fowler brothers, and toured with Walt as part of Diana Ross's touring band in late 1989. Immediately post-"Broadway", Wing was featured on Larry Carlton's *On Solid Ground* tour. As well as playing with the Mar Vista Philharmonic (though not on their *No Forest Fire*

CD), Wing played with Walt and Wackerman on the Mike Miller Quintet's *World Goes Round* album in 2008.

Kurt McGettrick (baritone sax, contrabass clarinet): According to Thunes, McGettrick was a "tall, thin, very old, alcoholic, cigarette smoker" who, on the "Broadway" tour, would "sit behind the bus driver with a bottle of wine and a map and follow our trip." McGettrick in turn allegedly thought Thunes "mentally ill". Post-'88, McGettrick played with B.B. King, Arthur Barrow and, as noted above, the Band From Utopia and the Mar Vista Philharmonic. He sadly passed away in 2007 due to "an aggressive cancer condition." McGettrick reportedly had a wonderfully dry sense of humour; Mann told the author, "he was a riot. Sober." Wackerman said, "I was shocked to hear the news that Kurt had passed away. I had such a great time working with him. We got to stretch and improvise together quite a lot on the BFU tour of the US some years ago. He played with a huge sound, and was very interesting rhythmically as an improviser. Because of the way he played when he improvised, he left space, and enjoyed lots of interaction. He was a monster of the baritone sax and all the low woodwinds. I'll miss him and his music."

Robert Martin (keyboards, sax, vocals): Since 1988, Martin has played with the Ban(ne)d From Utopia, Etta James, Stevie Nicks, Paul McCartney and Andy Williams. In 1995, he took part in a live tribute to Zappa in Belgium called *The Purple Cucumber*. Martin enjoyed a five-year relationship with the actress Cybill Shepherd, and became the musical director of her successful CBS sitcom, *Cybill*. Shepherd revealed in her autobiography that their engagement ended on 24th October 1998 when Martin (who she named 'Howard Roark') told her so during a couples' therapy session. In 2000, he made a guest appearance on *The Persuasions Sing Zappa - Frankly A Cappella*, along with Bruce Fowler and Keneally. Today, he plays with the World Rock Symphony Orchestra ("the greatest sing-along rock show in history!"), runs the Think Method music production company with Stephen Boyd, and provides an online crash course in getting yourself into shape, fast - producing a *Look Great Naked At Any Age* DVD. He appeared as a special guest at Zappanale in 2009, and again in 2010.

Mike Keneally (synth, vocals, guitar): For my money, Keneally is having the most thrilling post-"Broadway" career. While he has released many great solo albums and DVDs, he has also worked with Thunes, Dweezil and Ahmet in Z, toured with Steve Vai and Dethklok, reprised his 'Johnny Cash' voice for Nigey Lennon on her *Reinventing The Wheel* album, played guitar all over Napoleon Murphy Brock's first solo album *Balls*, led the rock band during Zappa's Universe and, after Zappa's death, briefly became the first Vaultmeister tasked with trawling the family Vault for nuggets. Keneally performed at Zappanale #13 in Germany (with Zappa alumni Bob & Thana Harris, Don Preston, Thunes, Willis and Jimmy Carl Black), and headlined the festival with a pick-up band the following year (2003). Sadly, he's unlikely to play there again until such time as the organisers align themselves with the Zappa Family Trust. In 2005/06, he played two gigs with Wackerman: one an evening of mainly eclectic covers (including 'songs' by Miles Davis, Thelonius Monk, John Coltrane, Neil Young, Radiohead, Bob Dylan and, of course, Zappa); the other, "in San Diego with (bassist) Doug Lunn - the gig was completely improvised music. We had a great time," Wackerman told the author in 2007. Also in 2007, Keneally performed a tribute to Zappa in Hungary with Mann as part of Budapest's Autumn Festival. More recently, Keneally played keyboards on guitarist Joe Satriani's *Black Swans And Wormhole Wizards* studio album and *Wormhole Tour* of Europe and North America 2010/11. There's oodles more to say about Keneally, but instead I strongly recommend that you add www.keneally.com to your favourites and tune in to www.radiokeneally.com with all good haste.

Chad Wackerman (drums, electronic percussion): Since the "Broadway" tour, Wackerman has released four solo albums (featuring contributions from Mann and Walt Fowler) and continued to regularly play with English guitarist Allan Holdsworth. 2009 saw a live double CD tribute to Tony Williams, *Blues For Tony*, with Holdsworth, Alan Pasqua and Jimmy Haslip. In 2010, Wackerman issued his first DVD - *Hits Live* - with his Trio, who headlined Zappanale in 2006. In the early nineties, Wackerman was the musical director for the short-lived late night TV talk show, *The Dennis Miller Show*. In the mid nineties, he and his family moved to Sydney and lived there for ten years (his wife is Australian). Wackerman occasionally tours with fellow ex-Zappa drummer, Terry Bozzio; their *Solos & Duets* live DVD features Zappa's *The Black Page*.

Ed Mann (vibes, marimba, electronic percussion): Post-"Broadway", Mann has released five solo albums featuring contributions from Wackerman, Walt & Bruce Fowler and Tommy Mars. He was the star turn at Zappanale in 2004, performing a number of Zappa tunes with some Charlie Mingus and Dizzy Gillespie thrown in for good measure, backed by Belgian avant-garde jazz fusion band The Wrong Object. Afterwards, he complained that no one could hear what the others were playing on stage, and told me it "was an experiment - my desire is to push the bounds of the traditional Zappa arrangements instead of reiterating them verbatim, but to do so in a way that maintains integrity. And so this requires knowing the Zappa material intimately, and also the ability to use that same material as essential components for improvisation. Anyway, it was an interesting first experiment - it worked well enough to tell me that this idea is worth pursuing (and to remind me that extensive sound checking is even more important with this approach!)" Mann was an on/off member of John Bergamo's Repercussion Unit (a collective of percussionists) for twenty years and, more recently, formed an experimental world-roots jazz and electronic reggae thang called The Dub Jazz Unit. Occasionally spanks some Frank with top US Zappa tribute band Project/Object. In 2009, Mann produced *Listen*, an album by Asani, the contemporary Aboriginal women's trio from Edmonton, Canada (where Mann currently resides).

Scott Thunes (electric bass, mini moog): After '88, Thunes toured with LA punk band Fear, Dweezil, Steve Vai and The Waterboys, and was a crucial part of the Zappa's Universe rock band with Keneally. He then kind of went into hibernation for a while. In 2002, he performed with his sister Stacy's band, The Lewinskys, as one of their special guests at Zappanale #13 - along with Willis, Keneally and original Mother Jimmy Carl Black (with whom he refused to perform Zappa's *Road Ladies*). He told the author he "jumped at the chance... free airfare, a week in Germany with some Euros in my pocket, time spent with Stacy and my niece Isabella, and a thousand Euros helped me to agree to leave my 'self-imposed exile' from music." Has thrice appeared as Zappa Plays Zappa's special guest (at Santa Rosa on 7th March 2009, Ventura on 10th June 2010, and as part of the Frank Zappa festival at London's Roundhouse on 6th November 2010), and recently appeared on Beyond The Holographic Veil, along with Mann and Martin... and (*cough*) this author, the second album by J21.* Of all the Zappa alums I have spoken to, he has proven to be the most outrageous and downright funny of them all; I can see what Zappa liked about him.

Frank Zappa (synth, lead guitar, vocals): Of course sadly passed away five years after the 'Broadway The Hard Way' tour, but did pick up the guitar again; most notably to play improvised solos with local musicians in Prague and Budapest in June 1991. He also participated in concerts with the Frankfurt-based Ensemble Modern in 1992, which resulted in his swan song, *The Yellow Shark*. His family now regularly issues previously unreleased material that he worked on during his lifetime, while Dweezil goes out spreading the word on his Zappa Plays Zappa tours - asking that we accept no substitutes; Frank's widow refutes Willis' assertion that her husband asked him to keep the music alive, and has issued a number of cease and desist orders trying to prevent his former musicians and tribute bands from doing just that.

---

* Joseph Diaz, a Zappa-loving stunt guitarist from Spain, whose first album (*Yellow Mind : Blue Mind*) featured Ed Mann.

APPENDIX I
Dates & Set-lists

This list includes all of the songs performed on the 'Broadway The Hard Way' tour. Some of the songs rehearsed, but not actually performed in concert, are also listed. Those who like their anoraks zipped all the way up should check Pat Buzby's *The Frank Zappa 1988 Tour Project* webpages for more. The list below also includes a comprehensive record of the Secret Words used, together with some of the stories behind them. As Paul Carman told me: "They were all about either news items of the day or things that happened to Frank or band members. From my standpoint, they didn't mean much... but if we happened to all be laughing about something in the green room it usually turned in to a secret word on stage... which made us laugh some more... it was really for us and not the audience." Zappa confirmed this when Den Simms mentioned the extensive use of 'cornhole' during the 25th May 1988 show in Germany and its possible alienating effect: "That's what the secret word is for. You just abuse it. How far can you take it? How many times can you stick in the wrong word in the middle of a song and literally change the meaning of the song? On one occasion, it gave us one of the worst reviews we ever got of a concert and it certainly baffled and alienated a large portion of the audience in Paris when in 1984, the secret word was 'Danger Will Robinson', from *Lost In Space*. The way Robbie the Robot's arms flop around... we were joking about that at the sound check and I remembered it and it cracked me up so much that through the whole show all I had to do is just a little of this and Ike was falling all over the place, and we really had a great time with it on stage. But the French critics thought that it was just this horrible show. They had no idea what it was and so we were, to use one of the words made popular by Jane Fonda, we were excoriated for doing *Lost In Space.*" So if you don't want to know the score, look away now.

2nd February, Palace Theatre, Albany, New York

Set One: *The Black Page (New Age Version), Packard Goose/Royal March From "L'Histoire Du Soldat"/Theme From The Bartók Piano Concerto #3/Packard Goose Reprise, Dickie's Such An Asshole, When The Lie's So Big, Planet Of The Baritone Women, Any Kind Of Pain, Jesus Thinks You're A Jerk, Sofa #1, Why Don't You Like Me?, The Torture Never Stops Part One/Theme From "Bonanza"/ Lonesome Cowboy Burt/The Torture Never Stops Part Two.*

Set Two: *Who Needs The Peace Corps?/I Left My Heart In San Francisco, We're Turning Again, King Kong, Stairway To Heaven.*

Encores: *Dancin' Fool, Whippin' Post, I Am The Walrus, Strictly Genteel*

4th February, Beacon Theatre, New York City, New York

Set One: *The Black Page (New Age Version), Dickie's Such An Asshole, When The Lie's So Big, Planet Of The Baritone Women, Any Kind Of Pain, Jesus Thinks You're A Jerk, Sofa #1, Packard Goose/Royal March From "L'Histoire Du Soldat"/Theme From The Bartók Piano Concerto #3/Packard Goose Reprise, The Torture Never Stops Part One/Theme From "Bonanza"/ Lonesome Cowboy Burt/The Torture Never Stops Part Two.*

Set Two: *Why Don't You Like Me?, Disco Boy, Teen-age Wind, Truck Driver Divorce, Who Needs The Peace Corps?/I Left My Heart In San Francisco, We're Turning Again, King Kong, Stairway To Heaven.*

Encores: *Dancin' Fool, Whippin' Post, I Am The Walrus, Strictly Genteel.*

5th February, Beacon Theatre, New York City, New York

Set One: *The Black Page (New Age Version), Chana In De Bushwop, Lucille Has Messed My Mind Up, Let's Make The Water Turn Black/Harry You're A Beast/The Orange County Lumber Truck/Oh No/Theme From Lumpy Gravy, More Trouble Every Day, Penguin In Bondage, Hot Plate Heaven At The Green Hotel, Montana, City Of Tiny Lites, A Pound For A Brown On The Bus.*

Set Two: *Dickie's Such An Asshole, When The Lie's So Big, Planet Of The Baritone Women, Any Kind Of Pain, Jesus Thinks You're A Jerk.*

Encore One: *Catholic Girls, Crew Slut, Andy, Inca Roads.*

Encore Two: *The Illinois Enema Bandit*

6th February, Beacon Theatre, New York City, New York

Set One: *Stink-Foot, I Ain't Got No Heart, Love Of My Life, Bamboozed By Love, Peaches En Regalia, Heavy Duty Judy, We're Turning Again, Packard Goose/Royal March From "L'Histoire Du Soldat"/Theme From The Bartók Piano Concerto #3/Packard Goose Reprise, When The Lie's So Big, Planet Of The Baritone Women, Any Kind Of Pain, Jesus Thinks*

You're A Jerk, Sofa #1.

Set Two: *Who Needs The Peace Corps?/I Left My Heart In San Francisco, The Torture Never Stops Part One/Theme From "Bonanza"/ Lonesome Cowboy Burt/The Torture Never Stops Part Two, King Kong, Stairway To Heaven.*

Encore One: *The Closer You Are/Johnny Darling, No No Cherry, The Man From Utopia Meets Mary Lou, Whippin' Post, Watermelon In Easter Hay.*

8th February, Warner Theatre, Washington, District of Columbia

Sound checked: *Sinister Footwear.*

Set One: *The Black Page (New Age Version), Dickie's Such An Asshole, When The Lie's So Big, Planet Of The Baritone Women, Any Kind Of Pain, Jesus Thinks You're A Jerk, Sofa #1, City Of Tiny Lites, A Pound For A Brown On The Bus, Cosmik Debris.*

Set Two: *Who Needs The Peace Corps?/I Left My Heart In San Francisco, We're Turning Again, The Torture Never Stops Part One/Theme From "Bonanza"/ Lonesome Cowboy Burt/The Torture Never Stops Part Two, King Kong, Stairway To Heaven.*

Encore One: *Packard Goose/Royal March From "L'Histoire Du Soldat"/Theme From The Bartók Piano Concerto #3/Packard Goose Reprise, I Am The Walrus.*

Encore Two: *Strictly Genteel, The Illinois Enema Bandit.*

Secret Word: Confinement loaf
Reason: "CNN ran a story last week about this new product that has been developed for our prison system. It is called 'Confinement Loaf'. Now what it is it's, uh, bean by-products compressed into a loaf, which is administered to problem prisoners. Their diet will be a slice of 'Confinement Loaf' and a cup of water, and it seems to mellow them out right away. So my question is: How long before 'Confinement Loaf' appears in United States High Schools?"[1]

9th February, Warner Theatre, Washington, District of Columbia

Sound checked: *What's New In Baltimore, Sinister Footwear, Marque-son's Chicken, Zomby Woof.*

Set One: *Stink-Foot, Hot Plate Heaven At The Green Hotel, Dickie's Such An Asshole, When The Lie's So Big, Planet Of The Baritone Women, Any Kind Of Pain, Jesus Thinks You're A Jerk, Sofa #1, Florentine Pogen, Andy, Inca Roads.*

Set Two: *Black Napkins, Montana, City Of Tiny Lites, A Pound For A Brown On The Bus, I Ain't Got No Heart, Love Of My Life, Bamboozled By Love, Peaches En Regalia.*

Encore One: *Catholic Girls, Crew Slut.*

Encore Two: *The Illinois Enema Bandit.*

Secret Word: Confinement loaf
Reason: See above.

10th February, Warner Theatre, Washington, District of Columbia

Sound checked: *Sinister Footwear.*

Set One: *It Ain't Necessarily So (incl. Danny Boy, Summertime, Aida, The Reader's Digest Classical Medley, There Goes My Baby), Peaches En Regalia, Dickie's Such An Asshole, When The Lie's So Big, Planet Of The Baritone Women, Any Kind Of Pain, Jesus Thinks You're A Jerk, Sofa #1, Let's Make The Water Turn Black/Harry You're A Beast/The Orange County Lumber Truck/Oh No/Theme From Lumpy Gravy.*

Set Two: *Sinister Footwear 2nd mvt., Bacon Fat, Stolen Moments, What's New In Baltimore, Who Needs The Peace Corps?/I Left My Heart In San Francisco, More Trouble Every Day, Penguin In Bondage, Hot Plate Heaven At The Green Hotel.*

Encores: *Whippin' Post, I Am The Walrus, Stairway To Heaven, Strictly Genteel*

12th February, Tower Theatre, Philadelphia, Pennsylvania

Sound checked: *Uncle Remus, Wonderful Wino, Ketchup Is A Vegetable.*

Set One: *The Black Page (New Age Version), Dickie's Such An Asshole, When The Lie's So Big, Planet Of The Baritone Women, Any Kind Of Pain, Jesus Thinks You're A Jerk, What's New In Baltimore, More Trouble Every Day, Penguin In Bondage, Hot Plate Heaven At The Green Hotel.*

Set Two: *Who Needs The Peace Corps?/I Left My Heart In San Francisco, City Of Tiny Lites, A Pound For A Brown On The Bus, Lucille Has Messed My Mind Up, Bamboozled By Love, Let's Make The Water Turn Black/Harry You're A Beast/The Orange County Lumber Truck/Oh No/Theme From Lumpy Gravy.*

Encore One: *Uncle Remus, Catholic Girls, Crew Slut.*

Encore Two: *Bobby Brown, Stairway To Heaven, Sofa #1.*

13th February, Tower Theatre, Philadelphia, Pennsylvania

Sound checked: *Big Swifty, Bacon Fat, Stolen Moments, Alien Orifice, Zomby Woof, Advance Romance.*

Set One: *Stink-Foot, We're Turning Again, Alien Orifice, Why Don't You Like Me?, Bacon Fat, Stolen Moments, I Ain't Got No Heart, Love Of My Life, Heavy Duty Judy, Zomby Woof.*

Set Two: *Chana In The Bushwhop, I Am The Walrus, Eric Dolphy Memorial Barbecue, Jezebel Boy, Jesus Thinks You're A Jerk, Big Swifty, Advance Romance, The Closer You Are/Johnny Darling, No No Cherry, The Man From Utopia Meets Mary Lou.*

Encores: *Watermelon In Easter Hay, Whippin' Post, Strictly Genteel.*

14th February, Tower Theatre, Philadelphia, Pennsylvania

Sound checked: *Zoot Allures, Honey,, Don't You Want A Man Like Me?, Sleep Dirt, Sofa.*

Set One: *The Black Page (New Age Version), I Ain't Got No Heart, Love Of My Life, Alien Orifice, Any Kind Of Pain, Jesus Thinks You're A Jerk, When The Lie's So Big, Planet Of The Baritone Women, City Of Tiny Lites, A Pound For A Brown On The Bus (incl. A Few Moments*

With Brother A. West).

Set Two: *Montana, Why Don't You Like Me?, Who Needs The Peace Corps?/I Left My Heart In San Francisco, The Torture Never Stops Part One/Theme From "Bonanza"/ Lonesome Cowboy Burt/The Torture Never Stops Part Two, King Kong, Stairway To Heaven.*

Encore One: *Zoot Allures, Peaches En Regalia.*

Encore Two: *The Illinois Enema Bandit.*

Secret Words: Bubbles The Chimp, The Love Boat
Reason: Bubbles was Michael Jackson's pet chimpanzee, erroneously referred to as 'the monkey' in *Why Don't You Like Me?* During the show, Den Simms sent up a request asking for, inter alia, Chad Wackerman to sing: when Frank held the microphone up, Chad sang the theme from *The Love Boat* (an American television series set on a cruise ship, which aired on the ABC Television Network from September 1977 until May 1986).

16th February, Bushnell Auditorium, Hartford, Connecticut

Sound checked: *Stick Together, My Guitar Wants To Kill Your Mama, Willie The Pimp, Joe's Garage, Why Does It Hurt When I Pee?, Filthy Habits, Cruisin' For Burgers.*

Set One: *The Black Page (New Age Version), Dickie's Such An Asshole, When The Lie's So Big, Planet Of The Baritone Women, Any Kind Of Pain, Jesus Thinks You're A Jerk, More Trouble Every Day, Penguin In Bondage, Hot Plate Heaven At The Green Hotel, Let's Make The Water Turn Black/Harry You're A Beast/The Orange County Lumber Truck/Oh No/Theme From Lumpy Gravy.*

Set Two: *What's New In Baltimore, Packard Goose/Royal March From "L'Histoire Du Soldat"/Theme From The Bartók Piano Concerto #3/Packard Goose Reprise, Alien Orifice, Inca Roads, Lucille Has Messed My Mind Up, Who Needs The Peace Corps?/I Left My Heart In San Francisco, King Kong, Stairway To Heaven.*

Encore One: *I Am The Walrus, Sofa #1, Cruisin' For Burgers.*

Encore Two: *Crew Slut, Strictly Genteel.*

17th February, Bushnell Auditorium, Hartford, Connecticut

Sound checked: *Find Her Finer, Eat That Question, Black Napkins, I Come From Nowhere, Sharleena, Marque-son's Chicken, Let's Move To Cleveland, Sleep Dirt, Bacon Fat, Stolen Moments, Goodbye Pork Pie Hat.*

Set One: *Stink-Foot, We're Turning Again, Alien Orifice, Why Don't You Like Me?, Bacon Fat, Stolen Moments, Montana, City Of Tiny Lites, A Pound For A Brown On The Bus, Cosmik Debris.*

Set Two: *Packard Goose/Royal March From "L'Histoire Du Soldat"/Theme From The Bartók Piano Concerto #3/Packard Goose Reprise, I Ain't Got No Heart, Love Of My Life, Any Kind Of Pain, The Torture Never Stops Part One/Theme From "Bonanza"/ Lonesome Cowboy Burt/The Torture Never Stops Part Two, Joe's Garage, Why Does It Hurt When I Pee?*

Encore One: *Watermelon In Easter Hay, Peaches En Regalia.*

Encore Two: *Eat That Question, Black Napkins.*

19th February, Orpheum Theatre, Boston, Massachusetts

Sound checked: *Tengo Ni Minchi Tanta, T'Mershi Duween, Why Don'tcha Do Me Right?, Brown Moses, Sinister Footwear II, Sy Borg, A Token Of My Extreme, Sinister Footwear II.*

Set One: *The Black Page (New Age Version), Who Needs The Peace Corps?/I Left My Heart In San Francisco, Dickie's Such An Asshole, When The Lie's So Big, Planet Of The Baritone Women, Any Kind Of Pain, Jesus Thinks You're A Jerk, Sofa #1, City Of Tiny Lites, A Pound For A Brown On The Bus.*

Set Two: *Let's Make The Water Turn Black/Harry You're A Beast/The Orange County Lumber Truck/Oh No/Theme From Lumpy Gravy, Bacon Fat, Stolen Moments, More Trouble Every Day, Penguin In Bondage, Hot Plate Heaven At The Green Hotel, What's New In Baltimore?*

Encores: *Whippin' Post, I Am The Walrus, Advance Romance, Stairway To Heaven, Strictly Genteel.*

20th February, Orpheum Theatre, Boston, Massachusetts

Sound checked: *Yo Cats, Find Her Finer, Disco Boy, Teen-age Wind, Truck Driver Divorce.*

Set One: *Stink-Foot, We're Turning Again, Alien Orifice, Inca Roads, Any Kind Of Pain, Sofa #1, Lucille Has Messed My Mind Up, Big Swifty, Packard Goose/Royal March From "L'Histoire Du Soldat"/Theme From The Bartók Piano Concerto #3/Packard Goose Reprise.*

Set Two: *Find Her Finer, Disco Boy, Teen-age Wind, Truck Driver Divorce, Why Don't You Like Me?, Outside Now, Joe's Garage, Why Does It Hurt When I Pee?*

Encore One: *Yo Cats, Catholic Girls, Crew Slut.*

Encore Two: *Strictly Genteel, The Illinois Enema Bandit.*

Secret Word : Just the tip
Reason: This is what Zappa postulated Jimmy Swaggart might have used if he did not fully consummate the sex act with a prostitute. On the day after the concert, a tearful Swaggart made his now infamous confession, stating "I have sinned against you, my Lord, and I would ask that your precious blood would wash and cleanse every stain until it is in the seas of God's forgiveness."

23rd February, Mid Hudson Civic Center, Poughkeepsie, New York

Sound checked: *The Deathless Horsie, Cocaine Decisions, Nig Biz, Stick It Out, What Kind Of Girl, 96 Tears, Andy, Tinsel Town Rebellion.*

Set One: *Stink-Foot, What's New In Baltimore, I Ain't Got No Heart, Love Of My Life, Florentine Pogen, Andy, Inca Roads, Eat That Question, Black Napkins.*

Set Two: *Packard Goose/Royal March From "L'Histoire Du Soldat"/Theme From The Bartók Piano Concerto #3/Packard Goose Reprise, Let's Move To Cleveland, Tinseltown Rebellion, More*

Trouble Every Day, Penguin In Bondage, Hot Plate Heaven At The Green Hotel, When The Lie's So Big, Jesus Thinks You're A Jerk, Sofa #1.

Encore One: *I Am The Walrus, Zomby Woof.*

Encore Two: *Stairway To Heaven.*

Encore Three: *Let's Make The Water Turn Black/Harry You're A Beast/The Orange County Lumber Truck/Oh No/Theme From Lumpy Gravy.*

Secret Word: Jimmy Swaggart
Reason: See above.

25th February, Syria Mosque, Pittsburgh, Pennsylvania

Sound checked: *Let's Move To Cleveland, The Man From Utopia Meets Mary Lou.*

Set One: *The Black Page (New Age Version), Who Needs The Peace Corps?/I Left My Heart In San Francisco, We're Turning Again, Alien Orifice, Why Don't You Like Me?, Dickie's Such An Asshole, When The Lie's So Big, Planet Of The Baritone Women, Any Kind Of Pain, Jesus Thinks You're A Jerk.*

Set Two: *The Torture Never Stops Part One/Theme From "Bonanza"/ Lonesome Cowboy Burt/The Torture Never Stops Part Two, Packard Goose/Royal March From "L'Histoire Du Soldat"/Theme From The Bartók Piano Concerto #3/Packard Goose Reprise, Lucille Has Messed My Mind Up, Bamboozled By Love, King Kong, Stairway To Heaven.*

Encore One: *Andy, Inca Roads.*

Encore Two: *I Am The Walrus, The Illinois Enema Bandit, Strictly Genteel.*

Secret Word: Jimmy Swaggart
Reason: See above.

26th February, Royal Oak Theatre, Detroit, Michigan

Sound checked: *The Man From Utopia Meets Mary Lou, Dumb All Over, Promiscuous.*

Set One: *The Black Page (New Age Version), When The Lie's So Big, Jesus Thinks You're A Jerk, Sofa #1, We're Turning Again, Alien Orifice, Any Kind Of Pain, I Ain't Got No Heart, Love Of My Life, Packard Goose/Royal March From "L'Histoire Du Soldat"/Theme From The Bartók Piano Concerto #3/Packard Goose Reprise.*

Set Two: *Montana, City Of Tiny Lites, A Pound For A Brown On The Bus, What's New In Baltimore, More Trouble Every Day, Penguin In Bondage, Hot Plate Heaven At The Green Hotel.*

Encore One: *Stairway To Heaven.*

Encore Two: *Promiscuous, The Illinois Enema Bandit.*

Encore Three: *Strictly Genteel.*

Secret Word: Jimmy Swaggart (all three nights)
Reason: See above.

27th February, Royal Oak Theatre, Detroit, Michigan

Sound checked: *What Kind Of Girl?, Time Is On My Side, Lucy In The Sky With Diamonds, Strawberry Fields Forever, Paperback Writer, Taxman, Norwegian Wood, Within You Without You, Sunshine Of Your Love, Hungry Freaks, Daddy.*

Set One: *Stink-Foot, Andy, Inca Roads, Uncle Remus, Outside Now, Disco Boy, Teen-age Wind, Truck Driver Divorce, Packard Goose/Royal March From "L'Histoire Du Soldat"/Theme From The Bartók Piano Concerto #3/Packard Goose Reprise.*

Set Two: *Eat That Question, Black Napkins, Find Her Finer, Who Needs The Peace Corps?/I Left My Heart In San Francisco, Norwegian Wood, King Kong, Lucy In The Sky With Diamonds.*

Encore One: *Joe's Garage, Why Does It Hurt When I Pee?*

Encore Two: *Montana, City Of Tiny Lites, A Pound For A Brown On The Bus.*

Encore Three: *I Am The Walrus, Crew Slut.*

28th February, Royal Oak Theatre, Detroit, Michigan

Sound checked: *Norwegian Jim (Norwegian Wood), Louisiana Hooker With Herpes (Lucy In The Sky With Diamonds), Texas Motel (Strawberry Fields Forever).*

Set One: *The Black Page (New Age Version), The Torture Never Stops Part One/Theme From "Bonanza"/Lonesome Cowboy Burt/The Torture Never Stops Part Two, Eric Dolphy Memorial Barbecue, Advance Romance, Let's Move To Cleveland, Tinseltown Rebellion, More Trouble Every Day, Penguin In Bondage, Hot Plate Heaven At The Green Hotel.*

Set Two: *Heavy Duty Judy, Why Don't You Like Me?, Any Kind Of Pain, When The Lie's So Big, Jesus Thinks You're A Jerk, Norwegian Jim (Norwegian Wood)/Louisiana Hooker With Herpes (Lucy In The Sky With Diamonds)/Texas Motel (Strawberry Fields Forever), Let's Make The Water Turn Black/Harry You're A Beast/The Orange County Lumber Truck/Oh No/Theme From Lumpy Gravy.*

Encore One: *Dancin' Fool, Whippin' Post, I Am The Walrus.*

Encore Two: *Watermelon In Easter Hay.*

1st March, Frauenthal Auditorium, Muskegon, Michigan

Sound checked: *Norwegian Jim (Norwegian Wood), Louisiana Hooker With Herpes (Lucy In The Sky With Diamonds), Texas Motel (Strawberry Fields Forever), What Kind Of Girl?*

Set One: *Stink-Foot, Who Needs The Peace Corps?/I Left My Heart In San Francisco, We're Turning Again, Alien Orifice, City Of Tiny Lites, A Pound For A Brown On The Bus, Lucille Has Messed My Mind Up, Florentine Pogen, Andy, Inca Roads.*

Set Two: *Bacon Fat, Stolen Moments, When The Lie's So Big, Jesus Thinks You're A Jerk, Norwegian Jim (Norwegian Wood)/Louisiana Hooker With Herpes (Lucy In The Sky With Diamonds)/Texas Motel (Strawberry Fields Forever), What Kind Of Girl?*

Encore One: *The Closer You Are/Johnny Darling, No No Cherry, The Man From Utopia Meets Mary Lou.*

Encore Two: *The Illinois Enema Bandit*.

Encore Three: *Watermelon In Easter Hay*.

3rd March, Auditorium Theatre, Chicago, Illinois

Sound checked: *Norwegian Jim (Norwegian Wood), Louisiana Hooker With Herpes (Lucy In The Sky With Diamonds), Texas Motel (Strawberry Fields Forever), What Kind Of Girl?, Filthy Habits, Sinister Footwear, Jezebel Boy*.

Set One: *The Black Page (New Age Version), We're Turning Again, Alien Orifice, Any Kind Of Pain, Why Don't You Like Me?, Norwegian Jim (Norwegian Wood)/Louisiana Hooker With Herpes (Lucy In The Sky With Diamonds)/Texas Motel (Strawberry Fields Forever), When The Lie's So Big, Jesus Thinks You're A Jerk, Sofa #1*.

Set Two: *Stolen Moments, Murder By Numbers, I Ain't Got No Heart, Love Of My Life, City Of Tiny Lites, A Pound For A Brown On The Bus, Stairway To Heaven*.

Encore One: *Whippin' Post, I Am The Walrus*.

Encore Two: *Catholic Girls, Crew Slut*.

Encore Three: *Strictly Genteel*.

4th March, Auditorium Theatre, Chicago, Illinois

Sound checked: *Sharleena, What Kind Of Girl?, The Untouchables, Ride My Face To Chicago, Cruisin' For Burgers, Cocaine Decisions, Nig Biz, Stick Together, My Guitar Wants To Kill Your Mama, Willie The Pimp*.

Set One: *Stink-Foot, When The Lie's So Big, Planet Of The Baritone Women, Any Kind Of Pain, What's New In Baltimore, Stick Together, My Guitar Wants To Kill Your Mama, Willie The Pimp, Montana, Inca Roads*.

Set Two: *Zoot Allures, Norwegian Jim (Norwegian Wood)/Louisiana Hooker With Herpes (Lucy In The Sky With Diamonds)/Texas Motel (Strawberry Fields Forever), What Kind Of Girl, Peaches En Regalia, The Torture Never Stops Part One/Theme From "Bonanza"/Lonesome Cowboy Burt/The Torture Never Stops Part Two*.

Encore One: *Yo Cats, Packard Goose/Royal March From "L'Histoire Du Soldat"/Theme From The Bartók Piano Concerto #3/Packard Goose Reprise*.

Encore Two: *Jesus Thinks You're A Jerk, The Illinois Enema Bandit*.

Secret Word : Llama

Reason: For the '88 tour, Zappa had rewritten the lyrics to *Tell Me You Love Me* to poke fun at llama owner, Michael Jackson. "They were advertising Willie Nelson albums on television just prior to that [concert], and one of the songs - they played just a little bit of each of these songs, and I don't even know what the name of this song is, but in it, Willie goes, 'Mama!'. [So] that's 'Mama!' turned into 'Llama!'"[2]

5th March, Music Hall, Cleveland, Ohio

Sound checked: *Satisfaction, Gloria, Last Train To Clarksville, Norwegian Wood, Honey, Don't You Want A Man Like Me?, Alien Orifice.*

Set One: *The Black Page (New Age Version), Dickie's Such An Asshole, When The Lie's So Big, Planet Of The Baritone Women, Any Kind Of Pain, Norwegian Jim (Norwegian Wood)/Louisiana Hooker With Herpes (Lucy In The Sky With Diamonds)/Texas Motel (Strawberry Fields Forever), Jesus Thinks You're A Jerk, Sofa #1.*

Set Two: *Let's Move To Cleveland, Packard Goose/Royal March From "L'Histoire Du Soldat"/Theme From The Bartók Piano Concerto #3/Packard Goose Reprise, King Kong, I Am The Walrus, Andy, Inca Roads.*

Encore One: *Peaches En Regalia, Stairway To Heaven.*

Encore Two: *Sharleena, Let's Make The Water Turn Black/Harry You're A Beast/The Orange County Lumber Truck/Oh No/Theme From Lumpy Gravy, The Illinois Enema Bandit.*

6th March, Veteran's Memorial Auditorium, Columbus, Ohio

Sound checked: *Shapes Of Things, Marque-son's Chicken, The Untouchables, Jesus Thinks You're A Jerk.*

Set One: *The Black Page (New Age Version), We're Turning Again, Alien Orifice, Any Kind Of Pain, City Of Tiny Lites, A Pound For A Brown On The Bus, The Untouchables, When The Lie's So Big, Jesus Thinks You're A Jerk, Sofa #1.*

Set Two: *Norwegian Jim (Norwegian Wood)/Louisiana Hooker With Herpes (Lucy In The Sky With Diamonds)/Texas Motel (Strawberry Fields Forever), Sharleena, Let's Make The Water Turn Black/Harry You're A Beast/The Orange County Lumber Truck/Oh No/Theme From Lumpy Gravy, Joe's Garage, Why Does It Hurt When I Pee?*

Encore One: *Whippin' Post, I Am The Walrus, The Illinois Enema Bandit, The Untouchables.*

Encore Two: *Strictly Genteel.*

8th March, Syria Mosque, Pittsburgh, Pennsylvania

Set One: *Stink-Foot, Peaches En Regalia, Stick Together, My Guitar Wants To Kill Your Mama, Willie The Pimp, Montana, City Of Tiny Lites, A Pound For A Brown On The Bus, When The Lie's So Big, Jesus Thinks You're A Jerk.*

Set Two: *Eat That Question, Black Napkins, Norwegian Jim (Norwegian Wood)/Louisiana Hooker With Herpes (Lucy In The Sky With Diamonds)/Texas Motel (Strawberry Fields Forever), Sharleena.*

Encore One: *Joe's Garage, Why Does It Hurt When I Pee?*

Encore Two: *Cruisin' For Burgers.*

Encore Three: *Uncle Remus, Let's Make The Water Turn Black/Harry You're A Beast/The Orange County Lumber Truck/Oh No/Theme From Lumpy Gravy.*

9th March, Shea's Theatre, Buffalo, New York

Set One: *The Black Page (New Age Version), Who Needs The Peace Corps?/I Left My Heart In San Francisco, Penguin In Bondage, Hot Plate Heaven At The Green Hotel, What's New In Baltimore, The Meek Shall Inherit Nothing, Advance Romance, Bobby Brown, When The Lie's So Big, Jesus Thinks You're A Jerk.*

Set Two: *Any Kind Of Pain, The Torture Never Stops Part One/Theme From "Bonanza"/ Lonesome Cowboy Burt/The Torture Never Stops Part Two, Norwegian Jim (Norwegian Wood)/Louisiana Hooker With Herpes (Lucy In The Sky With Diamonds)/Texas Motel (Strawberry Fields Forever), King Kong, Stairway To Heaven.*

Encores: *Watermelon In Easter Hay, The Untouchables, America The Beautiful.*

11th March, War Memorial Auditorium, Rochester, New York

Set One: *Chunga's Revenge, Packard Goose/Royal March From "L'Histoire Du Soldat"/Theme From The Bartók Piano Concerto #3/Packard Goose Reprise, Andy, Inca Roads, Lucille Has Messed My Mind Up, Big Swifty, Penguin In Bondage, Hot Plate Heaven At The Green Hotel, When The Lie's So Big, Jesus Thinks You're A Jerk.*

Set Two: *Heavy Duty Judy, Find Her Finer, Let's Make The Water Turn Black/Harry You're A Beast/The Orange County Lumber Truck/Oh No/Theme From Lumpy Gravy, Norwegian Jim (Norwegian Wood)/Louisiana Hooker With Herpes (Lucy In The Sky With Diamonds)/Texas Motel (Strawberry Fields Forever), Sofa #1.*

Encore One: *Whippin' Post, I Am The Walrus.*

Encore Two: *Peaches En Regalia, Stairway To Heaven.*

Encore Three: *America The Beautiful.*

12th March, Memorial Auditorium, Burlington, Vermont

Set One: *The Black Page (New Age Version), Dickie's Such An Asshole, Any Kind Of Pain, We're Turning Again, Alien Orifice, Advance Romance, Bobby Brown, Stolen Moments, When The Lie's So Big, Jesus Thinks You're A Jerk.*

Set Two: *Zoot Allures, I Ain't Got No Heart, Love Of My Life, Norwegian Jim (Norwegian Wood)/Louisiana Hooker With Herpes (Lucy In The Sky With Diamonds)/Texas Motel (Strawberry Fields Forever), City Of Tiny Lites, A Pound For A Brown On The Bus, Stairway To Heaven.*

Encore One: *The Closer You Are/Johnny Darling, No No Cherry, The Man From Utopia Meets Mary Lou.*

Encore Two: *The Untouchables, America The Beautiful.*

Secret Word : Eric Buxton
Reason: A died in the wool Zappa fan from Long Island, Buxton became a part of the entourage for the US leg of the tour and was regularly made fun of on stage - most notably the reference to his size 15 feet during *Zomby Woof* on the "*Best Band*" album ("like a reg'lar Buxton Hoof").

13th March, Civic Center, Springfield, Massachusetts

Sound checked: *Loops, Eric Dolphy Memorial Barbecue, Sofa, Stevie's Spanking, My Guitar Wants To Kill Your Mama, Willie The Pimp, Filthy Habits, Jesus Thinks You're A Jerk, Black Page #2, Royal March From "L'Histoire Du Soldat", Disco Boy, Teen-age Wind, Truck Driver Divorce, Advance Romance, You Are What You Is, Mudd Club, I'm The Slime, Loops, Stolen Moments, The Untouchables, Marque-son's Chicken, Zomby Woof.*

Set One: *Stink-Foot, Who Needs The Peace Corps?/I Left My Heart In San Francisco, Outside Now, Disco Boy, Teen-age Wind, Truck Driver Divorce, Packard Goose/Royal March From "L'Histoire Du Soldat"/Theme From The Bartók Piano Concerto #3/Packard Goose Reprise, Any Kind Of Pain, When The Lie's So Big, Jesus Thinks You're A Jerk.*

Set Two: *I Am The Walrus, City Of Tiny Lites, A Pound For A Brown On The Bus, Norwegian Jim (Norwegian Wood)/Louisiana Hooker With Herpes (Lucy In The Sky With Diamonds)/Texas Motel (Strawberry Fields Forever), Sofa #1.*

Encore One: *Peaches En Regalia, Stairway To Heaven.*

Encore Two: *Joe's Garage, Why Does It Hurt When I Pee?*

Encore Three: *The Illinois Enema Bandit.*

15th March, Cumberland County Civic Center, Portland, Maine

Sound checked: *Loops, Sofa, Boléro, Filthy Habits, King Kong.*

Set One: *The Black Page (New Age Version), Stainless The Maiden, Dickie's Such An Asshole, When The Lie's So Big, Planet Of The Baritone Women, Any Kind Of Pain, Penguin In Bondage, Hot Plate Heaven At The Green Hotel, What's New In Baltimore, Jesus Thinks You're A Jerk, Sofa #1.*

Set Two: *Let's Make The Water Turn Black/Harry You're A Beast/The Orange County Lumber Truck/Oh No/Theme From Lumpy Gravy, Packard Goose/Royal March From "L'Histoire Du Soldat"/Theme From The Bartók Piano Concerto #3/Packard Goose Reprise, Sharleena, Norwegian Jim (Norwegian Wood)/Louisiana Hooker With Herpes (Lucy In The Sky With Diamonds)/Texas Motel (Strawberry Fields Forever), Inca Roads.*

Encores: Montana, *City Of Tiny Lites, Peaches En Regalia, Stairway To Heaven.*

Secret Word: Stainless The Maiden
Reason: At the start of the show, Zappa was handed a devotional songbook with, among many other songs, the hymn *Stainless the Maiden*, which Robert Martin then sang and played.

16th March, Civic Center, Providence, Rhode Island

Set One: *Stink-Foot, I Ain't Got No Heart, Love Of My Life, Eat That Question, Black Napkins, The Meek Shall Inherit Nothing, Disco Boy, Teen-age Wind, Truck Driver Divorce, Packard Goose/Royal March From "L'Histoire Du Soldat"/Theme From The Bartók Piano Concerto #3/Packard Goose Reprise.*

Set Two: *The Torture Never Stops Part One/Theme From "Bonanza"/ Lonesome Cowboy*

Burt/The Torture Never Stops Part Two, Big Swifty (w/The Untouchables), Who Needs The Peace Corps?/I Left My Heart In San Francisco, Filthy Habits, Any Kind Of Pain, Jesus Thinks You're A Jerk, Sofa #1.

Encore One: *Norwegian Jim (Norwegian Wood)/Louisiana Hooker With Herpes (Lucy In The Sky With Diamonds)/Texas Motel (Strawberry Fields Forever), Sharleena.*

Encore Two: *Whippin' Post.*

17th March, Broome County Arena, Binghamton, New York

Set One: *The Black Page (New Age Version), Dickie's Such An Asshole, Stick Together, My Guitar Wants To Kill Your Mama, Willie The Pimp, Montana, City Of Tiny Lites, A Pound For A Brown On The Bus (incl. Make A Sex Noise), When The Lie's So Big, Jesus Thinks You're A Jerk.*

Set Two: *Florentine Pogen, Andy, Inca Roads, Lucille Has Messed My Mind Up, Let's Move To Cleveland, When Irish Eyes Are Smiling/Theme From The Godfather, Who Needs The Peace Corps?/I Left My Heart In San Francisco, Stairway To Heaven.*

Encore One: *Norwegian Jim (Norwegian Wood)/Louisiana Hooker With Herpes (Lucy In The Sky With Diamonds)/Texas Motel (Strawberry Fields Forever), Sofa #1.*

Encore Two: *The Illinois Enema Bandit.*

Secret Word : Training exercise, Nicaragua
Reason: Ed Mann "No stories except the obvious - stuff that FZ thought was funny which includes Nicaragua (Managua) and Nicaragua (political Iran/Contra)." See also 19th March 1988 (below).

19th March, Memorial Hall, Muhlenberg College, Allentown, Pennsylvania

Sound checked: *Stevie's Spanking, Sinister Footwear, Mr. Green Genes.*

Set One: *The Black Page (New Age Version), We're Turning Again, Alien Orifice, Find Her Finer, Sinister Footwear 2nd mvt., Stevie's Spanking, Any Kind Of Pain, Let's Make The Water Turn Black/Harry You're A Beast/The Orange County Lumber Truck/Oh No/Theme From Lumpy Gravy.*

Set Two: *When Irish Eyes Are Smiling/ "Godfather Part II" Theme, Packard Goose/Royal March From "L'Histoire Du Soldat"/Theme From The Bartók Piano Concerto #3/Packard Goose Reprise, Zomby Woof, King Kong, Mr. Green Genes, Florentine Pogen, Andy, Inca Roads/, Stairway To Heaven.*

Encore One: *Norwegian Jim (Norwegian Wood)/Louisiana Hooker With Herpes (Lucy In The Sky With Diamonds)/Texas Motel (Strawberry Fields Forever), The Untouchables.*

Encore Two: *Strictly Genteel.*

Secret Word: Golden pheasant
Reason: Operation Golden Pheasant was an emergency deployment of US troops to Honduras in March 1988, as a result of threatening actions by the forces of the then socialist Nicaraguans.

20th March, Rothman Center, Fairleigh Dickenson College, Teaneck, New Jersey

Set One: *Stink-Foot, The Untouchables, Stick Together, My Guitar Wants To Kill Your Mama, Willie The Pimp, Montana, City Of Tiny Lites, A Pound For A Brown On The Bus, Marqueson's Chicken, When The Lie's So Big, Jesus Thinks You're A Jerk.*

Set Two: *Zoot Allures, I Ain't Got No Heart, Love Of My Life, Big Swifty, The Torture Never Stops Part One/Theme From "Bonanza"/Lonesome Cowboy Burt/The Torture Never Stops Part Two, Peaches En Regalia, Stairway To Heaven.*

Encore One: *Norwegian Jim (Norwegian Wood)/Louisiana Hooker With Herpes (Lucy In The Sky With Diamonds)/Texas Motel (Strawberry Fields Forever), Whippin' Post.*

Encore Two: *Watermelon In Easter Hay.*

Secret Word: Golden pheasant
Reason: See above.

21st March, Landmark Theatre, Syracuse, New York

Set One: *The Black Page (New Age Version), Find Her Finer, Who Needs The Peace Corps?/I Left My Heart In San Francisco, Zoot Allures, Mr. Green Genes, Any Kind Of Pain, Stick Together, My Guitar Wants To Kill Your Mama, Willie The Pimp, Montana, City Of Tiny Lites.*

Set Two: *Eric Dolphy Memorial Barbecue, The Meek Shall Inherit Nothing, Sharleena, Norwegian Jim (Norwegian Wood)/Louisiana Hooker With Herpes (Lucy In The Sky With Diamonds)/Texas Motel (Strawberry Fields Forever), Sofa #1.*

Encore One: *Peaches En Regalia, Stairway To Heaven.*

Encore Two: *The Illinois Enema Bandit.*

Encore Three: *Boléro.*

23rd March, Towson Center, Towson, Maryland

Sound checked: *Boléro.*

Set One: *The Black Page (New Age Version), The Untouchables, Packard Goose/Royal March From "L'Histoire Du Soldat"/Theme From The Bartók Piano Concerto #3/Packard Goose Reprise, What's New In Baltimore, Who Needs The Peace Corps?/I Left My Heart In San Francisco, Any Kind Of Pain, Planet Of The Baritone Women, Let's Make The Water Turn Black/Harry You're A Beast/The Orange County Lumber Truck/Oh No/Theme From Lumpy Gravy, When The Lie's So Big, Jesus Thinks You're A Jerk, Sofa #1.*

Set Two: *I Am The Walrus, The Torture Never Stops Part One/Theme From "Bonanza"/Lonesome Cowboy Burt/The Torture Never Stops Part Two, Big Swifty, Keep It Greasy, Honey, Don't You Want A Man Like Me?, Inca Roads, Stairway To Heaven.*

Encore One: *Norwegian Jim (Norwegian Wood)/Louisiana Hooker With Herpes (Lucy In The Sky With Diamonds)/Texas Motel (Strawberry Fields Forever), Boléro.*

Encore Two: *The Illinois Enema Bandit.*

25th March, Nassau Coliseum, Uniondale, New York

Set One: *The Black Page (New Age Version), I Ain't Got No Heart, Love Of My Life, Inca Roads, Sharleena, Who Needs The Peace Corps?/ I Left My Heart In San Francisco, Dickie's Such An Asshole, When The Lie's So Big, Jesus Thinks You're A Jerk, Sofa #1.*

Set Two: *Packard Goose/Royal March From "L'Histoire Du Soldat"/Theme From The Bartók Piano Concerto #3/Packard Goose Reprise, The Torture Never Stops Part One/Theme From "Bonanza"/ Lonesome Cowboy Burt/The Torture Never Stops Part Two, City Of Tiny Lites, A Pound For A Brown On The Bus (w/Reverend A. West), Norwegian Jim (Norwegian Wood)/Louisiana Hooker With Herpes (Lucy In The Sky With Diamonds)/Texas Motel (Strawberry Fields Forever), Peaches En Regalia.*

Encore One: *Stairway To Heaven, I Am The Walrus, Whippin' Post.*

Encore Two: *Boléro, America The Beautiful.*

9th April, Le Stadium, Bourges, France

Sound checked: *Sofa, Strictly Genteel, Theme From The Bartók Piano Concerto #3, Lucy In The Sky With Diamonds, Norwegian Wood, When The Lie's So Big, Planet Of The Baritone Women, Boléro, Uncle Remus, Big Swifty, Catholic Girls, T'Mershi Duween.*

Set: *The Black Page (New Age Version), Who Needs The Peace Corps?/ I Left My Heart In San Francisco, Let's Make The Water Turn Black/Harry You're A Beast/The Orange County Lumber Truck/Oh No/Theme From Lumpy Gravy, The Torture Never Stops Part One/Theme From "Bonanza"/ Lonesome Cowboy Burt/The Torture Never Stops Part Two, Packard Goose/Royal March From "L'Histoire Du Soldat"/Theme From The Bartók Piano Concerto #3/Packard Goose Reprise, When The Lie's So Big, Planet Of The Baritone Women, Any Kind Of Pain, Jesus Thinks You're A Jerk, I Ain't Got No Heart, Love Of My Life, City Of Tiny Lites, A Pound For A Brown On The Bus, Inca Roads, Boléro.*

Encore One: *I Am The Walrus, The Illinois Enema Bandit.*

Encore Two: *Stairway To Heaven.*

10th April, Sportpalais, Gent, Belgium

Sound checked: *Sofa, Boléro, You Are What You Is, T'Mershi Duween, Zomby Woof, Advance Romance, Bobby Brown, Titties & Beer.*

Set: *The Black Page (New Age Version), Norwegian Jim (Norwegian Wood)/Louisiana Hooker With Herpes (Lucy In The Sky With Diamonds)/Texas Motel (Strawberry Fields Forever), Florentine Pogen, Andy, Inca Roads, Boléro, Stick Together, My Guitar Wants To Kill Your Mama, Willie The Pimp, Montana, Packard Goose/Royal March From "L'Histoire Du Soldat"/Theme From The Bartók Piano Concerto #3/Packard Goose Reprise, Any Kind Of Pain, Jesus Thinks You're A Jerk, Sofa #1.*

Encore One: *Joe's Garage, Why Does It Hurt When I Pee?*

Encore Two: *Stairway To Heaven.*

Encore Three: *Watermelon In Easter Hay.*

12th April, Deutschlandhalle, Berlin, West Germany

Sound checked: *T'Mershi Duween, Sofa, What's New In Baltimore?, The Closer You Are, Johnny Darling, America The Beautiful, When Yuppies Go To Hell, Eric Dolphy Memorial Barbecue, Loops.*

Set One: *The Black Page (New Age Version), Packard Goose/Royal March From "L'Histoire Du Soldat"/Theme From The Bartók Piano Concerto #3/Packard Goose Reprise, Any Kind Of Pain, Planet Of The Baritone Women, Eric Dolphy Memorial Barbecue, I Am The Walrus, I Ain't Got No Heart, Andy, Inca Roads, Boléro.*

Set Two: *Norwegian Jim (Norwegian Wood)/Louisiana Hooker With Herpes (Lucy In The Sky With Diamonds)/Texas Motel (Strawberry Fields Forever), The Torture Never Stops Part One/Theme From "Bonanza"/Lonesome Cowboy Burt/The Torture Never Stops Part Two, City Of Tiny Lites, A Pound For A Brown On The Bus, Stairway To Heaven.*

Encore One: *Bobby Brown, Whippin' Post.*

Encore Two: *Joe's Garage, Why Does It Hurt When I Pee?*

Encore Three: *Strictly Genteel.*

13th April, Stadthalle, Frankfurt, West Germany

Sound checked: *Sofa, Boléro, When Yuppies Go To Hell, Black Napkins, The Closer You Are, Johnny Darling, Jesus Thinks You're A Jerk, Zomby Woof, Disco Boy, Dancin' Fool, Chana In De Bushwop, Heavy Duty Judy.*

Set: *Stink-Foot, I Ain't Got No Heart, Love Of My Life, Heavy Duty Judy, Disco Boy, Teen-age Wind, Truck Driver Divorce, Let's Make The Water Turn Black/Harry You're A Beast/The Orange County Lumber Truck/Oh No/Theme From Lumpy Gravy, Advance Romance, Bobby Brown, Boléro, Big Swifty, Bamboozled By Love, Chana In De Bushwop, Sharleena, Sofa #1.*

Encore One: *Stairway To Heaven.*

Encore Two: *I Am The Walrus, The Illinois Enema Bandit.*

Encore Three: *Watermelon In Easter Hay.*

Secret Word: Bruce Fowler

Reason: When introducing the band members at the start of the show, Zappa was unable to come up with an adjective to describe Bruce Fowler, and so he became the Secret Word. For the record, Willis was 'the unbelievable'; Keneally 'the marginally incomprehensible'; Walt Fowler, 'the incredibly stimulating'; Carman, 'the incredibly piquant'; Wing, 'the disturbingly jolly'; McGettrick, 'the constantly appropriate'; Wackerman, 'the looking too young for his age'; Mann, 'the nimble, yet highly evolved'; Martin, 'the spandex bereft'; and Thunes, 'everybody's favourite bass player'.

14th April, Sporthalle, Cologne, West Germany

Sound check: *Sofa, What's New In Baltimore, Theme From The Bartók Piano Concerto #3, When Yuppies Go To Hell, Sinister Footwear, Joe's Garage, Paperback Writer, Lucy In The Sky With Diamonds.*

Set: *The Black Page (New Age Version), Inca Roads, When The Lie's So Big, Planet Of The Baritone Women, Any Kind Of Pain, Jesus Thinks You're A Jerk, City Of Tiny Lites, A Pound For A Brown On The Bus, When Yuppies Go To Hell, Packard Goose/Royal March From "L'Histoire Du Soldat"/Theme From The Bartók Piano Concerto #3/Packard Goose Reprise, The Meek Shall Inherit Nothing, The Torture Never Stops Part One/Theme From "Bonanza"/Lonesome Cowboy Burt/The Torture Never Stops Part Two, Disco Boy, Teen-age Wind, Bamboozled By Love, Sofa #1.*

Encore One: *Boléro.*

Encore Two: *I Am The Walrus, The Illinois Enema Bandit.E3 : Let's Make The Water Turn Black/Harry You're A Beast/The Orange County Lumber Truck/Oh No/Theme From Lumpy Gravy.*

Secret Word: Sheep (Sodomy, Mutton, Shepherds)
Reason: Mike Keneally: "Frank had told us a joke at the huddle which was: 'What do you call a New Zealander with many wives?' and the answer is: 'A shepherd.'"[3]

16th April, Brighton Centre, Brighton, England

Sound checked: *Sofa, When Yuppies Go To Hell, Sharleena, Easy Meat, More Trouble Every Day, Alien Orifice.*

Set One: *Stink-Foot, Packard Goose/Royal March From "L'Histoire Du Soldat"/Theme From The Bartók Piano Concerto #3/Packard Goose Reprise, Alien Orifice, Disco Boy, Teen-age Wind, Bamboozled By Love, Let's Make The Water Turn Black/Harry You're A Beast/The Orange County Lumber Truck/Oh No/Theme From Lumpy Gravy, When Yuppies Go To Hell, I Am The Walrus.*

Set Two: *Zoot Allures, When The Lie's So Big, Planet Of The Baritone Women, Any Kind Of Pain, Jesus Thinks You're A Jerk, City Of Tiny Lites, A Pound For A Brown On The Bus, Sharleena.*

Encore One: *Norwegian Jim (Norwegian Wood)/Louisiana Hooker With Herpes (Lucy In The Sky With Diamonds)/Texas Motel (Strawberry Fields Forever), Stairway To Heaven.*

Encore Two: *Boléro.*

18th April, Wembley Arena, London, England

Sound checked: *Sofa, Royal March, The Closer You Are, When Irish Eyes Are Smiling, Keep It Greasy, Boléro, When Yuppies Go To Hell, Cruisin' For Burgers, Stolen Moments, Dancin' Fool, The Torture Never Stops, The Dangerous Kitchen, Black Napkins, Mr. Green Genes, Let's Move To Cleveland, The Untouchables, Eat That Question, Alien Orifice.*

Set One: *The Black Page (New Age Version), Packard Goose/Royal March From "L'Histoire Du Soldat"/Theme From The Bartók Piano Concerto #3/Packard Goose Reprise, Mr. Green Genes, Florentine Pogen, Andy, Inca Roads, Disco Boy, Teen-age Wind, City Of Tiny Lites.*

Set Two: *I Ain't Got No Heart, Let's Move To Cleveland, Bamboozled By Love, Big Swifty, Who Needs The Peace Corps?/I Left My Heart In San Francisco, Peaches En Regalia, Stairway To Heaven.*

Encore One: *Boléro, I Am The Walrus, The Illinois Enema Bandit.*

Encore Two: *Strictly Genteel.*

19th April, Wembley Arena, London, England

Sound checked: *In France, T'Mershi Duween, Cruisin' For Burgers, When Yuppies Go To Hell, Chunga's Revenge, Crew Slut, Hot Plate Heaven At The Green Hotel, Crew Slut, Dumb All Over, Turning Again, Outside Now, King Kong.*

Set One: *Stink-Foot, Dickie's Such An Asshole, When The Lie's So Big, Planet Of The Baritone Women, Any Kind Of Pain, Jesus Thinks You're A Jerk, Cruisin' For Burgers, Outside Now, Let's Make The Water Turn Black/Harry You're A Beast/The Orange County Lumber Truck/Oh No/Theme From Lumpy Gravy.*

Set Two: *Norwegian Jim (Norwegian Wood)/Louisiana Hooker With Herpes (Lucy In The Sky With Diamonds)/Texas Motel (Strawberry Fields Forever), The Torture Never Stops Part One/Theme From "Bonanza"/ Lonesome Cowboy Burt/The Torture Never Stops Part Two, Stick Together, My Guitar Wants To Kill Your Mama, Willie The Pimp, Montana, Stairway To Heaven.*

Encore One: *Joe's Garage, Why Does It Hurt When I Pee?*

Encore Two: *Chunga's Revenge, Boléro.*

20th April, National Exhibition Centre, Birmingham, England

Set One: *Heavy Duty Judy, Cosmik Debris, I Ain't Got No Heart, Love Of My Life, Cruisin' For Burgers, Lucille Has Messed My Mind Up, Stolen Moments, More Trouble Every Day, Penguin In Bondage, Hot Plate Heaven At The Green Hotel.*

Set Two: *Eat That Question, Black Napkins, City Of Tiny Lites, A Pound For A Brown On The Bus, Peaches En Regalia, Stairway To Heaven.*

Encore One: *Keep It Greasy, Sharleena.*

Encore Two: *Dancin' Fool, Whippin' Post, I Am The Walrus.*

Encore Three: *Boléro.*

22nd April, Carl Diem Halle, Würzburg, West Germany

Sound checked: *Ring Of Fire, I Walk The Line, When Yuppies Go To Hell, Sofa, The Reader's Digest Classical Medley, The Untouchables, Alien Orifice, Oh No!, Dinah-Moe Humm, More Trouble Every Day.*

Set: *Heavy Duty Judy, Ring Of Fire, Packard Goose/Royal March From "L'Histoire Du Soldat"/Theme From The Bartók Piano Concerto #3/Packard Goose Reprise, Cosmik Debris, Who Needs The Peace Corps?/I Left My Heart In San Francisco, What's New In Baltimore, Inca Roads, Advance Romance, Disco Boy, Teen-age Wind, Bamboozled By Love, The Torture Never Stops Part One/Theme From "Bonanza"/ Lonesome Cowboy Burt/The Torture Never Stops Part Two, I Ain't Got No Heart, Love Of My Life, City Of Tiny Lites, A Pound For A Brown On The Bus, Stairway To Heaven.*

Encore One: *Ring Of Fire, Boléro.*

Encore Two: *Bobby Brown, Joe's Garage, Why Does It Hurt When I Pee?*

Encore Three: *Ring Of Fire, I Am The Walrus, The Illinois Enema Bandit.*

Secret Word: Ring Of Fire

Reason: "This afternoon at the hotel I was introduced for the first time to Johnny Cash, and Johnny was going to come to the concert tonight, and he was going to sing with us. Unfortunately his wife got sick so he can't come tonight, BUT...this afternoon we actually learned how to play a reggae version of *Ring Of Fire*, and we've been trying to decide whether or not we oughta play it even if Johnny's not gonna sing it."[4]

24th April, Stadthalle, Bremen, West Germany

Set: *The Black Page (New Age Version), Advance Romance, Any Kind Of Pain, Find Her Finer, Who Needs The Peace Corps?/I Left My Heart In San Francisco, Stick Together, My Guitar Wants To Kill Your Mama, Willie The Pimp, Montana, City Of Tiny Lites, A Pound For A Brown On The Bus (w/When Yuppies Go To Hell), Cosmik Debris, Cruisin' For Burgers, Keep It Greasy, Sofa #1*

Encore One: *Boléro, Crew Slut.*

Encore Two: *Joe's Garage, Why Does It Hurt When I Pee, Peaches En Regalia, Stairway To Heaven.*

Secret Words: Xenakis.

Reason: Zappa was the subject of a documentary, made for German television, called *Peefeeyatko*. "It's all about serious composition, and the guy who did it is a guy named Henning Lohner. And he came to Bremen before the show to meet with me, and he told me about the other things that he'd done. He'd done a documentary on Stockhausen, Cage, and Xenakis. We were talking backstage about Xenakis prior to the show."[5]

25th April, Falkoner Theater, Copenhagen, Denmark

Set One: *Heavy Duty Judy, Packard Goose/Royal March From "L'Histoire Du Soldat"/Theme From The Bartók Piano Concerto #3/Packard Goose Reprise, Alien Orifice, When The Lie's So Big, Planet Of The Baritone Women, Any Kind Of Pain, Jesus Thinks You're A Jerk, Norwegian Jim (Norwegian Wood)/Louisiana Hooker With Herpes (Lucy In The Sky With Diamonds)/Texas Motel (Strawberry Fields Forever), Sofa #1.*

Set Two: *The Torture Never Stops Part One/Theme From "Bonanza"/ Lonesome Cowboy Burt/The Torture Never Stops Part Two, Find Her Finer, Big Swifty, Bamboozled By Love, Boléro.*

Encore One: *Peaches En Regalia, Stairway To Heaven.*

Encore Two: *Mr. Green Genes, Florentine Pogen, Andy, Inca Roads.*

Secret Words: Air hose, Falcum

Reason: The air hose on one of the band's two tour buses broke down en route to

Copenhagen. Plus there are obvious phonetical similarities with the Danish town of Aarhus - indeed, during the show, Ed Mann asked "Is it Aarhus or air hose?". 'Falcum'" was how John Smothers (Zappa's former bodyguard) pronounced the arena they played in - as immortalised in *Dong Work For Yuda* on Zappa's *Joe's Garage* album.

26th April, Olympen, Lund, Sweden

Set: *The Black Page (New Age Version), Dickie's Such An Asshole, Stick Together, My Guitar Wants To Kill Your Mama, Willie The Pimp, Montana, City Of Tiny Lites, A Pound For A Brown On The Bus, The Dangerous Kitchen, What's New In Baltimore, Outside Now, Eat That Question, Black Napkins, Disco Boy, Teen-age Wind, Bamboozled By Love.*

Encore One: *Cruisin' For Burgers.*

Encore Two: *Boléro, I Am The Walrus, The Illinois Enema Bandit.*

Encore Three: *Stairway To Heaven.*

Secret Words: Haenna-Hoona-Haenna-Hoona
Reason: Zappa's take on The Swedish Chef from *The Muppet Show*. Börk, börk, börk!

27th April, Skedsmohallen, Oslo, Norway

Set: *Stink-Foot, I Ain't Got No Heart, Love Of My Life, Packard Goose/Royal March From "L'Histoire Du Soldat"/Theme From The Bartók Piano Concerto #3/Packard Goose Reprise, Alien Orifice, Sharleena, Let's Make The Water Turn Black/Harry You're A Beast/The Orange County Lumber Truck/Oh No/Theme From Lumpy Gravy, Advance Romance, Bobby Brown, Keep It Greasy, The Torture Never Stops Part One/Theme From "Bonanza"/Lonesome Cowboy Burt/The Torture Never Stops Part Two, Norwegian Jim (Norwegian Wood)/Louisiana Hooker With Herpes (Lucy In The Sky With Diamonds)/Texas Motel (Strawberry Fields Forever), City Of Tiny Lites, A Pound For A Brown On The Bus, Make A Sex Noise, Stairway To Heaven.*

Encore One: *Boléro, Rhymin' Man, Sofa #1.*

Encore Two: *Andy, Inca Roads.*

Encore Three: *Strictly Genteel.*

Secret Words: Sausage ("Shaushage!"), Fornebu
Reason: Mike Keneally: "That was a result of a story that someone had told Frank about this dog on British television that supposedly could actually say the word 'sausage' but in order to get it to emit that sound, they had to grab it by the throat and jaw and squeeze it and it would choke out the word, 'Shaushage! Naturally, that appealed to Frank, and it became part of the show."[6]

29th April, Isshallen, Helsinki, Finland

Set: *The Black Page (New Age Version), More Trouble Every Day, Penguin In Bondage, Hot Plate Heaven At The Green Hotel, What's New In Baltimore, Sinister Footwear 2nd mvt., Packard Goose/Royal March From "L'Histoire Du Soldat"/Theme From The Bartók Piano Concerto #3/Packard Goose Reprise, Big Swifty, Who Needs The Peace Corps?/I Left My Heart*

In San Francisco, Let's Make The Water Turn Black/Harry You're A Beast/The Orange County Lumber Truck/Oh No/Theme From Lumpy Gravy, Find Her Finer, Mr. Green Genes, Florentine Pogen, Andy, Inca Roads, Sofa #1.

Encore One: *Dancin' Fool, Whippin' Post, I Am The Walrus, The Illinois Enema Bandit.*

Encore Two: *Boléro.*

Encore Three: *Stairway To Heaven.*

1st May, Isstadion, Stockholm, Sweden

Sound checked: *Dragonmaster.*

Set: *Heavy Duty Judy, Packard Goose/Royal March From "L'Histoire Du Soldat"/Theme From The Bartók Piano Concerto #3/Packard Goose Reprise, Any Kind Of Pain, More Trouble Every Day, Penguin In Bondage, Hot Plate Heaven At The Green Hotel, Cosmik Debris, Inca Roads, Advance Romance, Bobby Brown, Keep It Greasy, The Torture Never Stops Part One/Theme From "Bonanza"/Lonesome Cowboy Burt/The Torture Never Stops Part Two, Big Swifty (incl. T'Mershi Duween), Joe's Garage, Why Does It Hurt When I Pee?*

Encore One: *Peaches En Regalia, Stairway To Heaven.*

Encore Two: *Whippin' Post, I Am The Walrus, Sofa #1.*

Secret Word: *Dragonmaster.*

Reason: *Dragonmaster* was a song Zappa had been working on with the band, who gave it a go at rehearsals that afternoon. Sadly, it never got played in concert by Frank... but Dweezil gave it a go a few years later: "Frank wrote the lyrics to it, I guess, in Stockholm. I heard it in various bits and pieces, but never in an arrangement that I thought was quite appropriate for it. Frank's not up on his thrash metal, so he suggested to me one night 'Why don't we do *Dragonmaster*?' So I wrote basically the ugliest music that I could possibly write. It's meant to be done as a bit of a joke, really. It's a send up of speed metal and all that stuff. It's pretty good though."[7]

3rd May, The Ahoy, Rotterdam, Netherlands

Set One: *The Black Page (New Age Version), I Ain't Got No Heart, Let's Make The Water Turn Black/Harry You're A Beast/The Orange County Lumber Truck/Oh No/Theme From Lumpy Gravy, Advance Romance, Find Her Finer, Big Swifty, Norwegian Jim (Norwegian Wood)/Louisiana Hooker With Herpes (Lucy In The Sky With Diamonds)/Texas Motel (Strawberry Fields Forever), Peaches En Regalia.*

Set Two: *Sinister Footwear 2nd mvt., Packard Goose/Royal March From "L'Histoire Du Soldat"/Theme From The Bartók Piano Concerto #3/Packard Goose Reprise, Heavy Duty Judy, More Trouble Every Day, Penguin In Bondage, Hot Plate Heaven At The Green Hotel, Boléro.*

Encore One: *Joe's Garage, Why Does It Hurt When I Pee?*

Encore Two: *Stairway To Heaven.*

Encore Three: *I Am The Walrus, The Illinois Enema Bandit.*

Secret Word: Fishbone

Reason: Zappa explained that, "Prior to the concert, Bobby Martin had eaten some fish backstage, gotten a fishbone wedged in his throat and had to be taken to the hospital to have it removed... and came onstage and sang the show that night!"[8] Coincidentally, Kurt McGettrick played baritone sax on the band Fishbone's 1986 album, In Your Face!

4th May, The Ahoy, Rotterdam, Netherlands

Set One: *Stink-Foot, Dickie's Such An Asshole, When The Lie's So Big, Planet Of The Baritone Women, Any Kind Of Pain, Jesus Thinks You're A Jerk, Mr. Green Genes, Florentine Pogen, Andy, Inca Roads.*

Set Two: *Eat That Question, Black Napkins, Sharleena, Dupree's Paradise, Marque-son's Chicken, City Of Tiny Lites, A Pound For A Brown On The Bus, The Torture Never Stops Part One/Theme From "Bonanza"/ Lonesome Cowboy Burt/The Torture Never Stops Part Two.*

Encore One: *Keep It Greasy, Cruisin' For Burgers.*

Encore Two: *Sofa #1, Crew Slut.*

Secret Word: Rehearsal
Reason: Before the show, a fan brought up Ed Mann's error during *Dickie's Such An Asshole* at the 19th April Wembley show, so Zappa had Ed rehearse the lick live on stage.

5th May, Westfalenhalle, Dortmund, West Germany

Set: *The Black Page (New Age Version), The Meek Shall Inherit Nothing, Alien Orifice, Who Needs The Peace Corps?/I Left My Heart In San Francisco, Outside Now, Eric Dolphy Memorial Barbecue, Bamboozled By Love, Zoot Allures, Cosmik Debris, Stolen Moments, Stick Together, My Guitar Wants To Kill Your Mama, Willie The Pimp, Montana, City Of Tiny Lites, A Pound For A Brown On The Bus, Cruisin' For Burgers.*

Encore One: *Dancin' Fool, Whippin' Post, I Am The Walrus, Strictly Genteel.*

Encore Two: *Watermelon In Easter Hay.*

Secret Word: Dildo
Reason: Unknown

6th May, CCH Halle, Hamburg, West Germany

Set: *The Black Page (New Age Version), Mr. Green Genes, Florentine Pogen, Andy, Inca Roads, Eat That Question, Black Napkins, Sharleena, Dupree's Paradise, Let's Move To Cleveland, I Ain't Got No Heart, Find Her Finer, Big Swifty, Lucille Has Messed My Mind Up, Let's Make The Water Turn Black/Harry You're A Beast/The Orange County Lumber Truck/Oh No/Theme From Lumpy Gravy, Stairway To Heaven.*

Encore One: *The Torture Never Stops Part One/Theme From "Bonanza"/ Lonesome Cowboy Burt/The Torture Never Stops Part Two.*

Encore Two: *I Am The Walrus, The Illinois Enema Bandit.*

Encore Three: *Boléro.*

8th May, Stadthalle, Vienna, Austria

Set One: *The Black Page (New Age Version), I Ain't Got No Heart, Packard Goose/Royal March From "L'Histoire Du Soldat"/Theme From The Bartók Piano Concerto #3/Packard Goose Reprise, Any Kind Of Pain, Cosmik Debris, Inca Roads, Advance Romance, Eric Dolphy Memorial Barbecue, Bamboozled By Love, Boléro.*

Set Two: *Eat That Question, Black Napkins, More Trouble Every Day, Penguin In Bondage, Hot Plate Heaven At The Green Hotel/, Peaches En Regalia, Stairway To Heaven.*

Encore One: *Sharleena.*

Encore Two: *Montana, City Of Tiny Lites, Whippin' Post.*

9th May, Rudi Sedlmayer Hall, Munich, West Germany

Set: *Stink-Foot, What's New In Baltimore, Heavy Duty Judy, Find Her Finer, Big Swifty (w/ classical excerpts), More Trouble Every Day, Penguin In Bondage, Hot Plate Heaven At The Green Hotel, Who Needs The Peace Corps?/I Left My Heart In San Francisco, Zomby Woof, King Kong, Mr. Green Genes, Florentine Pogen, Andy, Inca Roads, Cruisin' For Burgers.*

Encore One: *Rhymin' Man, Dupree's Paradise, Let's Move To Cleveland.*

Encore Two: *Whippin' Post, I Am The Walrus, Loops (Bavarian Sunset), Sofa #1.*

Secret Words: Mud Shark, Jazz Noise (Ayee!)
Reason: 'Mud Shark' was suggested by the 'secret word' banner bearers in the crowd and relates to the track of that name on The Mothers' album, Fillmore East - June 1971, during which Zappa talks about an infamous home movie made by Led Zeppelin's road manager and members of the Vanilla Fudge at the Edgewater Inn in Seattle, Washington on 28 July 1969. As for the jazz noises, Zappa later explained: "You ever heard of Errol Garner, jazz piano who mumbles along with what he plays? Moonglow was one of the most famous records he did. Anyway - "Ayee! Ayee!" - it's the whole concept of jazz musicians who make jazz noises while they perform. That was a good show."[9]

11th May, Hallenstadion, Zurich, Switzerland

Set One: *The Black Page (New Age Version), Packard Goose/Royal March From "L'Histoire Du Soldat"/Theme From The Bartók Piano Concerto #3/Packard Goose Reprise, Any Kind Of Pain, I Ain't Got No Heart, Outside Now, Let's Make The Water Turn Black/Harry You're A Beast/The Orange County Lumber Truck/Oh No/Theme From Lumpy Gravy, Cosmik Debris, Dupree's Paradise, Let's Move To Cleveland.*

Set Two: *More Trouble Every Day, City Of Tiny Lites, A Pound For A Brown On The Bus, The Torture Never Stops Part One/Theme From "Bonanza"/ Lonesome Cowboy Burt/The Torture Never Stops Part Two, Joe's Garage, Why Does It Hurt When I Pee?*

Encore One: *Boléro, Stairway To Heaven.*

Encore Two: *I Am The Walrus, The Illinois Enema Bandit.*

Secret Word: Paiste

Reason: On the afternoon of the show, Ed Mann and Chad Wackerman met some representatives from Paiste, the cymbal manufacturer, who presented them with corporate jackets. Mann wore his onstage that night, causing Zappa to introduce him as 'Ed Paiste'.

13th May, Velódromo, Bilbao, Spain

Set: *The Black Page (New Age Version), Packard Goose/Royal March From "L'Histoire Du Soldat"/Theme From The Bartók Piano Concerto #3/Packard Goose Reprise, I Ain't Go No Heart, Black Napkins, Sharleena, Inca Roads, Advance Romance, Find Her Finer, Big Swifty, The Torture Never Stops Part One/Theme From "Bonanza"/ Lonesome Cowboy Burt/The Torture Never Stops Part Two, Montana, City Of Tiny Lites, A Pound For A Brown On The Bus, Take Me Out To The Ball Game, Filthy Habits.*

Encore One: *Boléro, Elvis Has Just Left The Building, Sofa #1.*

Encore Two: *I Am The Walrus, The Illinois Enema Bandit.*

Encore Three: *Watermelon In Easter Hay.*

Secret Word: Baseball
Reason: Unclear, but perhaps the velodrome reminded the band of a baseball stadium, causing them to launch into an impromptu version of *Take Me Out To The Ball Game.*

14th May, Auditorio De La Casa De Campo, Madrid, Spain

Set: *The Black Page (New Age Version), Packard Goose/Royal March From "L'Histoire Du Soldat"/Theme From The Bartók Piano Concerto #3/Packard Goose Reprise, Alien Orifice, I Ain't Got No Heart, Love Of My Life, Cruisin' For Burgers, Find Her Finer, Big Swifty, More Trouble Every Day, Penguin In Bondage, Hot Plate Heaven At The Green Hotel, Cosmik Debris, Inca Roads, Sharleena, Bamboozled By Love.*

Encore One: *Boléro, Crew Slut.*

Encore Two: *The Closer You Are/Johnny Darling, Let's Make The Water Turn Black/Harry You're A Beast/The Orange County Lumber Truck/Oh No/Theme From Lumpy Gravy, Whippin' Post.*

Secret Word: Flight, Iberia Airlines
Reason: The band experienced 'airline difficulties' getting to Spain.

15th May, Prado De San Sebastian, Seville, Spain

Set: *The Black Page (New Age Version), Inca Roads, Advance Romance, Dupree's Paradise, Let's Move To Cleveland, Elvis Has Just Left The Building, Cosmik Debris, Stick Together, My Guitar Wants To Kill Your Mama, Willie The Pimp, Montana, City Of Tiny Lites, A Pound For A Brown On The Bus, I Ain't Got No Heart, The Torture Never Stops Part One/Theme From "Bonanza"/ Lonesome Cowboy Burt/The Torture Never Stops Part Two.*

Encore One: *Norwegian Jim (Norwegian Wood)/Louisiana Hooker With Herpes (Lucy In The Sky With Diamonds)/Texas Motel (Strawberry Fields Forever), Strictly Genteel.*

Encore Two: *Boléro, Stairway To Heaven.*

Encore Three: *Watermelon In Easter Hay, Whippin' Post.*

17th May, Palacio De Los Deportes, Barcelona, Spain

Set: *The Black Page (New Age Version), Packard Goose/Royal March From "L'Histoire Du Soldat"/Theme From The Bartók Piano Concerto #3/Packard Goose Reprise, Sharleena, Bamboozled By Love, Black Napkins, When The Lie's So Big, Planet Of The Baritone Women, Any Kind Of Pain, Jesus Thinks You're A Jerk, Sofa #1, Find Her Finer, Big Swifty, I Ain't Got No Heart, Love Of My Life, The Torture Never Stops Part One/Theme From "Bonanza"/ Lonesome Cowboy Burt/The Torture Never Stops Part Two.*

Encore One: *Boléro, Watermelon In Easter Hay, Whippin' Post, I Am The Walrus, The Illinois Enema Bandit.*

Encore Two: *Strictly Genteel.*

Secret Word: Raffle
Reason: See Chapter Four.

18th May, Le Zenith, Montpellier, France

Set One: *The Black Page (New Age Version), I Ain't Got No Heart, Love Of My Life, Let's Move To Cleveland, Lucille Has Messed My Mind Up, Dupree's Paradise, Oh No/Let's Make The Water Turn Black/Harry You're A Beast/The Orange County Lumber Truck/Theme From Lumpy Gravy.*
II : *Stick Together, My Guitar Wants To Kill Your Mama, Willie The Pimp, Montana, City Of Tiny Lites, Inca Roads, Peaches En Regalia, Stairway To Heaven.*

Encore One: *Boléro, Cruisin' For Burgers.*

Encore Two: *Joe's Garage, Why Does It Hurt When I Pee?*

Encore Three: *Loops, Bamboozled By Love.*

Secret Word: Jewellery
Reason: Zappa said "...I'm drawing a blank on that. It had to have something to do with something that one of the guys in the band did, or bought."[10]

19th May, Le Summun, Grenoble, France

Set: *The Black Page (New Age Version), More Trouble Every Day, Penguin In Bondage, Hot Plate Heaven At The Green Hotel, Cosmik Debris, Dupree's Paradise, Let's Move To Cleveland, Find Her Finer, Filthy Habits, Chana In De Bushwop, Who Needs The Peace Corps?/I Left My Heart In San Francisco, Easy Meat, King Kong, Sharleena, Bamboozled By Love.*

Encore One: *Peaches En Regalia, Stairway To Heaven.*

Encore Two: *Elvis Has Just Left The Building, Loops, Sofa #1.*

Secret Word: Hoop (later mutating into 'poop')
Reason: Robert Martin screwed-up just before the "hoop of real fire" line in *Penguin In Bondage*. Said Frank "Sometimes the secret word will get going just because

somebody will fuck up a song, and then you use the fuck-up as the secret word - because you don't always go on stage with a word in mind. Sometimes the shows won't have any at all. Things just get suggested, so the first part of the show could be really bland, and the second part could be outrageous depending on what popped up."[11]

20th May, Le Zenith, Paris, France

Set One: *The Black Page (New Age Version), Packard Goose/Royal March From "L'Histoire Du Soldat"/Theme From The Bartók Piano Concerto #3/Packard Goose Reprise, Any Kind Of Pain, Dupree's Paradise, Inca Roads, Advance Romance, Who Needs The Peace Corps?/I Left My Heart In San Francisco, The Torture Never Stops Part One/Theme From "Bonanza"/Lonesome Cowboy Burt/The Torture Never Stops Part Two.*

Set Two: *Eat That Question, Black Napkins, Find Her Finer, Big Swifty, I Ain't Got No Heart, Sharleena, Peaches En Regalia, Stairway To Heaven.*

Encore One: *Boléro, Bamboozled By Love.*

Encore Two: *Loops, I Am The Walrus, The Illinois Enema Bandit.*

Encore Three: *Strictly Genteel.*

Secret Word: Shellfish
Reason: Zappa explained, "Somebody had gotten ill from eating shellfish. One of the things you don't want to do when you're on the road is go out and gorge yourself on raw oysters in places where the bacteria count is high in the water. Like you want to commit suicide? Eat oysters in Naples."[12]

23rd May, Hall Tivoli, Strasbourg, France

Set: *Stink-Foot, Dickie's Such An Asshole, We're Turning Again, Alien Orifice, Mr. Green Genes, Florentine Pogen, Andy, Inca Roads, I Ain't Got No Heart, Love Of My Life, T'Mershi Duween, Dupree's Paradise, Find Her Finer, Filthy Habits, You Are What You Is, Marque-son's Chicken.*

Encore One: *Peaches En Regalia, Stairway To Heaven.*

Encore Two: *Boléro, Watermelon In Easter Hay.*

Encore Three: *Whippin' Post, Loops.*

Secret Word: Soup
Reason: Not known.

24th May, Liederhalle, Stuttgart, West Germany

Set: *Stink-Foot, What's New In Baltimore, Planet Of The Baritone Women, Any Kind Of Pain, I Ain't Got No Heart, I Ain't Got No Heart, Let's Move To Cleveland, Find Her Finer, Filthy Habits, Cosmik Debris, T'Mershi Duween, Dupree's Paradise, Marque-son's Chicken, Pick Me I'm Clean, Bamboozled By Love, Sofa #1.*

Encore One: *Bobby Brown, Sharleena.*

Encore Two: *Rhymin' Man, Elvis Has Just Left The Building, Boléro, Peaches En Regalia, Stairway To Heaven, Star Wars Won't Work, Whippin' Post.*

Secret Words: Summit, Star Wars
Reason: See Chapter Four

25th May, Mozarthalle, Mannheim, West Germany

Set: *The Black Page (New Age Version), We're Turning Again, Alien Orifice, When The Lie's So Big, Planet Of The Baritone Women, Any Kind Of Pain, Jesus Thinks You're A Jerk, Dupree's Paradise, Easy Meat, Sinister Footwear 2nd mvt., City Of Tiny Lites, A Pound For A Brown On The Bus, Outside Now, Let's Make The Water Turn Black/Harry You're A Beast/The Orange County Lumber Truck/Oh No/Theme From Lumpy Gravy, Bamboozled By Love.*

Encore One: *Ring Of Fire, Peaches En Regalia, Stairway To Heaven (incl. The Untouchables).*

Encore Two: *I Am The Walrus, The Illinois Enema Bandit.*

Secret Word: Cornhole
Reason: This 'traditional stupid, playground humour' word was originally heard on a Zappa album in 1979 as an ad-lib by bassist Patrick O'Hearn, captured for posterity in the song *Broken Hearts Are For Assholes* on *Sheik Yerbouti*. "I don't know how that one came up."[13] Zappa later said but, at this concert, Led Zeppelin's classic mutated into *Stairway To Cornhole.*

26th May, Stadthalle, Fürth, West Germany

Set: *The Black Page (New Age Version), Stick Together, My Guitar Wants To Kill Your Mama, Willie The Pimp (w/Ride Of The Valkyries), Purple Haze, Loops, Montana, City Of Tiny Lites, You Are What You Is, Marque-son's Chicken, Mr. Green Genes, Florentine Pogen, Andy, Inca Roads, Advance Romance, Bobby Brown, Stairway To Heaven.*

Encore One: *Boléro, Zoot Allures, Packard Goose/Royal March From "L'Histoire Du Soldat"/Theme From The Bartók Piano Concerto #3/Packard Goose Reprise.*

Encore Two: *The Closer You Are/Johnny Darling, No No Cherry, The Man From Utopia Meets Mary Lou.*

Encore Three: *Crew Slut.*

Secret Words: Shellfish, Moo-moo.
Reason: For 'shellfish, see 20th May 1988. The Bovine inspiration came from a large breasted audience member.

28th May, Sporthalle, Linz, Austria

Sound checked: *Purple Haze, Sunshine Of Your Love, When Yuppies Go To Hell.*

Set: *The Black Page (New Age Version), Inca Roads, Stick Together, My Guitar Wants To Kill Your Mama, Willie The Pimp, Montana, City Of Tiny Lites, You Are What You Is, Marque-son's Chicken, I Ain't Got No Heart, Love Of My Life, Cruisin' For Burgers, Bamboozled By Love, Find Her Finer, Big Swifty, Stairway To Heaven.*

Encore One: *Boléro, Joe's Garage, Why Does It Hurt When I Pee?*

Encore Two: *Sharleena.*

Encore Three: *I Am The Walrus, The Illinois Enema Bandit.*

Secret Word: Whinge, Scott's Face, Playground Psychotics
Reason: All inspired by the previous night's cake incident: see Chapter Five.

29th May, Eishalle Liebenau, Graz, Austria

Set: *The Black Page (New Age Version), Who Needs The Peace Corps?/I Left My Heart In San Francisco, Any Kind Of Pain, Dupree's Paradise, Find Her Finer, Pick Me I'm Clean, Cosmik Debris, More Trouble Every Day, Penguin In Bondage, Hot Plate Heaven At The Green Hotel, What's New In Baltimore, Mr. Green Genes, Florentine Pogen, Andy, Inca Roads, Bamboozled By Love.*

Encore One: *Stairway To Heaven.*

Encore Two: *Boléro, Whippin' Post.*

Encore Three: *Watermelon In Easter Hay.*

Secret Words: I'll be back, Hairpiece
Reason: 'I'll be back' is obviously a reference to Austrian American actor Arnold Alois Schwarzenegger's celebrated adage. Zappa revealed that 'hairpiece' was inspired by "that Cheech & Chong movie where they play these two Arab brothers"[14], *Things Are Tough All Over.* In one scene, Cheech gets a hair transplant and talks about his hairpiece; the shocked hair stylist asks "You have herpes, on your head?" "Of course I have it on my head! Where else would you have it - on your dick?" Cheech replies.

30th May, Palasport, Udine, Italy

Set: *The Black Page (New Age Version), Packard Goose/Royal March From "L'Histoire Du Soldat"/Theme From The Bartók Piano Concerto #3/Packard Goose Reprise, Zoot Allures, I Ain't Got No Heart, Love Of My Life, Filthy Habits, Stick Together, My Guitar Wants To Kill Your Mama, Willie The Pimp, Montana, City Of Tiny Lites, You Are What You Is, Marqueson's Chicken, The Torture Never Stops Part One/Theme From "Bonanza"/Lonesome Cowboy Burt/The Torture Never Stops Part Two, Peaches En Regalia, Stairway To Heaven.*

Encores: *Boléro, I Am The Walrus, The Illinois Enema Bandit.*

Secret Words : Turn off the lights, Popcorn
Reason: The house lights came on during *Love Of My Life*, causing Zappa to immediately change the lyric to "Turn off the lights..."; they remained on for a further 30 minutes. After they were switched off, Zappa's attentioned his focus on a popcorn vendor who is making his way through the audience while the band play.

1st June, Palasport, Padova, Italy

Set: *The Black Page (New Age Version), I Ain't Got No Heart, Love Of My Life, What's New In Baltimore, Who Needs The Peace Corps?/I Left My Heart In San Francisco, More Trouble Every Day, Penguin In Bondage, Hot Plate Heaven At The Green Hotel, Outside Now, Let's*

Make The Water Turn Black/Harry You're A Beast/The Orange County Lumber Truck/Oh No/Theme From Lumpy Gravy, Find Her Finer, Big Swifty, Packard Goose/Royal March From "L'Histoire Du Soldat"/Theme From The Bartók Piano Concerto #3/Packard Goose Reprise, Inca Roads, Sharleena.

Encore One: *Boléro, Bamboozled By Love.*

Encore Two: *Peaches En Regalia, Stairway To Heaven, Sofa #1.*

2nd June, Palatrussardi, Milan, Italy

Set: *The Black Page (New Age Version), Packard Goose/Royal March From "L'Histoire Du Soldat"/Theme From The Bartók Piano Concerto #3/Packard Goose Reprise, Any Kind Of Pain, Stick Together, My Guitar Wants To Kill Your Mama, Willie The Pimp, Montana, City Of Tiny Lites, A Pound For A Brown On The Bus, I Ain't Got No Heart, Love Of My Life, Inca Roads, Advance Romance, Bobby Brown, The Torture Never Stops Part One/Theme From "Bonanza"/ Lonesome Cowboy Burt/The Torture Never Stops Part Two.*

Encore One: *Joe's Garage, Why Does It Hurt When I Pee?*

Encore Two: *Boléro, Whippin' Post.*

Secret Words: Swatters
Reason: At a show in Milan in 1982, the band was attacked by a swarm of mosquitoes - an incident commemorated on the cover of *The Man From Utopia*. Fan Deepinder Cheema therefore threw two fly swatters up on stage six years later, which were used by Zappa as batons to conduct the band for the rest of the tour.

3rd June, Palasport, Torino, Italy

Set: *The Black Page (New Age Version), We're Turning Again, Alien Orifice, Cosmik Debris, Stolen Moments, Outside Now, Cruisin' For Burgers, When The Lie's So Big, Planet Of The Baritone Women, Any Kind Of Pain, Eat That Question, Black Napkins, Bamboozled By Love, Sharleena.*

Encore One: *The Closer You Are/Johnny Darling, No No Cherry, The Man From Utopia Meets Mary Lou.*

Encore Two: *Loops, Peaches En Regalia, Stairway To Heaven.*

Encore Three: *Boléro, Crew Slut.*

Secret Words: Don't drink the water
Reason: Not known, but likely to be related to incidents similar to those experienced after eating shellfish (see above).

5th June, Palasport, Modena, Italy

Set: *The Black Page (New Age Version), I Ain't Got No Heart, Love Of My Life, Let's Move To Cleveland, Find Her Finer, Marque-son's Chicken, Stick Together, My Guitar Wants To Kill Your Mama, Willie The Pimp, Dupree's Paradise, City Of Tiny Lites, You Are What You Is, More Trouble Every Day, Penguin In Bondage, Hot Plate Heaven At The Green Hotel.*

Encore One: *Sofa #1, Sharleena.*

Encore Two: *The Closer You Are/Johnny Darling, No No Cherry, Boléro.*

Encore Three: *Crew Slut.*

6th June, Palasport, Firenze, Italy

Set: *The Black Page (New Age Version), We're Turning Again, Alien Orifice, Mr. Green Genes, Florentine Pogen, Andy, Inca Roads, Advance Romance, Bobby Brown, What's New In Baltimore, Easy Meat, Let's Make The Water Turn Black/Harry You're A Beast/The Orange County Lumber Truck/Oh No/Theme From Lumpy Gravy, Sharleena, Peaches En Regalia, Stairway To Heaven.*

Encore One: *You Are What You Is, Whippin' Post.*

Encore Two: *I Am The Walrus, The Illinois Enema Bandit.*

Encore Three: *Boléro.*

7th June, Palaeur, Rome, Italy

Set: *The Black Page (New Age Version), Packard Goose/Royal March From "L'Histoire Du Soldat"/Theme From The Bartók Piano Concerto #3/Packard Goose Reprise, More Trouble Every Day, Hot Plate Heaven At The Green Hotel, Dupree's Paradise, Find Her Finer, Filthy Habits, I Ain't Got No Heart, Love Of My Life, Zoot Allures, City Of Tiny Lites, A Pound For A Brown On The Bus, Bamboozled By Love, Stairway To Heaven.*

Encore One: *Eat That Question, Black Napkins.*

Encore Two: *The Closer You Are/Johnny Darling, No No Cherry, Boléro, Arrivederci Roma.*

Encore Three: *Crew Slut.*

Secret Words: Home Shopping Network.
Reason: Unknown.

9th June, Palasport, Genoa, Italy

Set: *The Black Page (New Age Version), I Ain't Got No Heart, Love Of My Life, Marqueson's Chicken, Elvis Has Just Left The Building, Cruisin' For Burgers, Who Needs The Peace Corps?/I Left My Heart In San Francisco, Outside Now, Dupree's Paradise, Find Her Finer, Big Swifty, Rhymin' Man, Sinister Footwear 2nd mvt., City Of Tiny Lites, The Torture Never Stops Part One/Theme From "Bonanza"/ Lonesome Cowboy Nando/The Torture Never Stops Part Two.*

Encores: *Boléro, Whippin' Post, I Am The Walrus, The Illinois Enema Bandit.*

Secret Words: Pizza, Jellyfish
Reason: In 1982, the band's driver said he knew the best pizza place in town, only to return with some "frightening half-cooked sort of 'food simulation'"[15]. Also in the early 80s, Zappa fan Ferdinando ('Nando') Boero from Genoa got a job researching the taxonomy and ecology of the local fauna at the Bodega Marine Laboratory of the University of California. He identified and named a jellyfish - Phialella zappai - after

his hero as a way of getting to meet him. The two subsequently became friends. "The day after the Genoa concert (he called it the 'jellyfish concert'), I went to see him at the Hotel Splendido, at Portofino. He was grinning under his moustache (if you get what I mean) and he asked me if I liked the surprise he made for me. What do you say to FZ after he dedicated his last concert to you? He told me about his problems with the band, and that he would have to stop touring."[16]

APPENDIX II
The Official FZ 1988 Discography

Broadway The Hard Way

Official Release #53.
Originally Released: 25th October 1988

Tracklisting:

01. Elvis Has Just Left The Building (2:24)
02. Planet Of The Baritone Women (2:48)
03. Any Kind Of Pain (5:42)
04. Dickie's Such An Asshole (5:45)
05. When The Lie's So Big (3:38)
06. Rhymin' Man (3:50)
07. Promiscuous (2:02)
08. The Untouchables (2:26)
09. Why Don't You Like Me? (2:57)
10. Bacon Fat (1:29)
11. Stolen Moments (2:58)
12. Murder By Numbers (5:37)
13. Jezebel Boy (2:27)
14. Outside Now (7:49)
15. Hot Plate Heaven At The Green Hotel (6:40)
16. What Kind Of Girl? (3:16)
17. Jesus Thinks You're A Jerk (9:16)

Notes: Album originally released on vinyl and cassette in October 1988 minus tracks 9-16, but with an additional 'confinement loaf' intro rap at the start of *Dickie's Such An Asshole* from the 12th February Philadelphia show. Expanded CD version released 25th May 1989.

The Best Band You Never Heard In Your Life

Official Release #55.
Originally Released: 16th April 1991

Tracklisting:

DISC 1:
01. Heavy Duty Judy (6:04)
02. Ring Of Fire (2:00)
03. Cosmik Debris (4:32)
04. Find Her Finer (2:42)
05. Who Needs The Peace Corps? (2:40)
06. I Left My Heart In San Francisco (0:36)
07. Zomby Woof (5:41)
08. *Boléro* (5:19)
09. Zoot Allures (7:07)
10. Mr. Green Genes (3:40)
11. Florentine Pogen (7:11)
12. Andy (5:51)
13. Inca Roads (8:19)
14. Sofa #1 (2:49)

DISC 2:
01. Purple Haze (2:27)
02. Sunshine Of Your Love (2:30)
03. Let's Move To Cleveland (5:51)
04. When Irish Eyes Are Smiling (0:46)
05. "Godfather Part II" Theme (0:30)
06. A Few Moments With Brother A. West (4:01)
07. The Torture Never Stops Part One (5:20)
08. Theme From "Bonanza" (0:28)
09. Lonesome Cowboy Burt (Swaggart Version) (4:54)
10. The Torture Never Stops Part Two (10:47)
11. More Trouble Every Day (Swaggart Version) (5:28)
12. Penguin In Bondage (Swaggart Version) (5:05)
13. The Eric Dolphy Memorial Barbecue (9:18)
14. Stairway To Heaven (9:20)

Notes: Some European releases of this album omitted *Boléro* because the estate of Maurice Ravel objected to Zappa's treatment of the song. In Japan, the album featured different artwork by Cal Schenkel (used worldwide for the 1995 reissue, because Zappa had used a band picture on the original US and European version without the photographer's permission).

You Can't Do That On Stage Anymore, Vol. 4

Official Release #56.
Originally Released: 14th June 1991

Tracklisting:

DISC 1:
14. Take Me Out To The Ball Game (3:01)
15. Filthy Habits (5:39)

Make A Jazz Noise Here

Official Release #57.
Originally Released: 4th June 1991

Tracklisting:

DISC 1:
01. Stink-Foot (7:39)
02. When Yuppies Go To Hell (13:28)
03. Fire And Chains (5:04)
04. Let's Make The Water Turn Black (1:36)
05. Harry, You're A Beast (0:47)
06. The Orange County Lumber Truck (0:41)
07. Oh No (4:43)
08. Theme From Lumpy Gravy (1:11)
09. Eat That Question (1:54)
10. Black Napkins (6:56)
11. Big Swifty (11:12)
12. King Kong (13:04)
13. Star Wars Won't Work (3:40)

DISC 2:
01. The Black Page (New Age Version) (6:45)
02. T'Mershi Duween (1:42)
03. Dupree's Paradise (8:34)
04. City Of Tiny Lights (8:01)
05. Royal March From "L'Histoire Du Soldat" (0:59)
06. Theme From The Bartók Piano Concerto #3 (0:43)
07. Sinister Footwear 2nd mvt. (6:39)
08. Stevie's Spanking (4:25)
09. Alien Orifice (4:15)
10. Cruisin' For Burgers (8:27)
11. Advance Romance (7:43)
12. Strictly Genteel (6:36)

Note: Some European releases omitted *Royal March* From *"L'Histoire Du Soldat"* and *Theme From The Bartók Piano Concerto #3* due to concerns that the families of Stravinsky or Bartók might object to Zappa's treatment of these pieces. They didn't.

You Can't Do That On Stage Anymore, Vol. 6

Official Release #59.
Originally Released: 10th July 1992

Tracklisting:

DISC 1:
06. Honey, Don't You Want A Man Like Me? (4:01)
15. Make A Sex Noise (3:09)

DISC 2:
05. We're Turning Again (4:56)
06. Alien Orifice (4:16)
07. Catholic Girls (4:04)
08. Crew Slut (5:33)
12. Lonesome Cowboy Nando (5:09)

Notes: The coda for *Alien Orifice* is from an unknown '88 source, but the remainder is from a 1981 performance. *Lonesome Cowboy Nando* is from the final 9th June Genoa show, intercut with a performance from 1971 featuring Jimmy Carl Black.

Trance-Fusion

Official Release #79.
Released: 7th November 2006

Tracklisting:

01. Chunga's Revenge (7:01)
04. A Cold Dark Matter (3:31)
07. Scratch & Sniff (3:56)
08. Trance-Fusion (4:19)
09. Gorgo (2:41)
11. Soul Polka (3:17)
13. After Dinner Smoker (4:45)
15. Finding Higgs' Boson (3:41)
16. Bavarian Sunset (4:00)

Notes: This is an album of Zappa's 'air sculptures': *A Cold Dark Matter* is a guitar solo taken from an '88 performance of *Inca Roads*; *Scratch & Sniff* from *City Of Tiny Lites*; *Trance-Fusion* from *Marque-son's Chicken*; *Gorgo* and *After Dinner Smoker* from *The Torture Never Stops*; *Soul Polka* from *Oh No*; *Finding Higg's Boson* from *Hot Plate Heaven At The Green Hotel*; and *Bavarian Sunset* from *Loops*, a jam with Dweezil.

Anything Anytime Anywhere For No Reason At All

Exclusive download from iTunes. Released: 21st December 2006

Tracklisting:

04. Bamboozled By Love (5:41)

Note: Unlike the material edited together by Frank, this posthumous release contained a complete performance from the 8th May Vienna show.

Anything Anytime Anywhere For No Reason At All Again

Exclusive download from iTunes. Released: 21st December 2008

Tracklisting:

02. More Trouble Every Day (5:48)
05. America The Beautiful (3:35)

Note: Unlike the material edited together by Frank, this posthumous release contained complete performances from the 8th May Vienna and 25th March Uniondale shows.

Beat The Boots III - Disc Two

Exclusive download from AmazonMP3 and iTunes. Released: 25th January 2009

Tracklisting:

12. I Am the Walrus (03:43)
13. America the Beautiful (03:16)

Note: This posthumously released 'official bootleg' contained complete performances of two "Broadway" songs, from the 13th March Springfield and 12th March Burlington shows.

Anything Anytime Anywhere For No Reason At All, Again, Also

Exclusive download from iTunes. Released: 21st December 2010

Tracklisting:
07. My Guitar Wants To Kill Your Mama (3:34)
12. Stairway To Heaven (3:16)

Note: Unlike the material edited together by Frank, this posthumous release contained complete performances from the 21st March Syracuse and 9th March Buffalo shows.

APPENDIX III
The Easy Way

There was some initial reluctance on Zappa's part to releasing material recorded on the 1988 tour outside of the United States due to the political nature of some of the new songs. Consequently, initially, I and many others had to buy an import copy of the *Broadway The Hard Way* album and ponder how he could have even considered denying the rest of the world THAT guitar solo on *Any Kind Of Pain*. But non-Americans were still left a little mystified by some of the references in the lyrics. I therefore wrote the following article for the British Zappa fanzine, *T'Mershi Duween* (Issue #12) to help enlighten fellow fans. I figured most already knew enough about the dirty tricks of Richard Milhouse Nixon; the wit and wisdom of Ronald Reagan; the tears of clown Swaggart; and "the devil made me do it" antics of the Bakkers, so I uncovered a few stories behind some of the other c'a-rac-ters mentioned. I am therefore proud to re-present the following again one more time for the rest of the world (revised & revisited):

Charles G "Bebe" Rebozo: Miami businessman and Nixon's closest friend. Involved in raising money for the former US President's 'private fund', seeking contributions from the likes of John Paul Getty. Campaign money handed to Bebe by Howard Hughes is said to have mysteriously vanished. Rebozo was a frequent visitor to Nixon's Californian ocean front estate at San Clemente - nicknamed 'the Western White House' - from where the disgraced President issued his final statement accepting successor Gerald Ford's pardon.

Franklyn Curran "Lyn" Nofziger: Former White House political director. In 1967, while working as Californian Governor Reagan's press secretary, instigated a homosexual witch hunt in an attempt to discredit members of his own party and thus attain power for himself. The resultant scandal exposed at least two of the Governor's shirt-lifting aides, is said to have caused the Gipper to postpone his plans for the Presidency. Many years later, after leaving his Government post, Nofziger opened up a lobby firm and illegally sought, and obtained, help from former colleagues in securing a $32M Army contract for clients, the Wedtech Corporation. Was later indicted on four counts of violating the federal ethics law, fined $30K and sentenced to 90 days in jail.

Lieutenant Colonel Oliver Laurence North: Acted as the National Security Council's counter-terrorism co-ordinator from 1983-86 under the Reagan Administration. With help from Israel, he devised the 'neat' scheme of passing profits from Iranian arms sales to the Nicaraguan Contras - described as "the ultimate covert operation". As the scandal unfolded, poor Ollie was fired. However, his Oscar-nominated testimony at the televised Senate hearings brought a flood of endorsement offers, and Papazian Productions promptly made the Primetime Emmy-nominated TV movie, *Guts And Glory: The Rise and Fall Of Oliver North.*

Edwin Meese III: Reagan's Attorney General. First to make official disclosures of the Iran-Contra affair. Suspected of involvement in the Wedtech saga; while giving evidence during Nofziger's trial, Meese's memory failed him on 29 occasions. In 1984, was investigated for seemingly giving Government jobs, in exchange for financial assistance, to a real estate developer, a tax accountant and two senior bankers. Later accused of shirking his Attorney General responsibilities and of passing legislation to aid his suspect financial dealings. Meese nevertheless continued to receive the support of Reagan - his close friend for some 20 years.

Pat Robertson: Former television evangelist and Republican presidential candidate. Despite regularly preaching against sex before marriage, conceived first son out of wedlock, then fudged the date of his marriage to hide the fact. His résumé for the 1988 Presidential campaign referred to his "graduate studies at the University of London", which later turned out to be merely a summer arts course for American tourists. His claim of active duty in Korea was disputed by a combat veteran who said Robertson was never under fire or even near the front lines, his democratic father having pulled strings to keep his son away from the fighting. Robertson filed a libel suit, but subsequently dropped it as he himself dropped out of the Presidential race.

William J. Casey: Reagan's Presidential campaign manager in 1980 and CIA Director from 1981-87. In 1983, was investigated for insider trading of CIA contractors' stocks and for selling more than $600K worth of oil stocks shortly before oil prices plummeted. Was also ordered to pay damages over a plagiarism suit, and apparently lied to Congress about CIA involvement in the Iran-Contra scandal. He passed away, however, before the Senate hearings were concluded.

Vice Admiral John M. Poindexter: Involvement in the secret supply operation for the Nicaraguan Contras eventually forced him to resign his position as Reagan's National Security Adviser, Ollie North having been considered too junior to be a credible sacrifice. After the Senate hearings, Poindexter had a street named after him in Indiana.

Michael Deaver: One of Reagan's closest friends and his one-time Deputy Chief Of Staff. His lobby efforts on behalf of TWA shortly after quitting his Government position ultimately led to convictions on three counts of perjury.

Jesse Jackson: Former deputy to civil rights leader, Dr Martin Luther King Jr., and Democratic frontrunner during the 1988 Presidential campaign. Married Jacqueline Lavina Brown, then two months pregnant, in 1962. Subsequently romantically linked to a number of women, including singers Nancy Wilson and Roberta Flack. In 1968, when MLK was assassinated, Jackson, though in the parking lot one floor below King at the time, told reporters "I was the last man in the world he spoke to," wearing a blood-stained turtle-neck shirt. In spite of this inexcusable act, his renowned embrace of PLO leader Yasser Arafat, and the odd anti-Semitic statement (he referred to New York City as "Hymietown" in January 1984), Jackson surprisingly continues to be treated with kid-gloves by the media.

Louis Farrakhan: National Representative of the Nation of Islam, Farrakhan is an advocate for black interests and a critic of American society. He has referred to Judaism as "a gutter religion" and, following Jesse Jackson's 'Hymietown' comment, cautioned Jewish leaders, "If you harm this brother, I warn you in the name of Allah, it'll be the last one you ever harm."

APPENDIX IV
Notes

Unless noted, all quotes are taken from interviews with the author.

Chapter One - You Can't Do That On Stage Anymore

[1] *Does Humor Belong In Music?* by Frank Zappa (EMI Records CDP 7 46188 2, 1986).
[2] *Zappa's Inferno* by Noë Goldwasser (Guitar World, April 1987).
[3] *Father Of Invention* by Rick Davies (Music Technology, February 1987).
[4] Origin unknown, but reproduced in *Frank Zappa - A Visual Documentary* by Miles (Omnibus Press, 1993).
[5] *Sample This!* by Jim Aikin & Bob Doerschuk (Keyboard, February 1987).
[6] Ibid.
[7] *The Real Frank Zappa Book* by Frank Zappa with Peter Occhiogrosso (Simon & Schuster, 1990).
[8] *Happy Together* by Co de Kloet (Society Pages Issue #11, 30th October 1990).
[9] *They're Doing The Interview Of The Century* by Den Simms, Eric Buxton and Rob Samler (Society Pages, June 1990).
[10] *Happy Together* by Co de Kloet (Society Pages Issue #11, 30th October 1990).
[11] *A Mars A Day: Tommy Mars In Conversation* by Axel Wünsch and Aad Hoogesteger (T'Mershi Duween #20-21, July-September 1991).
[12] *Mars Needs Evil Princes* by Evil Prince (T'Mershi Duween #61, October 1997).
[13] *Little Band We Used To Play In* by Michael Davis (Keyboard, June 1980).
[14] Arthur Barrow's website, http://home.netcom.com/~bigear/Zappa.html#Clonemeister
[15] *Thomas Wictor's In Cold Sweat: Interviews With Really Scary Musicians* by Thomas Wictor (Limelight Editions, 2001).
[16] *The Real Frank Zappa Book* by Frank Zappa with Peter Occhiogrosso (Simon & Schuster, 1990).
[17] Ibid.
[18] *Beefheart: Through The Eyes Of Magic* by John 'Drumbo' French (Proper Music Publishing, 2010).
[19] Mike Keneally's website, http://www.keneally.com/allaboutmike.html
[20] Ibid.
[21] *They're Doing The Interview Of The Century* by Den Simms, Eric Buxton and Rob Samler (Society Pages, April 1990).
[22] Mike Keneally's website, http://www.keneally.com/allaboutmike.html
[23] Ibid.
[24] Ibid.
[25] Ibid.

[26] Ibid.

[27] Ibid.

[28] Ibid.

[29] Mike Keneally's website, http://www.keneally.com/allaboutmike.html

[30] *Thomas Wictor's In Cold Sweat: Interviews With Really Scary Musicians* by Thomas Wictor (Limelight Editions, 2001).

[31] *Remembering My Battle Against Fundamentalists* by Jim Luce (The Huffington Post, 6 July 2009).

Chapter Two - Welcome to the United States

[1] *20 Questions: Frank And Moon Unit Zappa* by David and Victoria Sheff (Playboy, November 1982).

[2] *Mom Redefined* by Moon Unit Zappa (from *Afterbirth: Stories You Won't Read In A Parenting Magazine*, St Martin's Press, 2009).

[3] *The Real Frank Zappa Book* by Frank Zappa with Peter Occhiogrosso (Simon & Schuster, 1990).

[4] Radio interview with Kevin Matthews (WLUP Chicago, 4 March 1988).

[5] *Thing-Fish Rap: Ike Willis Chats* by Evil Prince (T'Mershi Duween #54, October 1996).

[6] Ibid.

[7] Mike Keneally's website, http://www.keneally.com/allaboutmike.html

[8] *Thomas Wictor's In Cold Sweat: Interviews With Really Scary Musicians* by Thomas Wictor (Limelight Editions, 2001).

[9] *They're Doing The Interview Of The Century* by Den Simms, Eric Buxton and Rob Samler (Society Pages, June 1990).

[10] *A Talk With Frank Zappa* by Bill Camarata (Scene, March 1988).

[11] *1988 Was A Million Years Ago: Mike's Zappa Tour Diaries*, http://www.keneally.com/1988/1988.html

[12] *The Frank Zappa 1988 Tour Project* webpage by Pat Buzby, http://members.shaw.ca/fz-pomd/1988/index.html

[13] *1988 Was A Million Years Ago: Mike's Zappa Tour Diaries*, http://www.keneally.com/1988/1988.html

[14] Ibid.

[15] *Chatting With A. Wing And A Prayer* by Fred Banta (T'Mershi Duween #63, March 2000).

[16] *A Talk With Frank Zappa* by Bill Camarata (Scene, March 1988).

[17] *1988 Was A Million Years Ago: Mike's Zappa Tour Diaries*, http://www.keneally.com/1988/1988.html

[18] *Panty Rap* by Frank Zappa (from *Tinsel Town Rebellion*, Barking Pumpkin Records, 1981)

[19] Washington Call-In, February 1988

[20] *Speak Up, Ike, An' 'Spress Yourself* by Matthew Galaher (Society Pages, May 1990)

[21] *Dickie's Such An Asshole (The San Clemente Magnetic Deviation)* by Frank Zappa (from *Broadway The Hard Way*, Barking Pumpkin Records, 1988).

[22] *Thing-Fish Rap: Ike Willis Chats* by Evil Prince (T'Mershi Duween #54, October 1996).

[23] *The Real Frank Zappa Book* by Frank Zappa with Peter Occhiogrosso (Simon & Schuster, 1990).

[24] *1988 Was A Million Years Ago: Mike's Zappa Tour Diaries*, http://www.keneally.com/1988/1988.html

[25] *Mike Keneally With Frank Zappa*, http://www.keneally.com/discography/zappa.html

[26] *1988 Was A Million Years Ago: Mike's Zappa Tour Diaries*, http://www.keneally.com/1988/1988.html

[27] *They're Doing The Interview Of The Century* by Den Simms, Eric Buxton and Rob Samler (Society Pages, April 1990).

[28] *Project Documentation* by Den Simms.

[29] *1988 Was A Million Years Ago: Mike's Zappa Tour Diaries*, http://www.keneally.com/1988/1988.html

[30] Ibid.

[31] Ibid.

[32] *Dr. Dot! Buttnaked And Backstage: Diary Of A Rock & Roll Masseuse* (©2003 Dr. Dot & Mike Halverson).

[33] *Thing-Fish Rap: Ike Willis Chats* by Evil Prince (T'Mershi Duween #54, October 1996).

[34] *1988 Was A Million Years Ago: Mike's Zappa Tour Diaries*, http://www.keneally.com/1988/1988.html

[35] Radio interview with Kevin Matthews (WLUP Chicago, 4th March 1988).

[36] *Frank Zappa* by Barry Miles (Atlantic Books, 2004)

[37] *Record Collector* #93, May 1987.

[38] Radio interview with Kevin Matthews (WLUP Chicago, 4th March 1988).

[39] *1988 Was A Million Years Ago: Mike's Zappa Tour Diaries*, http://www.keneally.com/1988/1988.html

[40] Radio interview with Kevin Matthews (WLUP Chicago, 4th March 1988).

[41] *1988 Was A Million Years Ago: Mike's Zappa Tour Diaries*, http://www.keneally.com/1988/1988.html

[42] *They're Doing The Interview Of The Century* by Den Simms, Eric Buxton and Rob Samler (Society Pages, April 1990).

[43] *A Talk With Frank Zappa* by Bill Camarata (Scene, March 1988).

[44] *The Real Frank Zappa Book* by Frank Zappa with Peter Occhiogrosso (Simon & Schuster, 1990).

[45] *King Kong* by Frank Zappa (from *Make A Jazz Noise Here*, Barking Pumpkin Records, 1991).

[46] *The Trombone's Connected To The Lip Bone: Bruce Fowler Interview* by Evil Prince (T'Mershi Duween, #55-57, November 1996 - March 1997).

[47] *1988 Was A Million Years Ago: Mike's Zappa Tour Diaries*, http://www.keneally.com/1988/1988.html

[48] Radio interview with Kevin Matthews (WLUP Chicago, 4th March 1988).

[49] *1988 Was A Million Years Ago: Mike's Zappa Tour Diaries*, http://www.keneally.com/1988/1988.html

[50] Ibid.

[51] Ibid.

[52] *Thomas Wictor's Thomas Wictor's In Cold Sweat: Interviews With Really Scary Musicians* by Thomas Wictor (Limelight Editions, 2001).

[53] *They're Doing The Interview Of The Century* by Den Simms, Eric Buxton and Rob Samler (Society Pages, April 1990).

[54] *1988 Was A Million Years Ago: Mike's Zappa Tour Diaries*, http://www.keneally.com/1988/1988.html

[55] *The Immortals - The Greatest Artists of All Time: 71) Frank Zappa* by Trey Anastasio (Rolling Stone, April 2005).

[56] *Mike Keneally With Frank Zappa*, http://www.keneally.com/discography/zappa.html

[57] *Thomas Wictor's In Cold Sweat: Interviews With Really Scary Musicians* by Thomas Wictor (Limelight Editions, 2001).

[58] Ibid.

[59] Ibid.
[60] Ibid.
[61] Ibid.
[62] Ibid.
[63] Ibid.
[64] Ibid.

Chapter Three - Playground Psychotics

[1] *The Frank Zappa 1988 Tour Project* webpage by Pat Buzby,
http://members.shaw.ca/fz-pomd/1988/index.html
[2] *The Real Frank Zappa Book* by Frank Zappa with Peter Occhiogrosso
(Simon & Schuster, 1990).
[3] *Thomas Wictor's In Cold Sweat: Interviews With Really Scary Musicians* by Thomas Wictor
(Limelight Editions, 2001).
[4] *Dr. Dot! Buttnaked And Backstage: Diary Of A Rock & Roll Masseuse*
(©2003 Dr. Dot & Mike Halverson).
[5] *A Life In The Day: Dr Dot, Masseuse To The Stars* (The Sunday Times, 16th March 2003).
[6] *They're Doing The Interview Of The Century* by Den Simms, Eric Buxton and Rob Samler
(Society Pages, April 1990).
[7] *The Frank Zappa 1988 Tour Project* webpage by Pat Buzby,
http://members.shaw.ca/fz-pomd/1988/index.html
[8] *They're Doing The Interview Of The Century* by Den Simms, Eric Buxton and Rob Samler
(Society Pages, April 1990).
[9] *Thomas Wictor's In Cold Sweat: Interviews With Really Scary Musicians* by Thomas Wictor
(Limelight Editions, 2001).
[10] Ibid.
[11] *They're Doing The Interview Of The Century* by Den Simms, Eric Buxton and Rob Samler
(Society Pages, June 1990).
[12] Ibid.
[13] *Dr. Dot! Buttnaked And Backstage: Diary Of A Rock & Roll Masseuse*
(©2003 Dr. Dot & Mike Halverson).
[14] Ibid.

Chapter Four - Shall We Take Ourselves Seriously?

[1] *They're Doing The Interview Of The Century* by Den Simms, Eric Buxton and Rob Samler
(Society Pages, April 1990).
[2] *Playboy Interview: Frank Zappa* (Playboy Volume 40 Number 4, April 1993).
[3] *Somebody Up There Doesn't Like Me* by Elin Wilder (High Times, December 1989).
[4] *1988 Was A Million Years Ago: Mike's Zappa Tour Diaries,*
http://www.keneally.com/1988/1988.html
[5] *Cosmik Debris: The Collected History And Improvisations Of Frank Zappa*
("The Son Of Revised" edition) by Greg Russo (Crossfire Publications, 2002).
[6] Ibid.
[7] *The Real Frank Zappa Book* by Frank Zappa with Peter Occhiogrosso
(Simon & Schuster, 1990).
[8] *The Drummers Of Frank Zappa: Roundtable Discussion And Performance - More Stories And Chad's
Audition* (Drum Channel DVD Collection: Vol. One, 2009).

⁹ *Say Waat?* (Making Music, May 1988).

¹⁰ *1988 Was A Million Years Ago: Mike's Zappa Tour Diaries*,
http://www.keneally.com/1988/1988.html

¹¹ *Live Reviews: Brighton Centre 16.4.88* by Matthew Johns (T'Mershi Duween #2, Summer 1988).

¹² *The Frank Zappa 1988 Tour Project* webpage by Pat Buzby,
http://members.shaw.ca/fz-pomd/1988/index.html

¹³ Radio interview with Kevin Matthews (WLUP Chicago, 4th March 1988).

¹⁴ *1988 Was A Million Years Ago: Mike's Zappa Tour Diaries*,
http://www.keneally.com/1988/1988.html

¹⁵ *They're Doing The Interview Of The Century* by Den Simms, Eric Buxton and Rob Samler
(Society Pages, June 1990).

¹⁶ Ibid.

¹⁷ *1988 Was A Million Years Ago: Mike's Zappa Tour Diaries*,
http://www.keneally.com/1988/1988.html

¹⁸ Ibid.

¹⁹ *Packard Goose* by Frank Zappa (from *Joe's Garage Act III*, Zappa Records, 1979).

²⁰ *Say Waat?* (Making Music, May 1988).

²¹ *Live Live Live: Wembley Wembley And Birmingham* by Fred Tomsett
(T'Mershi Duween #1, May 1988).

²² *1988 Was A Million Years Ago: Mike's Zappa Tour Diaries*,
http://www.keneally.com/1988/1988.html

²³ *Thirteen* by Frank Zappa
(from *You Can't Do That On Stage Anymore, Vol. 6*, Barking Pumpkin Records, 1992).

²⁴ *1988 Was A Million Years Ago: Mike's Zappa Tour Diaries*,
http://www.keneally.com/1988/1988.html

²⁵ *Mike Keneally With Frank Zappa*, http://www.keneally.com/discography/zappa.html

²⁶ From Ole M. Lysgaard's liner notes for the posthumous Zappa album, *Joe's Menage*
(Vaulternative Records, 2008).

²⁷ *1988 Was A Million Years Ago: Mike's Zappa Tour Diaries*,
http://www.keneally.com/1988/1988.html

²⁸ *The Frank Zappa 1988 Tour Project* webpage by Pat Buzby,
http://members.shaw.ca/fz-pomd/1988/index.html

²⁹ *1988 Was A Million Years Ago: Mike's Zappa Tour Diaries*,
http://www.keneally.com/1988/1988.html

³⁰ *Montana (Whipping Floss)* by Frank Zappa (from *You Can't Do That On Stage Anymore, Vol. 2:
The Helsinki Concert*, Barking Pumpkin Records, 1988).

³¹ *Meeting Mr Zappa* by Morgan Ågren, http://www.morganagren.com/zappa/zappa1.asp

³² *1988 Was A Million Years Ago: Mike's Zappa Tour Diaries*,
http://www.keneally.com/1988/1988.html

³³ *Zappa's Universe* press statement, read by Moon Unit Zappa
(Ritz Theatre, New York, 7th November 1991).

³⁴ "Grandstand" by Monty Python's Flying Circus (Series Three, Episode 39, January 1973).

³⁵ *Being In Zappa's Universe* by Morgan Ågren,
http://www.morganagren.com/zappa/zappa2.asp

³⁶ *Happy Birthday, Frank!* by Robert L. Doerschuk (Keyboard, February 1992).

³⁷ *Frank Zappa* (Musician, February 1994).

³⁸ *1988 Was A Million Years Ago: Mike's Zappa Tour Diaries*,
http://www.keneally.com/1988/1988.html

³⁹ *Stink-Foot* by Frank Zappa (from *Make A Jazz Noise Here*, Barking Pumpkin Records, 1991).

⁴⁰ Ibid.
⁴¹ *They're Doing The Interview Of The Century* by Den Simms, Eric Buxton and Rob Samler (Society Pages, April 1990).
⁴² *Thomas Wictor's In Cold Sweat: Interviews With Really Scary Musicians* by Thomas Wictor (Limelight Editions, 2001).
⁴³ Ibid.
⁴³ *They're Doing The Interview Of The Century* by Den Simms, Eric Buxton and Rob Samler (Society Pages, April 1990).
⁴⁵ *Mike Keneally With Frank Zappa*, http://www.keneally.com/discography/zappa.html
⁴⁶ Ibid.
⁴⁷ *54 Albums Later, Zappa Tells His Life Story From Z To A* by George Varga (San Diego Union, 18th December 1988).
⁴⁸ *Mother! Is The Story Of Frank Zappa Story* by Michael Gray (Proteus Book, 1984).
⁴⁹ *Zappa!* (Keyboard/Guitar Player Magazine Special, 1992).
⁵⁰ *Really, Keneally? Mike Responds To Friendly Interrogation*, http://www.keneally.com/reallykeneally.html
⁵¹ *Hey Frank, Where You Goin' With That Guitar in Your Hand?* by Alan di Perna (Musician, September 1988).
⁵² *Thomas Wictor's In Cold Sweat: Interviews With Really Scary Musicians* by Thomas Wictor (Limelight Editions, 2001).
⁵³ *They're Doing The Interview Of The Century* by Den Simms, Eric Buxton and Rob Samler (Society Pages, September 1990).
⁵⁴ *The Complete History Of The Last Few Weeks Of The Mothers Of Invention* by Frank Zappa (Reprise circular, Vol. 4, No. 40, 9th October 1972)
⁵⁵ *Star Wars Won't Work* by Frank Zappa (from *Make A Jazz Noise Here*, Barking Pumpkin Records, 1991).
⁵⁶ *They're Doing The Interview Of The Century* by Den Simms, Eric Buxton and Rob Samler (Society Pages, April 1990).
⁵⁷ *The Frank Zappa 1988 Tour Project* webpage by Pat Buzby, http://members.shaw.ca/fz-pomd/1988/index.html
⁵⁸ *They're Doing The Interview Of The Century* by Den Simms, Eric Buxton and Rob Samler (Society Pages, June 1990).
⁵⁹ *Thomas Wictor's In Cold Sweat: Interviews With Really Scary Musicians* by Thomas Wictor (Limelight Editions, 2001).

Chapter Five - Why Don't You Like Me?

¹ *Thomas Wictor's In Cold Sweat: Interviews With Really Scary Musicians* by Thomas Wictor (Limelight Editions, 2001).
² Ibid.
³ Email from Ferdinando Boero to Pat Buzby, June 1999.
⁴ *Mike Keneally With Frank Zappa*, http://www.keneally.com/discography/zappa.html
⁵ *Unholy Mother* by David Mead (Guitarist, June 1993).
⁶ *Ode To Gravity - Frank Zappa: World Affairs Commentator* by Charles Amirkhanian (KPFA radio interview, 15th April 1991).
⁷ *Hey Frank, Where You Goin' With That Guitar in Your Hand?* by Alan di Perna (Musician, September 1988).
⁸ *Ode To Gravity - Frank Zappa: World Affairs Commentator* by Charles Amirkhanian (KPFA radio interview, 15th April 1991).

[9] *Chatting With A. Wing And A Prayer* by Fred Banta (T'Mershi Duween #63, March 2000).

[10] *54 Albums Later, Zappa Tells His Life Story From Z To A* by George Varga
(San Diego Union, 18th December 1988).

[11] *Scott Thunes/The Demise Of The Band* (KMPC-FM radio interview, 8th January 1989).

[12] *Poetic Justice: Frank Zappa Puts Us In Our Place* by Matt Resnicoff (Musician, November 1991).

[13] *Thomas Wictor's In Cold Sweat: Interviews With Really Scary Musicians* by Thomas Wictor
(Limelight Editions, 2001).

[14] Ibid.

[15] *Unholy Mother* by David Mead (Guitarist, June 1993).

[16] *Be A Little Civic Hellraiser* by Jeff Newelt (telephone interview from 3rd April 1991,
excerpts of which were published in Philadelphia periodical, 34th Street)

[17] *The Real Frank Zappa Book* by Frank Zappa with Peter Occhiogrosso
(Simon & Schuster, 1990).

[18] *Playboy Interview: Frank Zappa* (Playboy Volume 40 Number 4, April 1993).

[19] *The Real Frank Zappa Book* by Frank Zappa with Peter Occhiogrosso
(Simon & Schuster, 1990).

[20] *They're Doing The Interview Of The Century* by Den Simms, Eric Buxton and Rob Samler
(Society Pages, April 1990).

[21] *The Real Frank Zappa Book* by Frank Zappa with Peter Occhiogrosso
(Simon & Schuster, 1990).

[22] *They're Doing The Interview Of The Century* by Den Simms, Eric Buxton and Rob Samler
(Society Pages, April 1990).

[23] *The Real Frank Zappa Book* by Frank Zappa with Peter Occhiogrosso
(Simon & Schuster, 1990).

[24] *Thing-Fish Rap* by Evil Prince (T'Mershi Duween, #54, October 1996).

[25] *What Can You Do That's Fantastic?* by Mitch Myers (Downbeat, January 2004).

[26] *Mike Keneally With Frank Zappa*, http://www.keneally.com/discography/zappa.html

[27] *Uptight: The Velvet Underground Story* by Victor Bockris and Gerard Malanga
(Omnibus Press, 1983)

[28] Dweezil & Ahmet Zappa interviewed for (but rejected by) *The Wire* at Music For Nations,
102 Belsize Lane on 30th September 1992 by Danny Houston and Ben Watson. This author
forwarded excerpts from the interview - with Watson's permission - for publication in the
Dweezil Zappa Fan Club magazine.

[29] *Beauty Queen* by Leather Dynamite (from *Testicular Manslaughter*, Quicksand Music, 2002).

Chapter 6 - A Very Nice Body

[1] *Mike Keneally With Frank Zappa*, http://www.keneally.com/discography/zappa.html

[2] *They're Doing The Interview Of The Century* by Den Simms, Eric Buxton and Rob Samler
(Society Pages, April 1990).

[3] *Would You Like Some Fries With That Interview?* by Martin De Jong, Piet Doelder,
Aad Hoogesteger, Uli Mrosek and Axel Wünsch (Society Pages USA, May 1991).

[4] *The Best Band You Never Heard In Your Life* by Frank Zappa (Barking Pumpkin Records, 1991).

[5] Posted at The Official Frank Zappa Messageboards on Thursday 2nd August 2007
at 12:15pm (Topic: 'Frank Zappa>Randomonium>WTF? Gail').

[6] *The Best Band You Never Heard In Your Life* by Frank Zappa (Barking Pumpkin Records, 1991).

[7] *Would You Like Some Fries With That Interview?* by Martin De Jong, Piet Doelder,
Aad Hoogesteger, Uli Mrosek and Axel Wünsch (Society Pages USA, May 1991).

[8] *He's A Human Being, He Has Emotions Just Like Us* by Den Simms and Rob Samler

(Society Pages USA, September 1991).
[9] *I Am Ozzy* by Ozzy Osbourne with Chris Ayres (Sphere, 2009).
[10] *He's A Human Being, He Has Emotions Just Like Us* by Den Simms and Rob Samler (Society Pages USA, September 1991).
[11] *Thomas Wictor's In Cold Sweat: Interviews With Really Scary Musicians* by Thomas Wictor (Limelight Editions, 2001).
[12] *Mike Keneally With Frank Zappa*, http://www.keneally.com/discography/zappa.html
[13] *Caravan With A Drum Solo: The Chad Wackerman Interview* by Ben Watson (T'Mershi Duween #25, June 1992).
[14] *1988 Was A Million Years Ago: Mike's Zappa Tour Diaries*, http://www.keneally.com/1988/1988.html
[15] *Frank Zappa's "Alien Orifice" Scott Thunes's Complete Bass Line* by Bryan Beller (Bass Player magazine, 1st April 2009).
[16] Ibid.
[17] Ibid.

Chapter Seven - When No One Was No One

[1] *Zappa 89-7* by Deborah Paris (Rhythm, July 1989).
[2] *Ike Willis Joins Project/Object... To Keep The Music Alive For Frank* by Rusty Pipes (Cosmic Debris, 2001).

Appendix I - Dates & Set-lists

[1] *Dickie's Such An Asshole (The San Clemente Magnetic Deviation)* by Frank Zappa (from *Broadway The Hard Way*, Barking Pumpkin Records, 1988).
[2] *They're Doing The Interview Of The Century* by Den Simms, Eric Buxton and Rob Samler (Society Pages, April 1990).
[3] *1988 Was A Million Years Ago: Mike's Zappa Tour Diaries*, http://www.keneally.com/1988/1988.html
[4] *Heavy Duty Judy* by Frank Zappa (from *The Best Band You Never Heard In Your Life*, Barking Pumpkin Records, 1991).
[5] *They're Doing The Interview Of The Century* by Den Simms, Eric Buxton and Rob Samler (Society Pages, April 1990).
[6] *1988 Was A Million Years Ago: Mike's Zappa Tour Diaries*, http://www.keneally.com/1988/1988.html
[7] *"No dude... don't say that!"* by Andrew Greenaway (T'Mershi Duween #21, May 1991).
[8] *They're Doing The Interview Of The Century* by Den Simms, Eric Buxton and Rob Samler (Society Pages, April 1990).
[9] Ibid.
[10] Ibid.
[11] Ibid.
[12] Ibid.
[13] Ibid.
[14] Ibid.
[15] *You Can't Do That On Stage Anymore Vol. 1* liner notes by Frank Zappa (Rykodisc, 1988).
[16] Email from Ferdinando Boero to Onno Gross.

ACKNOWLEDGEMENTS

Thanks to:

My family: Julie, Chris, Emma and Lizzy (for love and laughs - and for putting up with all my vacant looks as I worked on this); Mum, Steve, Lynn, Paul, Michelle, Trevor and Simon...and all the rest - love ya.

My friends: Canadian John and Uncle Ian (for being loyal travelling companions and more); Amaretto Mick; Heather; Jo & Kim.

The contributors: Scott Thunes, Ed Mann, Mike Keneally, Ike Willis, Robert Martin, Albert Wing, Walt Fowler and Paul Carman (and thanks for the music too); Tom Fowler; Howard Kaylan; Lorraine Belcher Chamberlain; Fabio Treves; Billy James; Al Stone; Morgan Ågren; the late Harry Andronis (RIP); Dr Dot; Den Simms; Bill Lantz; Jon Larsen; Pat Buzby; Jerry Bloom; Tina Grohowski; Rob Samler; Maki Galimberti; Michelle Greenaway, Lisa Popeil; Deepinder Cheema; Ken Windish; Chris Coulson; and last, but by no means least, Patrice "Candy" Zappa-Porter (I can't thank you enough for the great words)...

And not forgetting: Bruce & Chad (maybe next time?); Nathan & Ryan (take good care of my babies); Anton & Jan; Dave McMann & Lesley; André Cholmondeley; the late Gamma (RIP); Mary B; Jamie and Jazzman Dave; Greg Russo; Alan Jenkins; the Slick family; Pete Brunelli & Stephen Chillemi; Wolfhard Kutz, Thomas Dippel & Thomas Reinicke; Roddie Gilliard; Kilissa Cissoko; Jerry Outlaw; Richard Hemmings; Luis Gonzalez; FrazKnapp; Michel Delville; Joseph Diaz; Princess Helen & the Amazing Mr Bickerton; Kevin Armstrong (who first introduced me to Frank's music, all those years ago); Peter van Laarhoven; Todd Grubbs; Lorraine & Kim; Clinton Morgan; Erik Palm; Mark McInnes; John Kaminski; Ben & Esther; Hans Annellsson; Stacy Thunes; Jürgen Verfaillie; Nigey Lennon & John Tabacco; Paul Green; Ryan Heinz; and too many Zappateers to mention.

And finally: thanks to Frank.

AFTERWORD

When Frank hung up his guitar after the 1988 'Broadway The Hard Way tour', he explained he was fed up with endless squabbles between members of his band. But was this the real reason he cancelled the rest of the tour? Could it have been an excuse, a cover up for something else - Frank's failing health perhaps? Could Frank have been feeling increasingly unfit to cope with relentless concerts across America and Europe night after night - 81 in all over 127 days, in other words, one concert every one and a half days, including travel? When I met him in April, midway through the tour, he certainly did look tired and drawn.

An interview for *Radio 210* was the perfect excuse to meet up again. It was sixteen years since I'd stopped working for Frank in Hollywood, an astonishing, riveting, extraordinary four-year period between 1968 to 1972 which I detail in my own book, *Freak Out! My Life With Frank Zappa (Plexus Books, 2011)*. A few fleeting visits in between had reignited our bond, but in London in 1988 the whole afternoon stretched before us.

Always polite and respectful, he answered my questions with honesty, even when I quizzed him about his sex life. He had often told me that, after music, lust was the most important thing in his life, so I was astonished to hear him say, "when you think about sex, about what's actually going on, it's just silly." Later, Lorraine Belcher confirmed to me that she'd spent a loving, platonic night with Frank during the tour and when Frank organised prostitutes for his band members he had shown no interest in groupies for his own needs. It would be wrong to draw concrete conclusions from such flimsy evidence, but it does appear that this man who was so into lust all his life, was suffering from sapped energy and a loss of libido. Rock stars, Frank always proclaimed, do not tour because they love music but because they love a constant supply of 'nookie'. Frank was no different - so could it be that touring had suddenly lost its base appeal?

Zappa The Hard Way shows how eleven men lived and played in harmony through dozens of concerts because of their respect and admiration for Frank. And what astonishing concerts they were too. Andrew manages to convey the brilliance and uniqueness of this band not only through his own descriptions but also from the band members' own praise for the astonishing variety of music they created. But even this respect could not stop cracks opening up and, let's face it, any group of people locked together without a break for this period of time would snap. To my mind, it is surprising not that they imploded but that they endured as long as they did.

Through interviews with the surviving band members, Andrew has pieced together the evidence and teased out the truth. Now every Zappa fan, because of this meticulously researched book, has a better understanding of why 'Broadway The Hard Way' was Frank Zappa's final tour.

Pauline Butcher
October 2011

ABOUT THE AUTHOR

Andrew Greenaway was born in Orpington, Kent, in 1958. He is editor of the UK's only Zappa website, www.idiotbastard.com, and has compiled two albums of "deranged" versions of Zappa songs: *20 Extraordinary Renditions (Cordelia Records, 2008)* and *21 Burnt Weeny Sandwiches (Cordelia Records, 2010)*. A third long player, featuring some of the songs Frank covered on the 'Broadway The Hard Way' tour, is in the pipeline.

As well as writing regularly for the British Zappa fanzine, *T'Mershi Duween*, and a monthly 'From A to Z' column for the now defunct *Dweezil Zappa Fan Club Magazine*, Andrew has also contributed to *The Freedonia Gazette, Society Pages, The Chelsea Independent* and *1001 Songs You Must Hear Before You Die (Octopus Books, 2010)*. He also helped write *Onside - The True Story Of Football's Mr Fix-It*, Anton Johnson's forthcoming autobiography.

Excerpts from his interviews with various Zappa-alumni conducted during the past twenty years have appeared in numerous biographies, and he is currently one of the key contributors to ZappaCast - The Frank Zappa Podcast. Andrew also made a guest appearance - along with Robert Martin, Scott Thunes and Ed Mann - on J21's album *Beyond The Holographic Veil (Floating World Records, 2011)*.

Andrew has three children, four cats, one dog, and lives with his wife Julie in Essex where, for the last twenty three years, he has confused his local Chinese takeaway by phoning through orders using the names of Frank's last touring band.

His hobbies include watching films, football & speedway, smiling, reading books and, of course, listening to music.

Index

The index does not include references to appendices.
Album titles are in italics; song, film and video titles in quotation marks.

Also available from Wymer Publishing

WP
WYMER
PUBLISHING

BOOKS

The More Black than Purple Interviews (compiled and edited by Jerry Bloom)
For over ten years the Ritchie Blackmore magazine, More Black than Purple has featured many interviews within its pages. Wymer Publishing has collected the best and most riveting of these in to one book. There are also previously unpublished interviews, and additional, previously unpublished parts to some of the others.
Each interview also includes background information and some amusing tales surrounding the stories behind them. The book is bolstered further by a selection of b/w photos, many of which have never been published before.
• Includes interviews with: Don Airey° • Ritchie Blackmore (x3) • Graham Bonnet • Tony Carey* • Mark Clarke • Bob Daisley* • Glenn Hughes* • John McCoy° • Steve Morse • Cozy Powell.
° Part, previously unpublished * Previously unpublished
ISBN 978-0-9557542-0-3
Paperback 149x210mm, 180pp, 33 b/w images. **£14.99**

Rock Landmark's: Rainbow's Long Live Rock 'n' Roll (Jerry Bloom)
This book, the first in a series on landmark albums is an in-depth look at the classic Rainbow album 'Long Live Rock 'n' Roll'. The full story behind the making of the album; track by track analysis, recollections by the band and crew, all combined in a full colour CD size book designed to sit on your CD shelf alongside the album as its perfect companion.
ISBN 978-0-9557542-2-7
Paperback 125x140mm, 64pp (8 x colour). **£7.99**

Sketches Of Hackett - The authorised Steve Hackett biography (Alan Hewitt)
The first full and authorised biography of former Genesis guitarist Steve Hackett. Written by Alan Hewitt, a recognised authority on Genesis, whose previous writings include the critically acclaimed Genesis Revisited. Hewitt is also editor of the Genesis web fanzine The Waiting Room. First edition hardback plus 90 min DVD.
ISBN: 978-0-9557542-3-4
Hardback, 234 x 156 mm, 320pp (16 b/w, 43 colour images). **£24.95**

Rock Landmark's: Judas Priest's British Steel (Neil Daniels)
The second in our series of landmark albums looks at the sixth album by the British heavy metal band Judas Priest, recorded at Tittenhurst Park, home of former Beatle John Lennon. It is arguably the album that really defined heavy metal and is regarded as the band's seminal recording.
Written and researched by respected Judas Priest authority Neil Daniels, author of the first full Judas Priest biography, Defenders Of The Faith.
Foreword by Ron "Bumblefoot" Thal
ISBN 978-0-9557542-6-5
Paperback, 125x140mm, 72pp, including 17 b/w images. **£4.99**

A Hart Life- Deep Purple & Rainbow's tour manager's Life Story (Colin Hart)
Hart devoted over thirty years of his life to these great rock musicians. This is his story and indeed theirs. A tale of excess in terms of greed, petulance, anger and devotion. It is counter balanced by extremes of pure talent, showmanship and, of course musicianship. He was the constant 'man in the middle' through all of the break ups, make-ups and revolving door line-up changes. A story of two of the most innovative, often copied, rock bands; seen through the eyes, ears and emotions of their 'mother hen' as Jon Lord described him. He was their minder, chauffeur, carer, provider, protector, father confessor & confidant. In truth he is the only one who can tell this tale of both bands as he was the only one there on the road throughout the life of, not one, but both gigantic bands.
ISBN: 978-0-9557542-7-2
Hardback, 234 x 156 mm, 288pp (15 b/w, 73 colour images). **£19.95**

Hart's Life- 1971-2001 (Colin Hart)
Limited edition, deluxe slipcase version of 'A Hart Life' with bonus book, 'Hart's Life 1971-2001'; 80 pages of photos and memorabilia from Colin's collection including reproductions of tour itineraries, faxes and letters. Also includes a facsimile of the 'Burn' 1974 tour programme.
ISBN: 978-0-9557542-8-9 (plus ISBN: 978-0-9557542-7-2)
Paperback, 240 x 160 mm, 80pp (plus A Hart Life, 288pp). **£35.00**

Zermattitis: A Musician's Guide To Going Downhill Fast (Tony Ashton)
Written in 1991, Tony Ashton's incredible tales of his career with Ashton Gardner & Dyke, Paice Ashton & Lord, bankruptcy, skiing in Zermatt, Switzerland and many other adventures within the heady world of the music business are documented in this hilarious roller coaster of a ride. His writings have laid unpublished for twenty years, but in conjunction with Tony's wife this wonderful and unbelievably amusing story will now finally see the light of day. With a delightful and moving foreword from his dear friend Jon Lord, this is truly the last word from a man who sadly died in 2001, but whose life enriched so many. Although Tony wasn't a household name, within the entertainment world his numerous friends read like a who's who, including Dave Gilmour, John Entwistle, Eric Clapton and George Harrison. Foreword by Jon Lord (endorsed by Billy Connolly and Ewan McGregor)
ISBN: 978-0-9557542-9-6
Hardback, 234 x 156 mm, 192pp (Limited edition with DVD)* **£24.95**
*The DVD contains previously unreleased Ashton Gardner & Dyke material including a live performance from the Gala Rose of Montreux in 1970; a rare promo film, and a performance of their biggest hit 'Resurrection Shuffle'. The DVD also includes Tony's song 'Big Freedom Dance' written about John Lennon and filmed at Air Studios by TV presenter Chris Evans.

Sketches Of Hackett - The authorised Steve Hackett biography (Alan Hewitt)
The first full and authorised biography of former Genesis guitarist Steve Hackett. Written by Alan Hewitt, a recognised authority on Genesis. Revised with additional chapters taking the story up to end of 2011 with the release of Beyond The Shrouded Horizon.
ISBN: 978-1-908724-01-4
Paperback, 234 x 156 mm, 320pp (59 b/w images). **£14.95**

Norfolk Rebels: Fire In The Veins (Joanna Lehmann-Hackett)
Stories of Norfolk's rebels, from Boudicea to modern day rebels. Many of them linked and weaved into the vibrant tapestry of rebellion that is our inheritance. With a foreword by one of Norfolk's most well-known modern day rebels Keith Skipper, and another, beautifully written by Joanna's husband, former Genesis *guitarist* Steve Hackett, *this book depicts the many fine men and women of Norfolk who through the centuries have defended their ways, as only Norfolk people can.*
ISBN: 978-1-908724-02-1
Paperback, 246 x 189 mm, 100pp **£9.99**

All titles can be ordered online at our webstore- www.wymeruk.co.uk/Store
or from any decent retailer by quoting the relevant ISBN.

MAGAZINES

More Black than Purple
Established in 1996 this is the leading Ritchie Blackmore magazine, documenting the Man In Black's exploits with Rainbow, Deep Purple & Blackmore's Night.
ISSN 1478-2499
More info at: www.moreblackthanpurple.co.uk

Autumn Leaves
The official magazine of Mostly Autumn, established in 2000. This A4 magazine published twice a year is the official spokespiece for York's finest band, and arguably one of the greatest British bands to have emerged over the past decade.
*I*SSN: 1473-7817
More info at: www.autumn-leaves.co.uk

The Good Old Boys - Live At The Deep Purple Convention

Catalogue No: TSA1001. Released 13th July 2009

The Good Old Boys is: Nick Simper (Deep Purple); Richard Hudson (The Strawbs); Pete Parks (Warhorse); Simon Bishop (Renaissance) & Alan Barratt (Jo Jo Gunne).

Recorded live 3rd May 2008 at the Deep Purple Convention to celebrate the 40th Anniversary of the formation of Deep Purple. A unique performance that showcases their rock 'n' roll roots and musicianship. This 13-track CD includes a blistering version of Hush, the song that launched Deep Purple all those years ago. It also comes with a 12-page booklet with full band history, behind the scenes stories and previously unpublished photos from the actual performance and soundcheck.

Tracks: I'm Ready / A Fool For Your Stockings / My Way / Shakey Ground / Sleepwalk / Twenty Flight Rock / Somebody To Love / Don't Worry Baby / C'mon Everybody / Shakin' All Over / Oh Well / Hush / All My Rowdy Friends Are Comin' Over Tonight //

Nick Simper & Nasty Habits - The Deep Purple MKI Songbook

Catalogue No: TSA1002. Released: 16th August 2010

The Deep Purple MKI Songbook is up to date re-workings of Deep Purple songs from the first three albums performed by original Purple bassist Nick Simper with Austrian band, Nasty Habits. Powerful and hard-hitting arrangements of Deep Purple songs that have largely been over-looked since Deep Purple first had success in America with these songs. This initial release is a special limited edition (1,000 copies only) enhanced CD with bonus video footage including a Nick Simper interview.

Reissued as standard CD without video, 19th September 2011 (TSA1004)

Tracks: And The Address / The Painter / Mandrake Root / Emmaretta / Chasing Shadows / Lalena / Wring That Neck / The Bird Has Flown / Why Didn't Rosemary / Kentucky Woman / Hush //

Nick Simper & Nasty Habits - Roadhouse Blues

Catalogue No: NOR500. Released: 16th August 2010

Three track single with storming version of the Doors' Roadhouse Blues, plus The Painter and alternative version of Hush (unavailable elsewhere).

Liam Davison - A Treasure Of Well-Set Jewels

Catalogue No: TSA1003. Released: 21st March 2011

The debut solo album by Mostly Autumn guitarist Liam Davison is a cornucopia of aural delights. Guests include fellow Mostly Autumn band mates, Heather Findlay, Anne-Marie Helder, Iain Jennings and Gavin Griffiths plus Paul Teasdale (Breathing Space) and Simon Waggott. The first edition strictly limited to 1,000 copies, is an enhanced CD with bonus tracks and video footage.

Tracks: Ride The Seventh Wave / The Way We Were / Emerald Eternity / Eternally Yours / In To The Setting Sun / Once In A Lifetime / Heading Home / Picture Postcard / Bonus tracks: A Moment Of Silence / Immortalized // Bonus video: Liam's Treasure //

Amy Leeder - Fisticuffs With Cupid

Catalogue No: TSA1005. To be released: Late 2011

With this album we have broken with our own policy of only releasing works by established artists. Just 18, Amy has been writing songs since she was 14 and we believe she is destined for stardom. The maturity in her songs belie her age. Songs such as Chavs Of 2023 and Rough Around The Edges will resonate with people of all ages.

All titles can be ordered online at our webstore- www.wymeruk.co.uk/Store

or from any decent retailer. Also visit Wymer Records at http://records.wymeruk.co.uk

CPSIA information can be obtained at www.ICGtesting.com
Printed in the USA
LVOW111025200613

339485LV00002B/7/P